MINOR MIRACLES

MINOR MIRACLES:
The Legend & Lure of Minor League Baseball

by DAVID PIETRUSZA

DIAMOND COMMUNICATIONS, INC.
SOUTH BEND, INDIANA
1995

Minor Miracles

© 1995 by David Pietrusza

10 9 8 7 6 5 4 3 2 1

Manufactured in the United States of America

Diamond Communications, Inc.
P.O. Box 88
South Bend, Indiana 46624
Editorial: (219) 299-9278 or FAX (219) 299-9296
Orders Only: (800) 480-3717

Library of Congress Cataloging-in-Publication Data
Pietrusza, David, 1949—
   Minor miracles : the legend & lure of minor league baseball / by
David Pietrusza.
      p.   cm.
   Includes bibliographical references.
   ISBN 0-912083-82-4
   1. Minor league baseball--United States--History.   I. Title.
GV875.A1P545 1995
796.357'0973--dc20   95-8592
                                                                CIP

CONTENTS

To
John Thorn,
a big league guy,
a giant of baseball research,
and
a true friend

ACKNOWLEDGMENTS

Any project of this sort requires the help of a large number of individuals and organizations, and this one is certainly no exception.

I would like to thank the following for their help: the Society for American Baseball Research, Ralph Kiner, Howard Green, Tom Leip of the Northern League, Cappy Gagnon, Bill Gilbert, the Catholic Diocese of Ogdensburg (NY), Jay Acton, Joe Overfield, Jim Overmyer, Tom Heitz and the staff of the National Baseball Library, A. E. Rausch, Bob Bluthardt of SABR's Ballparks Committee, Andy McCue of SABR's Bibliographical Committee, Bill McCaffrey and the management of the Bowie BaySox, Mort Bloomberg of the New Haven Ravens, and Margaret McCahill of *USA Today Baseball Weekly*.

I'd particularly like to salute Scott & Mike McKinstry and Chuck Hershberger of *OldTyme Baseball News*, who provided me with a regular outlet for chronicling the greats of minor league history and who continue to publish one of baseball's finest publications.

I would also like to thank Jim and Jill Langford for their support of this project and the tremendous work they have done in furthering baseball publishing in general.

David Pietrusza

THE MINORS:
Where the Pros Begin

The Bushes. The Minors. Hardly anyone refers to them by their proper name, the National Association of Professional Baseball Leagues. Yet that varied collection of circuits provides nearly all the new blood the major leagues get as well as showcasing an affordable, quality brand of the National Pastime to scores of communities. The minors, the major leagues' often forgotten stepchildren, perform both functions exceedingly well.

Perhaps the most frustrating thing one can hear at a minor league park is an offhand comment about the "pros"?: "Do you think these guys will make the " 'pros'?"

The "pros"?

Who do these so-called fans think they are watching? Irradiated, mutant tee-ball players? From the Gulf Coast Rookie League to the International League, minor leaguers are professionals in every sense of the word. They get *paid to do this*. Granted, most of the time not much. But they meet the basic criteria of professionalism: they are good enough to draw a check for what they do.

They are also approximately one hundred times better than the best competition *you* ever faced, let alone *were*. It takes a certain level of skill—a very high one—just to be invited to sign a minor league contract. Every player who receives that honor was a star somewhere. In high school. In college. In Legion ball. They were all *big* fish in little diamond-shaped ponds all across North and South America.

Yet, the competition is so tough, that most wash out. Not just fail to make the majors, but fail in the entry level of minor league ball. It's a tough racket, and those who have worn the sneering title of "bush leaguer" really have nothing to be ashamed of at all.

So how have these leagues come to exist and how do they operate? Some may think the minors started out with Branch Rickey and his idea of a farm system. That was hardly the case. The bushes have a long and—sometimes even—proud history, stretching back, as they say, to the very dawn of professional baseball.

The first minor league, the ramshackle International Association, was born just 11 months after the founding of the National League—on February 20, 1877. Under the presidency of W.A. "Candy" Cummings, reputed inventor of the curveball, the fledgling circuit consisted of seven clubs: Rochester, New York; Allegheny of Pittsburgh; Manchester, New Hampshire; the Live Oaks of Lynn, Massachusetts; the Buckeyes of Columbus, Ohio; the Tecumsehs of London, Ontario; and the Maple Leafs of Guelph, Ontario.

Despite the fact that an International Association franchise cost just $10, it was a fast circuit, giving as good as it got against National League competition. Some modern historians even believe it deserves big league status, one contending that it "included many players who could have played in the National League if they had wished to do so but who preferred the more relaxed and easy atmosphere of the International." Supporting this theory, is the fact that in 1879 the International Association's Buffalo Bisons and Syracuse Stars easily made the jump to National League membership. The Bisons, featuring such stars as Jack Rowe, Hardy Richardson, and Pud Galvin, finished third in the National League; the Stars came in seventh, beating out the hapless Troy Trojans.

In 1877 other nascent minor leagues formed, including the New England League and the Midwest-based League Alliance (which pledged fealty to the National League). Yet only the International Association followed a set (albeit very short) schedule and was bound by a strict code of rules.

Soon still more circuits appeared, the Northwestern League in 1879 and the Eastern Championship Association (featuring the first version of the New York Mets) in 1881. When the National League and the upstart major league American Association went to war in 1882, both found minor circuits to side with them. The Northwestern League aligned itself with the Nationals while the Interstate Association found itself in the AA's corner.

2

An agreement between the National League, the American Association, and Northwestern League President Elias Mather not only cemented peace between the two competing major leagues but also formed the cornerstone of what we now know as organized baseball. This " Tripartite Agreement" allowed each league control over its internal affairs, but the three circuits would now stand together on such vital concerns as player control, outside competition, and territoriality.

Minor leagues existed throughout the 19th century. The Western League formed in November 1883 with annual dues of just $40. Gate receipts were divided as follows: "the visiting club to receive 40 percent..., or a guarantee of $60.00." The International League (the minors' oldest surviving circuit) began in 1884 as the "Eastern League," first becoming known by its current name in 1886 after merging with a Canadian circuit. Under the tutelage of famed Atlanta newspaper editor, Henry W. Grady, the Southern League commenced play in 1885. The Texas League started in 1888 and was reorganized by former St. Louis Browns manager Ted Sullivan in 1895.

Other notable, although less familiar, early circuits included the New York State League, the Illinois-Indiana League, the Southern Michigan League, the Ohio State League, the Iron and Oil League, the Connecticut State League, and the Eastern Inter-State League.

Furthering the stability of minor loops was an 1887 amendment to the National Agreement which eliminated the right of big league clubs to sign any minor leaguer they chose at season's end. Thenceforth, any bush league club could reserve up to 14 players. The idea was originally proposed by *Sporting Life* editor Francis Richter, one of the 19th century's most influential sportswriters. Richter was not entirely moved by concern for the minors.

"Reservation must be granted the minor leagues by the big leagues as a matter of self-preservation, aside from the toning-down effect it will have on salaries," Richter argued. "The fact that players can get as much salary in a minor league, under less severe discipline and without reservation, as they can get in a big league, where the work is continuously exacting and reservation from year to year certain, is certainly not calculated to easily land young players in big leagues or to make old players in big leagues anxious to retain their places therein, or at least indifferent thereto; and to just that extent is discipline loosened. The truth of this was illustrated during the last season when many players were made dissatisfied or indifferent by communications from old confreres who had gone into minor leagues descriptive of the 'very soft snaps' they were enjoying; and is further illustrated at the present time when we see so many players who give every indication of future greatness resolutely refusing the most flattering offers from big clubs, preferring to cast their lot with the minor leagues where the pay is nearly equal, and their work less likely to be over-shadowed. Of course, the minor leagues should not pay these excessive salaries so damaging to themselves and the entire business, but they cannot help themselves so long as they are driven into competition season after season with the big leagues...Reservation will cure this evil."

It was at the beginning of the 1891 season that the minors began to assume the familiar alphabet structure we know today. A second National Agreement established a definite pecking order, with high level circuits able to genteelly raid lower ones for talent.

"Class A has protection for contract and reservation," noted the *Philadelphia Press*, "Class B has protection but any club in the three major leagues can at any time during the season draw on this league for a player, with the latter's consent, and by paying a stipulated price. Class C gives protection for contract only. Class D protects a contract, but any of the grades above it can draw on it for a player during the season by paying a stipulated sum."

The American League began as a minor circuit, the old Western League. Hard-drinking Cincinnati sportswriter Ban Johnson took over the circuit in the early 1890s, when it was a tottering structure on the verge of collapse. He quickly transformed it into the minors' most stable circuit. Featuring such Midwestern aggregations as the St. Paul Saints, Minneapolis Millers, Kansas City Blues, Grand Rapids Gold Bugs, and Toledo Swamp Angels, the league eventually shifted eastward to larger cities as it moved toward major league status in 1901.

In the struggle that ensued between the American and National Leagues, the Senior Circuit, badly in need of playing talent, callously abrogated its former agreements with the minors. In defense, most minor leagues banded together in a new protective grouping, the National Association, which was, for the first time in its history, totally independent from major league control.

4

Formed on September 5, 1901, its original members were:

League	President
Western League	Mike Sexton
Eastern League	P.T. Powers
New York State League	John H. Farrell
Pacific Northwest League	W.H. Lucas
New England League	Tim Murnane
Three-I League	Mike Sexton
Western Association	William Meyers

The National Association chose the Eastern League's Patrick T. Powers as its first president; John H. Farrell became its first secretary. The organization's founders thrashed out a variety of issues—salaries, reserve rules, arbitration, drafting procedures, and continuing the classification of circuits into the "A," "B," "C," and "D" system. Statements of support quickly came from the Southern Association, the North Carolina League, the Connecticut League, and the California League.

Wrote Francis Richter, who now seemed more concerned about the minors' interests: "If the minor leagues hold together and perfect their present organization, we shall have a novel and ideal condition; for, with the major leagues operating under a new agreement and all the minor leagues working under their own agreement, there will be between the two great divisions of the baseball world—the major and minor—such an exact balance of power as will compel mutual respect, tolerance, and fair dealing, and thus open up the happiest era baseball has ever enjoyed."

The new organization displayed its muscle early on. The Western League and Thomas Hickey's American Association found themselves squabbling over certain territories, and the National Association vigorously—although as it turned out, only temporarily—booted the AA out as punishment.

By 1903, 19 minor leagues had come together under the National Association banner. The chastened American Association was readmitted, and a Class A "Pacific National League" had formed on the West Coast.

The National Association might have continued as an independent body, but with peace coming between the American and National

Leagues, it ratified a fourth version of the National Agreement and again opted for subservience to the majors.

For a decade the minors grew steadily, reaching a peak of 51 circuits in 1910-11. But many were ramshackle operations. Crowd control and umpire safety were hit-and-miss. Stories of violence were all too common. Typical was umpire "Steamboat" Johnson's experience in the New York State League. In Troy, New York, the local second baseman took a swing at Johnson but missed. Johnson counterpunched and knocked him back, but the Trojan catcher landed his mask over Johnson's right eye.

"As I was lying there with the players milling about over me," Johnson wrote in his autobiography, "I found blood was streaming from my cut eye. I put my handerchief over my eye and held it in place with my cap. Then I sat up and ordered five players out of the game. I scrambled to my feet and ordered the game to go on. I finished the rest of the game with one eye, as the blood was obscuring the sight of the other."

Not only violence but poor finances plagued the minors. "There is a certain precariousness to the minor league situation," wrote the 1909 *Spalding's Guide*, "which will exist until the control of minor leagues is grounded on common sense principles and the members of minor leagues, individually, will faithfully live up to the rules of their organizations."

Trouble was brewing. In 1911, 10 circuits folded in mid-season; in 1912, 11 out of 47 collapsed in mid-campaign. The outbreak of the Federal League War of 1914-15 caused the demise of numerous circuits, and American participation in World War I resulted in the wholesale extinction of even more. By 1918, a mere 10 leagues started the season, and only the International League survived till season's end.

With Armistice Day, confidence was restored. By January 1919, the minors had regrouped and went so far as to manfully reassert their independence, demanding an end to player options and the major league draft. Big league clubs retaliated by abrogating whatever primitive working agreements they had with the bushes.

Five minor leagues—the International League, the American Association, the PCL, the Western League, and the Three-I League—were vehemently opposed to any form of player draft. In January 1921 a draft was nonetheless restored, although the IL, AA, and PCL still remained exempt from it.

Newly designated commissioner Kenesaw Mountain Landis was four-square in favor of the draft, viewing it as a players' rights issue. "A situation," he expounded, "where a group of ballplayers can be boxed into a minor league, and can advance only at the whim of their employer is intolerable and un-American. So long as I am in this job, I will fight for full restoration of the draft."

In 1931, thanks in part to depression-era economics, the draft was finally extended to all minor leagues.

But there was another factor in the draft's extension, the passing of one of the minor leagues' giants—Baltimore's Jack Dunn. From 1919 to 1925 his International League dynasty captured seven straight pennants. In 1921, his Orioles won 119 games while losing just 47.

Dunn bought into the Orioles in 1910, but during the Federal League's incursion in Baltimore (they literally built a park across the street from his) he was forced to move his club to Richmond. When the Feds folded, International League President Ed Barrow barred Dunn from moving his franchise back to Baltimore. Instead, he demanded that Dunn buy the Jersey City franchise and transfer it to Baltimore. Dunn did so, but in retaliation, Dunn forced Barrow out of the league presidency—an actual favor to the man, as Barrow was soon hired as Red Sox general manager.

Dunn was a great judge of talent. It was he who discovered Babe Ruth. "He's Jack Dunn's babe," said the other players about the young southpaw, and the nickname stuck.

But Ruth was only the *most* famous player Dunn developed. He later sold such stars as Lefty Grove, Frank Baker, Joe Boley, Max Bishop, Fritz Maisel, Bob Shawkey, Ben Eagan, Jack Bentley, Johnny Ogden, and George Earnshaw to major league clubs. For Bentley alone he got $65,000 from the New York Giants. Grove went to Dunn's old friend Connie Mack for over $100,000.

Grove, a native of Lanconing, Maryland, made his professional debut in 1920 with the Class C Blue Ridge League. Dunn obtained him from Martinsburg for $3,500 plus another pitcher. Grove was 12-2 for Baltimore the rest of the year, then went 25-10, 18-8, 27-10, and 26-6 for the Orioles.

The Giants offered $75,000 for Grove, but Dunn wouldn't budge. Finally—faced with the threat of the draft—he sold the great southpaw to Mack for $106,000. The extra $6,000 was to ensure this the most expensive cash purchase in diamond annals—topping the $100,000 the Yankees had paid the Red Sox for Babe Ruth. In fact, it was *so* expensive, Mack had to pay Dunn on the installment plan.

"We were satisfied to stay there," Grove contended about his extended Baltimore tenure, "We were getting bigger salaries…than lots of clubs were paying in the big leagues. So why leave? We couldn't get $750 to $1,000 a month in the big leagues in those days. Not in lots of clubs but that's what we were getting in Baltimore. And Dunnie was good to us. We'd play exhibition games with the big league teams, and all the money was pooled and we got a cut. Plus we got Little World Series money every year. I started off there at $250 a month, and by the time I got sold to Connie I was up over $750. We did fine."

In 1921 Dunn's boys had gone 119-47 for a .717 percentage. As a team they hit .313 and early in the season pealed off 27 consecutive victories. Righthander Jack Ogden had a remarkable season. The Swarthmore-educated 25-year old went 32-8 with a 2.01 ERA, winning 18 games in a row including three 3-hitters, two 4-hitters, and four 5-hitters. Versus Joe McCarthy's Louisville Colonels in that year's Junior World Series, he won three more contests.

Teammate Jack Bentley went 12-1 with a 2.35 ERA. Not bad— particularly for a first baseman who paced the league with a .412 average and 24 home runs. No wonder he was known as the "Babe Ruth of the International League." Inexplicably, when he was sold to the New York Giants, John McGraw chose to employ him as pitcher and *not* as a hitter.

Sitting on such talent, Dunn bitterly fought the player draft and it was not until following his death in October 1928 that Landis could develop momentum for overturning the higher leagues' draft exemption. Dunn was a titan of his era, and the minors have not seen his like since.

One reason we have not was Branch Rickey's creation of the farm system. For the first two decades of the century the St. Louis Cardinals were a woebegone franchise unable to compete with wealthier clubs such as the Giants, Yankees, or Cubs in buying players from the minors. So in 1919 Rickey, then Cardinals general manager, decided to develop them himself. Using part of the $350,000 proceeds from the sale of the Cards' ancient home park, Robison Field, he started his scheme by purchasing 18 percent of the Texas League's Houston

Buffs. By 1925 he had full control of the club. In short order he gobbled up clubs in Fort Worth, Syracuse, Sioux City, Joplin, and Springfield. The system was soon producing quality players like Jim Bottomley, Chick Hafey, Pepper Martin, Rip Collins, the Dean brothers, Joe Medwick, and Terry Moore. In less than a decade the Cardinals were transformed from perennial also-rans into World Champions.

At its peak in 1940, the Red Bird farm system boasted 32 teams (16 of which it owned outright) and 600 farmhands. "There were 20 Class D Leagues in the United States in 1940, and the Cardinals had a team in each of them," said Cardinals Farm director Arthur Feltzner. "One actually had to go out of the country to find a Class D league in Organized Baseball in which we weren't represented; that was the Canadian [Cape Breton] Colliery League, which operated in New Brunswick."

But as early as 1924, Commissioner Landis had expressed grave doubts about this new order, contending that local ownership and control of clubs were more desirable. A 1931 court case involving the Browns and their Milwaukee Brewers farm club validated the legality of the system, but this in no way lessened Landis' hostility. In March 1938, in the so-called "Cedar Rapids Case," he emancipated 91 Cardinal farmhands, including future big leaguers Pete Reiser and Skeeter Webb; fined two Cardinal-controlled clubs; and leveled several verbal blasts at Branch Rickey for entering "into arrangements for complete control of the lower classification clubs through secret understandings."

Cardinal magnate Sam Breadon shot back that Rickey's farm system had saved the minors from extinction. "There was a time in baseball history when there was over 50 minor leagues," he noted. "About 1930, the number had dropped to 13 or 14. The ten years preceding had been boom years, yet the minor leagues reached the low mark when only seven or eight leagues could be counted on to start in the Spring of 1931. Minor league baseball was dying and was almost a thing of the past. What was done about it? Was anything attempted? Nothing at all…

"After…the added interest of…major league clubs in the minors, the minors took on new life and their rebirth took place during the dark days of 1931 and 1932 on down to the present time, and today there are approximately 40 leagues…Branch Rickey should receive a vote of thanks from the Commissioner's office for what he had done for baseball, not censure."

On January 14, 1940, however, Landis struck again, emancipating 91 Detroit farmhands and ordering payments of $47,250 to 15 other Tiger-owned players. Landis' main complaint was that Detroit had violated regulations on the number of players it could legally hold on option. Among the 87 liberated minor leaguers was righthander Johnny Sain. Also freed were major leaguers Roy Cullenbine, Benny McCoy, Lloyd Dietz, and Steve Rachunok. The Tigers suffered an estimated property loss of $500,000, and club president Walter O. "Spike" Briggs was so disheartened he sold off all but a dozen or so of his farm teams.

The self-satisfied Yankees were somewhat slow to adopt the concept, yet ironically their first farm director, George Weiss, was one of the best. Starting his baseball career in 1919 as manager of a semi-pro nine in New Haven, Weiss' business sense was such that the town's Eastern League franchise wilted under Weiss' competition as he cagily booked such novelties as all-Chinese teams, Bloomer Girl teams, and even such stars as Ty Cobb and Babe Ruth. Eastern League owners quickly sold out to him. Later, he replaced Jack Dunn at Baltimore, and in 1932 Ed Barrow and Yankee owner Jacob Ruppert hired him to supervise the Yankee farm system. "He knows more about the minors than anyone else," praised Barrow. Before long the sagging Yankees were rejuvenated. Weiss eventually became Yankee general manager and a Hall-of-Famer.

The Yankees' first farm club had been at Chambersburg, Pennsylvania, in 1930. It was hardly a great success as it folded with the rest of the Blue Ridge League at season's end. But in November 1931 Ruppert purchased the Newark Bears for $600,000 and placed Weiss in charge. A product of Weiss' handiwork was Newark's 1937 squad, whom many contend was the greatest minor league club of all time. Newark won the International League flag by $25\frac{1}{2}$ games and the playoffs and Little World Series in eight straight contests. Every team member but one eventually made the majors—including: George McQuinn, Buddy Rosar, Babe Dahlgren, Charlie Keller, Joe Gordon, Marius Russo, Atley Donald, and Spud Chandler. Even the manager, Oscar Vitt, reached the big leagues.

Night baseball was successfully introduced to the minors in 1930. The first night baseball game had occurred less than a year after Thomas Edison had perfected the incandescent bulb—on Nantasket Beach in Hull, Massachusetts, in October 1880. The first minor league team to play under the lights had performed in an arclit exhibition at Fort Wayne, Indiana, in 1883. Throughout the decades that followed, bush league clubs flirted with night ball, yet the breakthrough had to wait until April 28, 1930, when Muskogee played at Independence in a Class C Western Association contest.

M.L. Truby's Independence Producers had stolen the thunder of E. Lee Keyser's Class A Western League Des Moines Demons. Keyser had announced his plans at the preceding Winter Meetings, but Truby had beaten him to the punch with a crude operation. Nonetheless, it was Keyser's $19,000 system that all of baseball saw as its guide. In just a matter of weeks, arc lights shone throughout the bushes.

Also aiding the minors' salvation in the desperate days of the depression were two other factors: structural reforms promulgated by newly installed National Association President William G. Bramham and the institution of the popular "Shaughnessy Playoffs." Under Bramham, fly-by-night franchises were weeded out. Leagues were stabilized. Players' salaries were protected. Under the Shaughnessy Plan, late-season fan interest was rejuvenated and greater revenue was generated.

As a consequence of these innovations, minor league baseball bounced back. In 1933—even though the Depression still ravaged the nation—every circuit that started the season finished it. Only four times in minor league history (1883, 1903, 1921, and 1927) had that previously happened.

In Tinsel Town it even became fashionable to hold stock in the local minor league club. Bing Crosby, Barbara Stanwyck, Robert Taylor, Cecil B. DeMille, Gary Cooper, and George Raft all owned a piece of the Pacific Coast League's Hollywood Stars and added glamour to proceedings at new 12,987-seat Gilmore Field.

By 1940 there were 44 leagues and 310 clubs in operation. Pearl Harbor short-circuited such success. League after league closed up shop. By 1943 the National Association had shrunken to 10 circuits and just 66 clubs.

Following V-J Day, the minors, like all of baseball, experienced unprecedented boom times. The peak was reached in 1949—59 leagues, 448 teams, 9,000 players under contract, and 41,872,762 paid admissions. Then came television and the Korean War and a long, steady decline began. Particularly along the East Coast, television's effects were devastating. Such fabled franchises as the Newark

Bears and the Jersey City Giants quickly disappeared. Entire leagues, such as the Colonial, the North Atlantic, the Middle Atlantic, and the Canadian-American simply vanished.

Broadcasts and telecasts of big league games were the big factor. Radio coverage had begun back in 1921, with Graham McNamee's coverage of the Yankee-Giants World Series. Then in 1924, Chicago's WMAQ initiated the first steady transmission of regular season games when it signed a contract with the Cubs. By 1959 over a thousand stations were blanketing the nation with live Major League Baseball—a privilege for which sponsors paid $40 million. The Mutual Network alone had 500 stations doing daily baseball, and even Gordon McLendon's shoestring Liberty Network boasted 431 stations airing announcer Lindsey Nelson's re-creations. National Association President George Trautman noted that in one Pacific Coast League city five games per day were on the radio, from 10:30 in the morning till 11 at night.

Television had an even deeper impact. The first telecast was on August 26, 1939, featuring Red Barber with a Reds-Dodgers doubleheader from Ebbets Field. After World War II, the novelty caught fire. Even though the New York Metropolitan area had just 500 sets in 1946, the fledgling Dumont Network willingly paid the Yankees $75,000 for video rights. By 1950 television rights for the World Series alone fetched $6,000,000 annually.

But while this was a bonanza for the majors, it proved an unmitigated disaster for their affiliates. The big leagues showed some inclination to soften the blows. For a short time, a 50-mile broadcast-free zone was set up around minor league cities but was soon scrapped, as the majors claimed it might jeopardize their anti-trust exemption.

Commissioner Ford Frick contended that the threat of federal action kept the majors from protecting the minors. "We eliminated [restrictions on broadcasting] because we were high-pressured by the Department of Justice at a time when we were already faced with five or six litigations," he testified before Congress, "and we did not want litigation by the Department of Justice and the United Stated Government to come in and be added to this terrific pile which we already faced, and not because at any time we had the slightest doubt as to the legality of our position."

But it wasn't only radio and television that was killing minor league franchises. The Korean War was also part of the problem, draining the talent pool available to big league scouting systems. Basically, however, the minors had overextended themselves. In 1950 there were 232 independent clubs operating, the highest number since the 1910s. There were nine full leagues in which not a single franchise possessed a major league working agreement. Many of these unaffiliated clubs were simply matters of local boosterism, failing to have either an artistic or economic *raison d'etre*.

By 1956 there were only 28 minor leagues operating, and Commissioner Ford Frick organized a "Save the Minors Committee" of major league club owners. They instituted a $500,000 stabilization fund, but it was clearly not enough. In 1959 the minors had shrunk to just 21 circuits (just a third of their 1949 total), and the fund increased to $1 million. A more permanent remedy was required, and in May 1962, the "Player Development Plan" was unveiled. The minors, which had added the "AA" rating in 1908, "A-1" in 1936, and "AAA" in 1946 were reclassified once more. The new plan lumped most lower (B,C, and D) leagues into Class A, and created a special category of "Rookie" circuits. Player salaries were totally subsidized in some cases and partially subsidized in the remainder. All spring training costs and all minor league managers' salaries were now borne by parent clubs.

The situation slowly improved. Each major league team was required to carry five (a figure later reduced to four) farm clubs. Even a few independent teams reappeared (such as the Pioneer League's very successful Salt Lake City Trappers). *Baseball America* publisher Miles Wolff even founded a very prosperous and totally independent (i.e., non-National Association) circuit in 1993, the Northern League. Other independent leagues were quick to follow Wolff's lead.

Minor league attendance, which dipped to a low of 9,963,174 in 1963, rose to over 33 million in 1993. It was the first time that the minors had topped the 30-million mark since 1950, when 446 clubs had taken the field. Average per-game National Association attendance in 1994 was 3,364, the highest in history. In 1993 eight circuits (the International, Eastern, Southern, California, Carolina, South Atlantic, Northwest, and Appalachian leagues) attained all-time attendance marks. The International League set a record for the highest minor league attendance ever—4.6 million fans. In 1994, 33,355,199 fans again trooped through bush league turnstiles, with the Eastern,

Southern, Texas, California, Midwest, South Atlantic, New York-Penn, and Northwest leagues setting circuit records.

The trend had been building for at least a decade. In 1982 the Denver Bears attracted 65,666 to a July 4th Fireworks Night. That same year A. Ray Smith's Louisville Redbirds drew 868,418 paying customers. Prior to 1982 only eight minor league clubs had ever drawn more than 500,000 in a single season: San Francisco (PCL), 670,543, 1956; Oakland (PCL), 634,311, 1956; Baltimore (IL), 620,726, 1946; Los Angeles (PCL), 576,372, 1948; Nashville (SL), 575,676, 1980; Denver (AA), 565,214, 1980; Columbus (IL), 546,074, 1980; and Hollywood (PCL), 513,056, 1946.

The next season Smith poured $750,000 into further improvements for Louisville's Cardinal Stadium and became the first minor league club to top the million attendance mark, when his team drew 1,052,438. Despite the American Association's truncated 136-game schedule, the Redbirds outdrew the major league Indians, Twins, and Mariners. They were not far behind the Reds and Mets.

In 1988 Bob Rich's Buffalo Bisons topped Louisville's record by drawing 1,186,651. The Bisons' first 22 dates that season sold out, and they drew over a million fans every year through 1993. Aiding their accomplishment was spectacular Pilot Field, which sparked a resurgence of interest in downtown ballparks. "Since they moved into the new ballpark, Buffalo has been one of the great success stories," commented Baltimore General Manager Roland Hemond. "It has all the features of a first-class major league ballpark." Not coincidentally, Baltimore was soon featuring its own downtown park.

It's once again become fashionable to own shares in a minor league team. Such celebrities as Bill Murray, Pia Zadora, Tony Orlando, Roger Kahn, the late Don Drysdale, Jimmy Buffett, Darrell Evans, George Brett, and the late Conway Twitty have all gotten a piece of the action in recent seasons.

Franchises have accordingly skyrocketed in value. The PCL's Tucson Toros sold for $3 million. The Eastern League's Waterbury Indians were purchased in 1986 for $345,000, moved to another city, and sold again in 1988, this time for $1.5 million. The Southern League's Memphis Chicks fetched $2 million in 1988 and $3 million when they were peddled once more just a season later. In 1990 the Vancouver Canadians went for $5.5 million. The following year, it was reported that Nashville Sounds owner Larry Schmittou had turned down a $10 million bid for his Triple-A franchise.

In 1993-94 the enterprising Schmittou even hosted two teams at Nashville's Herschel Greer Stadium. Fellow owner George Shinn could not find a home for his Double-A Charlotte Knights which had been displaced by International League expansion to Charlotte. Schmittou took a gamble. Although Shinn retained ownership of the Knights (now renamed the Xpress), Schmittou took all financial risks. The gamble paid off. In 1993 Schmittou estimated that before debt service he had cleared $245,000 on operating the Xpress.

Actually, two teams in one city was not unique. In 1972, the Southern League's Charlotte Hornets and the Western Carolinas League's Charlotte Twins shared Charlotte's Griffith Park. In 1993, the Eastern League's Bowie BaySox found themselves with no stadium. They moved into Baltimore's old Memorial Stadium and shared the town with the parent Orioles. And back during the Federal League war Cleveland ownership moved the American Association's Toledo Mud Hens into Cleveland's League Park to provide "continuous ball" for local fans and discourage a Federal League incursion.

In the boom years of the 1980s and early 90s, even the Japanese took time out from gobbling up Rockefeller Center and Pebble Beach to invest in the American minors. In 1989, Japan Sports Systems U.S.A. purchased the California League's Visalia Oaks. In February 1990, a partnership that included Suntory, Inc., the Japanese beverage, food, and restaurant combine acquired the Southern League's Birmingham Barons. The price tag: $3 million.

The question before the house is: just how many hot dogs can one sell? How many wieners and nachos do you *have* to peddle to get your money back when franchises go for *that* much money?

In a very large sense, however, that is *not* the question. Money is *not* made from ticket sales or concessions or parking. Money can only be made by reselling the franchise to another group of investors. In that sense, what we are seeing now is a giant pyramid scheme.

Seeing all this money changing hands made the majors jealous of the minors. Jealousy was compounded by resentment. By 1989, the average major league club put $5.5 million per year into player development, footing the bill not only for minor league player salaries but also for sundry items such as bats and balls and travel accommodations.

The major league clubs would successfully cut themselves in on the minors' new found prosperity. Pressure coming out of Commissioner Fay Vincent's office was immense, as he instructed the majors to cancel every working agreement they could. In August 1990, 56 were dropped. The minors had to knuckle under and accept a new agreement—or minor league ball would collapse in a heap.

"There's no doubt all this is coming from Vincent," said veteran minor league operator Jack Tracz. "They want to control us, and now they can. When Vincent came in, everybody thought he was a good man who wanted to carry on Bart Giamatti's legacy. Now, we can all see he has no inclination to do that. I can't figure out the major leagues. They pay millions of dollars to mediocre players, they pay millions for collusion, and they fight with umpires. They can't win one, so now they're coming after the minors—the little people."

In December 1990, the minors grudgingly accepted a new Professional Baseball Agreement (PBA) which, among other things, called for them to surrender 5 percent of their revenues to the majors as well as to give up their historic—but small—share of Major League Baseball's television revenues.

But perhaps the PBA's most onerous provision involved ballpark standards. Nit-picking seemed an apt description of its bureaucratic standards, defining everything from the number of urinals to the height of outfield fences. Even sparkling new Harry Grove Stadium, built at a cost of $3 million and designed by the parent Orioles, was in violation of the new standards. So was the Orioles' new Camden Yards facility—its seven-foot high fence falling one foot shy of the minimum.

Grandfathering was possible but exceedingly rare. "The major league teams' primary objective is to get the best facilities for their players. They are not in favor of granting waivers," commented Professor Arthur Johnson, author of *Minor League Baseball and Local Economic Development.* "They don't have any interest in the welfare of the small communities. They know other cities want them."

Summed up veteran minor league statistician and historian Bill Weiss: "For 90 years, being a member of the National Association afforded a league and its members protection: territorial, player-contract rights, etc. What you have now is major league tyranny, not minor league protection."

But even with the new PBA placing new burdens on minor league owners, there is no shortage of those trying to get into the club.

The Minors

"Why, all of a sudden, is minor league baseball so popular?" pondered one-time minor league magnate Joe Vellano. "I [was] involved in the middle of it, and I have no friggin' idea. Is it sensible? No, it makes no sense."

A LITTLE MORE
HISTORY:
A Player's Life

For minor league players life can often be a grim existence. For some, it is the first time away from family, and it is almost standard policy not to play a youngster near his hometown. The level of competition is a quantum leap from high school or college ball. Making the transition can be traumatic.

Physical conditions as well as psychological ones are also factors. Salaries are small; tiny allowances for meals guarantee a steady diet of greasy cheeseburgers; hotels can be second-rate; and the buses—oh, those buses—can be an ordeal.

Rides in the low minors can take 19 or 20 hours. Breakdowns have not been unknown. Once on the West Palm Beach team bus, a gearshift broke, and a player, armed with a screwdriver, was jammed into the engine compartment. "When the [bus driver] had to shift gears," recalled the manager, "he'd holler, and the guy with the screwdriver would move it with the thing. Every once in a while, we'd stop and let the guy out for air."

For Latin Americans the torture takes the form of the language barrier. Outfielder Jose Cardenal, a native Cuban, remembers his difficulties in deciphering American menus: "Breakfast, lunch, and dinnertime, I had ham and eggs. It took me a week to order something different. Next thing I learned was 'Steak and potatoes.' Then 'hamburger' and 'hot dog.' After a while I started to rotate." Cardenal was clearly in the tradition of fellow Cuban Bobby Estalella who developed a strange rash which was finally diagnosed as the result of eating nothing but eggs for three weeks.

Visa problems are also endemic for Latin American players. A few years ago at Hamilton, Ontario, second baseman Jose Trujillo and his pet ferret were attempting to enter Canada. The ferret's papers were in order; Jose's weren't.

Yet not too bleak a picture should be painted. Many young minor league players have married local girls and permanently settled in their first or second minor league town. Some cities and fans clearly take the players to their hearts. "I didn't want to leave. I told them they would have to carry me out," were the words of one Bristol Red Sox fan who suffered a heart attack during a game and refused to be hospitalized until the seventh inning. Was he waiting for the seventh-inning stretcher?

And conditions aside from fan support can often be surprisingly pleasant. A spurt of new stadium construction in the 1980s and '90s gave the minors such excellent facilities as Buffalo's Pilot Field, Scranton-Wilkes-Barre's Lackawanna County Multi-Purpose Stadium, Norfolk's Harbor Park, Binghamton's Municipal Stadium, and Frederick's Harry Grove Stadium. Nineteen ninety four saw two new structures in New Jersey alone: Skyland Park, housing the New York-Penn League's New Jersey Redbirds, and $12.2 million Mercer County Stadium, home to the Eastern League's Trenton Thunder.

Each of these new parks either propelled infant franchises off the ground or boosted attendance for existing teams. And the Florida State League is the grateful beneficiary of spring training, using often excellent parks meant for big leaguers' pre-season activities such as St. Petersburg's Al Lang Stadium or (briefly) the magnificent Baseball City complex in remote Davenport, Florida. Baseball City boasted larger and more opulent facilities than those found in many major league parks.

The minors have their own legends. In the 1960s Baltimore farmhand Steve Dalkowski impressed everyone with his blazing fastball. It's estimated he threw at over 100 miles an hour and was quite possibly the fastest hurler ever, but control was his downfall. In nine years he fanned 1,396 batters in just 995 innings but managed to walk 1,354.

Some say his wildness stemmed from a fear of hitting anyone. Others placed the blame on drinking and riotous living. After leaving baseball, Dalkowski, in fact, became a derelict and now works as a farm laborer in California.

To fellow unsuccessful bushers, observed author Pat Jordan, himself a once-promising minor league pitcher, "Dalkowski will always symbolize every frustration and every elation they have ever felt because of their God-given talent."

A minor league pitching legend of a different sort was "Kewpie Dick" Barret. Hindered, like Dalkowski, by control problems, this diminutive southpaw spent 10 full years in the bushes before finally hitting his stride. In fact, he holds the minor league career record for bases on balls. But after he joined the Pacific Coast League's Seattle Indians in 1935 he rattled off eight 20-win seasons.

His control remained somewhat remiss, however. When Barrett would take the mound at Seattle's then-new $150,000 Sicks Stadium, play-by-play announcer Leo "Mr. Baseball" Lassen would recite the following ditty:

"Roses are red, violets are blue,
"Barrett's pitching, three and two!"

In 1937 Barrett had a clause inserted in his Seattle contract, promising him an extra $500 if he won 20 games. The 5'9" southpaw went into a doubleheader against Sacramento on the last day of the season with 18 wins. Indians manager Johnny Bassler was determined to give Kewpie his chance. Barrett won the first game, and owner "Bald Bill" Klepper stormed into the clubhouse, screaming: "I want you to pitch Marion Oppelt in the second game."

"I'm the manager, and Barrett's pitching," snapped Bassler—and so he did.

As Barrett was defeating the Solons in the second game, things *really* got exciting. A combination of federal, state, and Seattle tax men raided the stadium box office, seizing assets left and right for back payment of taxes.

Barrett got his $500, though.

Joe Bauman's performance for the Roswell Rockets of the 1954 Class C Longhorn League was as sweet a season as one player could ask for. Joe clouted 72 homers, hit .400, drove in 224 runs, walked 150 times, and compiled a fabulous .916 slugging percentage. Bauman steadily closed in on Joe Hauser's all-time home run mark of 69, drawing near with a four-homer effort on September 1. "I wasn't really trying for home runs, but after I hit those four, I really got conscious of the durned record," Bauman later recalled. "It went from an impossibility to a possibility in one night."

He had built up to his big year by slamming 48 homers in 1946, 38 in 1947, 50 in 1952, and 53 in 1953. In 1955 he fell off to a mere 46 round-trippers and 132 RBI. Yet, despite his awesome displays of power, the 6'5"; 235-pound first baseman never played so much as an inning of major league ball. While Babe Ruth and Hank Aaron went on to Cooperstown, Bauman went on to work for a beer distributor.

Bauman accomplished his gargantuan feats in the low minors, but Joe Hauser was just as good at the Triple-A level. From 1930 to 1936 he clouted 302 four-baggers, including 69 for the 1936 Minneapolis Millers and 63 for the 1930 Baltimore Orioles. Yet somehow, Hauser too, despite a lifetime .285 major league average and a 1924 season spent with Connie Mack's Philadelphia Athletics, could not find steady employment.

Ike Boone was still yet another terror with a bat. The only player in modern Texas League history to bat .400, he also hit at a .402 pace for the Southern Association in 1923 and twice topped the .400 mark (.407 in 1929 and .448 in 1930) with Mission in the Pacific Coast League. Yet despite a .315 average for four major league teams, he too could not find a permanent niche in either the NL or AL.

Slugger Luscious Luke Easter enjoyed three different careers, starting in the Negro Leagues, moving on to the majors and ending up in the minors. No matter *where* he played he could hit. "I just hit 'em and forget 'em," bragged Easter, who in Negro League competition in 1947 hit an estimated 75 homers.

Bad knees ended Easter's major league career. Starting in 1956 for Buffalo, Easter began his third career. That year he paced the International League in homers (35) and RBI (106). At Buffalo's old Offerman Stadium on August 6 of that year, Easter clubbed one of the most prodigious blasts in minor league history—a 550-foot homer that landed not one but two streets out of the park. In 1957 Easter led the league in homers (40), total bases (300), and RBI (128). It is no wonder that the 6' 4½" first baseman was one of the most beloved players in Buffalo Bisons history.

But even beloved personnel get released. Buffalo cut Easter loose in May 1959. Still, the aged slugger spent six more seasons in the high minors—with the nearby Rochester Redwings—and was just as popular in that city. Although Easter didn't start his minor league career in earnest until age 29 (he had earlier played 80 games for San Diego), he still collected 269 bush league homers.

Luke Easter's end was a violent one. In March 1979 he was working at the TRW, Inc., plant near Cleveland. After cashing his fellow employees' paychecks at a local bank, Easter was shot dead when he refused to hand over the cash he had just received for the checks.

Most of the outstanding minor league position players were fearsome hitters but butchers in the field. The exception to the rule was long-time Los Angeles Angels center fielder "Jigger" Statz, who was known as one of the finest flyhawks in all baseball history. Statz, who spent his entire 18-season bush league career with Los Angeles, was such a good fielder that whenever any other Angels outfielder would fail to make a play, chagrined Los Angeles fans would scream, "Jigger would have had it."

He could also hit. Statz collected 200 or more safeties in 10 separate Angels seasons and still holds career Pacific Coast League marks for games played (2,790), runs scored (1,996), hits (3,356), doubles (595), and triples (137). He is also fourth in the all-time minor league list for runs scored and sixth in hits.

The multi-talented Statz was also one of the finest golfers ever to play baseball, and obtained his nickname from one of his favorite irons, an implement known as a "jigger."

That Statz could not find a niche in the majors is somewhat amazing. In his only full major league season (1931), he batted .313 and slugged .538 with 18 homers in 121 games. Granted, 1931 was a hitter's year, but one would think a club might find a spot for a defensive specialist with a .313 average.

On another level is the fame attained by a player known just as "Wilson." This young outfielder joined Junction City of the Class D Central League before World War I. He slashed the ball hard, compiling a .355 average, and ran the bases with abandon. Then he suddenly disappeared. Ordinarily this would be the end of the story, except for one thing—this busher was West Point cadet Dwight Eisenhower. Appropriately the Junction City club was known as the "Soldiers."

It's been said that every major league record—save that of Lou Gehrig's 2,130 game playing streak—has been bettered in the minors.

Even the schedule was larger than life in the bushes. Blessed with good warm weather, the Pacific Coast League could play from mid-March to mid-November—and often did. "The best thing about a long season," recalled slugger Dale Long, "was that you had a short off-season; there were less days you had to carry a lunch bag to the factory."

In 1903 the PCL carded a 225-game schedule and former major league outfielder George Van Haltren batted an amazing 941 times. The year before, Los Angeles coasted to a 133-78 record, and in 1925 the Salt Lake City Bees' Tony Lazzeri drove home 225 runs while smashing 60 homers.

An excellent trick question: Joe DiMaggio holds the record for most consecutive games, one or more base hits, in baseball history. How many games, for what team, and when? The answer is *not* 56 games, the New York Yankees, 1941. In 1933, with San Francisco, DiMaggio connected in 61 straight contests. So such feats were old hat to DiMag by the time he reached Yankee Stadium.

Even the times of games go to fantastic lengths. On September 19, 1910, the Southern Association's Mobile Sea Gulls and Atlanta Crackers decided to see just how fast nine innings could be played. The answer was 32 minutes, and Mobile even turned a triple play to keep things moving along. Ironically, on the same day, in the same league, Chattanooga and Nashville played a game lasting only 42 minutes.

As for the *longest* game, look no further than the 33-inning marathon that began at Pawtucket's McCoy Stadium on April 18, 1981. The PawSox and the visiting Rochester Red Wings battled to a 2-2 deadlock, until the game was suspended after 32 innings at 4:07 A.M. on April 19. When the action resumed on June 23, it took only 18 minutes to come to a decision, with Dave Koza scoring on a Marty Barrett single. Bob Ojeda got the win. Future superstars Cal Ripken, Jr., (with Rochester) and Wade Boggs (with Pawtucket) went an aggregate 6-for-25. Time of game: eight hours and seven minutes.

And trades can be interesting, too. While not being able to shake the baseball world by exchanging players of the Jose Canseco or Fred McGriff category, there *is* room for more imaginative swapping. Chattanooga Lookouts owner Joe Engle proved that when he dealt shortstop Johnny Jones to Charlotte of the Sally League for a 25-pound turkey.

But Engel's swap was by no means unique in minor league annals. In 1913, infielder Buzzy Wares was left behind by the St. Louis

Browns at Montgomery when they couldn't pay for renting the Black Sox' ballpark. Omaha's Barney Burch once bartered two players for an airplane.

In 1928, the Mississippi Valley League's Rock Island Islanders sent infielders Frank Walczak and Sammy Schwartz to the Moline Plowboys for second sacker Karl "Peanuts" Swanson and his pet terrier "Rusty." Named to play DH ("Designated Hound") by Moline manager Pat Patterson, "Rusty" helped spark a couple of rallies with his obnoxious yelping. League president Beldon Hill responded by barring the pooch from the Plowboys' dugout.

Similar trades involved Booth Hopper, whom Pongo Joe Contillon once exchanged for a bird dog, and southpaw Glenn Darrough, whom the Dallas Steers' Fred McJunkin also swapped for a hunting dog.

McJunkin also once tendered pitcher Joe Martina of Dallas his release for two barrels of oysters. Martina wanted to leave Dallas to accept a managerial post in the Cotton States League.

In September 1930, San Antonio Texas League magnate Homer Hammond dispatched infielder Mike Dondero to Dallas for 12 doughnuts. After completing the deal, Dallas owners—George and Julius Schepps—allegedly consumed three of the fry cakes. In 1989 the California League's Reno Silver Sox traded pitcher Tim Fortugno to the Brewers' system for $2,500, plus a gross of baseballs.

As trades are a little different, so are some of the games. On July 12, 1952 the Fitzgerald Pioneers of the Class D Georgia State League being shellacked, 13-0, by the rival Statesboro Pilots. Enemy fans taunted: "Put in the batboy." Fitzgerald's new manager, Charlie Ridgeway, figured things couldn't get any worse and signalled 12-year-old batboy Joe Reliford to pinch hit for the team's leading slugger. The black Reliford slashed a seeing-eye hit between third and short and then went out to right field where he made a spectacular diving catch of a ball hit by Statesboro player-manager Charlie Quimby, thus ending Quimby's 21-game hitting streak.

League president Bill Estroff was not amused. He fined Ridgeway and fired umpire Ed Kubick, who had allowed the stunt.

C.B. DeWitt wasn't 12 years old, but he was the owner's son, and, on June 15, 1902, the boss insisted that he get a chance to pitch. Manager Cy Mulkey did just that, leaving him in for a full nine innings as the Corsicana Oil Citys defeated Texarkana, 51-3. That Texas League contest saw Corsicana hammer out 53 hits, including 21 homers. Part of the reason for the slugfest was a ban on Sabbath ball in Texarkana. The game in question had been moved out of that city to nearby Ennis, whose ballpark was decidedly on the cozy side.

Corsicana's catcher, a 19-year old Canadian named Justin "Nig" Clarke, hit eight homers in eight times at bat, scored eight runs and had 16 RBI and 32 total bases—all professional records. Not surprisingly, Texarkana disbanded early the following month.

On the last night of the 1942 Piedmont League season, manager Harry Smythe decided to totally juggle his lineup and sent catcher Odell Barberry to the mound. Barberry, whose contract had just been purchased by Washington, had long boasted to his team's hurlers about his legendary high school pitching record. Now he was put to the test. After a shaky start he settled down and began to routinely mow down the Asheville Hornets' batters. The game went into extra innings with the score tied 3-3. He continued to pitch, inning after inning, until his teammates finally pushed across a run in the last of the 22nd. Barberry had hurled the longest game in the history of the Piedmont League, damaging his arm in the process. When the game was over, he had a small confession to make to his teammates. "I'll have to tell you the truth," he drawled, "I never pitched a game before today in my life."

Just before the delivery was banned, Dallas spitballer Snipe Conley was working against the Wichita Falls Spudders in the Texas League. Around about the third inning his tongue began to swell up savagely, and by the fifth it was so painfully swollen and burnt that he left the game. Texas A&M's chemistry department later discovered that Wichita Falls had applied a creosote derivative to the ball to stymie Conley.

Former major league infielder Rocky Bridges managed for quite some time in the minors. Once, as he was coaching third, he suddenly started giving signals while standing on his head. The batter, a fellow named Ethan Allen Blackaby, fell into the spirit of the event and promptly stood on *his* noggin to receive the signs.

When Bill Veeck and Charlie Grimm were running the American Association's Milwaukee Brewers, they were thoroughly miffed by the poor level of lighting at rival Columbus' ballyard. The Brewers, after all, could barely hit pitching they *could* see, let alone connect in semi-darkness with the hard-throwing St. Louis farmhands' serves. To protest, the Milwaukee players wore miners' caps on the field, the coaches took lanterns to their stations, and second baseman "Packy" Rogers spent his spare time in the infield taking readings on a light meter.

At Indianapolis, the next stop on the Brewers' schedule, the team found the situation even worse. The Indians refused to turn the lights on at all for Brewers batting practice. Fortunately, the team still had their lanterns. They set them up on the batting cage and nonchalantly went about their business.

Some famous folks have toiled in the minors before reaching their stardom—and we are not talking about going to the majors. Country-and-western singer Charlie Pride performed in the Reds' and Yankees' chains and he paid his own way to spring training with the 1962 Mets, but Casey Stengel refused to take a look at him. On the way home he stopped off at Nashville, and the rest was history.

United States Senator Pete Dominici pitched briefly in the West Texas-New Mexico League, going 0-1 in three games with the Albuquerque Dukes. Once he was reminiscing to a Washington political reporter about legendary home run king Joe Bauman and how, while Joe could easily collect four-baggers for Roswell, he could never hit at a higher classification. "Once around the league," advanced Dominici, "and Joe was on the Trailways, with a sack of ham sandwiches big enough to get him across Texas. He couldn't hit Southern Association pitching."

The he thought again, and admitted: "Well, he could hit mine."

In 1952 former St. John's University star M. Matthew Cuomo was offered a $2,000 bonus to play for Pittsburgh. They sent him down to Brunswick in the Class D Georgia-Florida League where he was hitting a solid .353 before crashing into an outfield fence and injuring his wrist. He kept playing, going 0-for-32. That August, Cordele's John Barbier drilled him in the back of the head with a pitch. Cuomo was knocked out cold. Someone ran out with a cup of water for Cuomo. The umpire drank it.

A blood clot formed near Cuomo's brain, and he was hospitalized for two weeks. By season's end his average had slumped to .244. Like Charlie Pride, M. Matthew Cuomo (aka Mario M. Cuomo) went on to another career.

Comedian Dick Shawn pitched in the White Sox' chain in the 1950s. Screenwriter Ron Shelton (he created *Bull Durham* and *Cobb*) played in the Oriole system. Actor Kurt Russell was with the Sacramento Bees and the Portland Beavers before injuring his shoulder.

Soap opera star Drake Hogestyn (Roman Brady on *Days of Our Lives*) played for the New York-Penn League's Oneonta Yankees in the early 1970s under the name Donald Drake Hogestyn.

Famed Western novelist Zane Grey performed for a number of minor league clubs in the 1890s while he was preparing at the University of Pennsylvania for a career—dentistry. Signed in 1895 by Ed Barrow for Wheeling of the Interstate League, he got as far as Toronto of the Eastern (International) League in 1899. Outfielder Grey went on to write three baseball tomes—*The Shortstop*, *The Red-Headed Outfielder*, and *The Pitcher*. His brother, Romer Carl Grey played one game for Pittsburgh in 1903, going 1-for-3.

One of the least likely minor leaguers was songwriter Harry Ruby. Ruby, who penned Groucho Marx's theme song "Hooray for Captain Spalding!," had a reputation as baseball's greatest fan. That might very well have been true. A rabid Giants rooter, he transferred his loyalties to the PCL's Hollywood Stars when he moved west in the 1930s. In 1935 Ruby signed a contract with Stars owner Bill Lane, which had a few extra clauses thrown in:

> Player must report in perfect condition. Fines will be imposed on said player as follows: $50 for each time striking out with men on base; $100 for sleeping on the grass around second base; $20 for each error; $300 for each point under .300.

In the last game of the 1935 season, the Stars were losing to the visiting Mission Reds. It was 14-7, with two out and none on in the bottom of the ninth. Two thousand fans saw manager Frank Shellenback send Ruby up as a pinch hitter. Not to be outdone, the Missions' pilot called in screen comedian Joe E. Brown to pitch. Brown motioned his outfielders in to the mound, then calmly fanned the 40-year old Ruby.

Ruby killed not only the inning, the game, and the season—he killed the franchise. A few months later the Angels moved to San Diego and became the Padres.

Some minor leaguers have turned to other sports. Randy Poffo appeared at Orangeburg in the Western Carolinas League before transforming himself into wrestling's Randy "Macho Man" Savage. NHL great Doug Harvey played four seasons with Ottawa of the

Class C Border League. Basketball Hall-of-Famer Bill Sharman hit .288 with Pueblo of the Western League. Carl Braun, an early Knicks star, pitched in the Yankee chain for the Canadian-American League's Amsterdam Rugmakers. "Funny thing about Carl Braun," recalled teammate Bunny Mick, "was, as great a basketball player as he was, usually a guy that has that kind of ability is a great competitor. Boy, he could find a way to lose a game!...If he was winning, 2-1, in the seventh inning, you could pretty well figure he was planning on losing. Unbelievable." Going the other way, heavyweight champion Gentleman Jim Corbett played in one game for the Eastern League's Rochester Brownies in 1897. He went 0-for-4.

It was a minor league club that gave CBS newsman Charles Kuralt his start in journalism. At age 13 Kuralt moved from Atlanta to Charlotte, transferred his loyalties from the Atlanta Crackers (and a young announcer by the name of Ernie Harwell) to the local Hornets. The next year Kuralt entered a contest sponsored by the *Charlotte News*. He won, and his prize was a road trip with the Hornets and the opportunity to file a series of stories on the team. His work so impressed the Hornets' radio outlet they hired the teenager as their color man.

So, the first time Charles Kuralt went "On The Road," it was for a bush league nine.

Some minor leaguers become known for a single incident. In June 1991 Vancouver Canadians right fielder Rodney McCray literally crashed through to his 15 minutes of fame. In the seventh inning at Portland's Civic Stadium, McCray was galloping full-tilt after a flyball when he ran straight through a park's plywood fence. He didn't catch the ball, but video of his daring-do went across both Canada and the USA. Luckily, he was not seriously injured, merely incurring a small cut over his right eye and staying in the field for the rest of the inning.

"I was really just concentrating on catching the ball and had no idea I was that close to the fence," McCray admitted. "I didn't hear anything from [center fielder] Aubrey Waggoner. Usually you communicate, but this particular time there wasn't any."

For his efforts the advertiser whose sign he demolished munificently bestowed on McCray some golf balls, a jacket, and a hat as well as making a $1,000 donation in his honor to the United Negro College Fund.

"If he had hit the Coca-Cola sign, he'd never have to work the rest of his life," chortled Vancouver pitching coach Moe Drabowsky.

Then there was Williamsport Bills catcher Dave Bresnahan. On Labor Day 1987, Bresnahan successfully (well, almost successfully) developed a new variation on the old hidden-ball trick—the hidden-potato trick.

The Reading Phillies' Rick Rudblad was on third when Bresnahan (a relative of Hall-of-Famer Roger Bresnahan) attempted a pick-off throw. His toss went into left field, and Rudblad scampered home. When he arrived, Bresnahan had the ball waiting for him, since what he had thrown seconds earlier was no horsehide-covered spheroid, but instead a peeled potato.

The umpire ruled Rudblad safe. The official scorer gave Bresnahan an error, and the Eastern League fined him $50. "I thought it'd be a do-over," theorized Bresnahan.

The Philadelphia Phillies failed to find such inventiveness amusing and released Bresnahan the following day. Perhaps his .149 batting average influenced their decision. The local ballclub, however, wasn't about to mash such an opportunity for a promotion and announced they would admit any fan into the park for one dollar—plus a potato. Bresnahan was on hand to autograph each potato with the inscription: "This spud's for you."

Yes, there is a sense of deviltry in the minors, but yet there is a sense of nobility—of men toiling in some great lost cause or just for the love of a child's game. "Aside from the glory, the fame, the money, the groupies, or the status," wrote Howard Senzel, "was the internal drama of the game. In the minor leagues, the game was played mostly by grown men who would never be famous and would never be rich, men who would travel by rented school bus and always stay in flea-bag hotels. They were grown men who had to sacrifice money and comfort in order to play. And that is the kind of heroism that is larger and more noble than any kind of superhuman dexterity."

FUN AND GAMES

In the majors nowadays you need two things to make money:
1. A winning team
2. A payroll somewhere under $30 million

Minor league franchises have no problems with point two, but even a pennant-winning club can plunge pretty deeply in the red ink. In the majors, after all, fans are bombarded with information about their team's players: on TV, radio, in newspapers, around the water cooler at work. In the minors the cast is always shifting and is invariably unknown. Even if you win the Eastern League or American Association championship, it's a sad fact that no one beyond the stadium parking lot may know—or care.

That's where the promotion department comes in. In Shakespeare the play's the thing. In the minors it's also the concessions, the business-sponsored buyouts, the giveaways, the mascots, and the celebrity appearances. In fact, most of the time it seems it's anything *but* the game of baseball. Make it a happening. Pump up the volume on the PA system and turn the park into a party zone is the philosophy. Make it fan-friendly, keep it cheap, and, above all, remember that the fans can watch major league ball for free in air-conditioned comfort at home.

Buffalo Bisons General Manager Mike Billoni will never be mistaken for Bill Veeck or Joe Engel. He isn't colorful; he's just the most successful minor league operator (in terms of putting fannies in the seats) of all time. It's a shame nobody's ever heard of him, but each year from 1988 through 1993 Buffalo attracted over a million fans per season and saw their streak severed in 1994 only because of an abysmal last-place team and two rain outs which saw their total stall at 982,493. From 1988 through 1991 the Bisons outdrew at least one big league franchise. In 1988 the Bisons outpaced three: the Braves, White Sox, and Mariners:

Year	Bisons	White Sox	Mariners	Braves	Indians	Expos
1988	1,147,651	1,115,525	1,020,354	848,089	1,411,610	1,478,659
1989	1,116,441	1,045,651	1,298,456	984,930	1,285,542	1,783,533
1990	1,174,358	2,555,688	1,509,705	980,129	1,225,241	1,373,087
1991	1,188,972	2,934,154	2,147,905	2,140,217	1,051,863	978,045

"We know we don't have superstar players, so the concessions are our superstars," said Bisons owner Bob Rich, a fellow whose fortune not coincidentally comes from the food industry. "We know a team is going to lose about half of its games and the fans will be disappointed about half the time. In addition to baseball, we want them to have some other attraction. So even if the team doesn't win, we want the fan to say, 'That was the best Italian sausage sandwich I ever had and I'll be back for another one.' "

Bob Rich's sausage sandwiches notwithstanding, the Hagerstown Suns (now in the South Atlantic League, but for many years an Eastern League franchise) boast having the best chow in the minors. They just might be right, featuring awesome homemade barbecue pork sandwiches, funnel cakes, steamers ("Hagerstown's Answer to the Sloppy Joe"), one-third-of-a-pound burgers for just two bucks and—for you fast-food junkies—Pizza Hut Pan Pizza.

Hagerstown, however, cannot lay claim to discovering a simple idea that has resulted in many calories and even more profits: the concept of selling ice cream in a souvenir plastic batting helmet. That honor goes to the Nashville Sounds' Larry Schmittou, who came up with the idea back in the late '70s.

Many franchises enjoy local specialties such as catfish sandwiches at Jackson (MS), chicken spiedies (chicken marinated and then barbecued) at Binghamton, salt potatoes (delicious new potatoes boiled in salt) at Syracuse, beef on a weck (a roast beef sandwich on a salted hard roll) in Buffalo and boiled peanuts at Columbus, Georgia. Local calories have clearly augmented local color.

Enclosed restaurants, such as Pilot Field's Pettibones Grill, Tuft's at Ottawa's Rosenblatt Stadium, or the Cub Club at Iowa's Sec Taylor

Stadium are increasingly more commonplace—and more opulent. Even El Paso's open-air Hardball Cafe serves such delicacies as filet mignon and swordfish. Of course, where lavish facilities are lacking, imaginative fans have been known to make their own atmosphere. Each night, two fans at Pittsfield's old, wooden Wahconah Park sip fine wine and munch grapes by the light from candlesticks balanced on the ledge of their front row seats.

Does the Pittsfield Fire Department know about this?

It's sad to say, but fear of cholesterol has even invaded the sacred confines of America's minor league ballparks, where unhealthy eating is a glorious way of life. Pushing aside the humble hot dog and whatever that stuff is atop the nachos, are such nutritious (but somehow emotionally unsatisfying) items as the vegetable platter that was offered at Salt Lake City's Derks Field. "We are a health-conscious community in Salt Lake," explained General Manager Dave Baggot. "When people bring their kids out to a ball game, they don't want 'em filling up on junk food. It sounds kind of bland, but dip 'em in ranch sauce and it tastes quite nice."

As someone once snorted: "I say it's spinach, and I say the hell with it."

And, in a world where vendors at movie theaters ask: "Would you like the $10 or $15 popcorn?" all the razzmatazz of a minor league experience can be had at bargain basement prices—including admission. The Hagerstown Suns typified how cheaply one can gain entrance to a minor league venue. During five homestands the local Wal-Mart made available $2 general admission tickets. Every Wednesday, one could sneak in for half-price, courtesy of Wendy's. Tuesdays and Thursdays were Knothole Gang Nights, with members admitted for two bits.

"One of the principles is getting you to come out there and then keeping you coming back," remarked former Eastern League president Charlie Eschbach, "Instead of the old days where some fans owned and operated the team, we're getting businessmen who can better operate it.

"But the basic fact is, [minor league baseball] is a good economic buy. If you've spent $20 at a game, you've spent a lot. At some places, they won't park your car for less than $20."

Said former Frederick Keys general manager Keith Lupton: "Once we get the people to the ballpark and they say, 'Gee, isn't this a pretty stadium, and look how close we are to the action,' they'll see ballplayers who make $1,000 a month and enjoy signing autographs, without the super big egos.

"They will also be able to buy a hot dog for a buck and a soft drink for 75 cents, and that's why we will draw close to a quarter-million people."

And, of course, minor league promoters provide far more than baseball to amuse their fans. Everything from cow-milking contests to camel races have been given a try. Allegedly the first minor league promotion was held in the 1890s at Dayton, when a woman parachuted out of a hot air balloon and into the ballpark. Her aim was far better than that of Mitch Williams, and she landed right at second base.

The stunts have not slowed down since. At Schenectady, New York, in August 1946 popular outfielder Lee Riley (father of basketball coach Pat Riley) was awarded a pig. Young Pat and his five siblings feasted on pork and ham and bacon for much of the off-season.

There have been the aforementioned camel races, plus greased pig races and horse races. In 1977 at Modesto in the California League, A's outfielder Rickey Henderson (then a minor leaguer) was matched against a horse. He lost.

Then there are appeals to human greed—always a guaranteed draw. Like many franchises, the Hagerstown Suns have sponsored "Diamond Digs," an amusing celebration of distaff rapacity. Under this promotion, a local jeweler donates a diamond, which is buried under the mound. After the game, female fans descend on the field and proceed to rip the mound—and often each other—apart in search of buried treasure.

Good fun for everyone.

The Carolina League's Prince William Cannons have attempted their own version of the diamond dig. The Cannons hand out ice cubes to the first 500 ladies attending their promotion. Inside 499 are cubic zirconiums. Inside one, a real diamond, valued at $2,000.

In yet another variation on the "Diamond Dig," money was simply scattered around the diamond, and the some lucky fans get the chance to battle over it. The Tacoma club once staged a "Dash for Cash Night" in which a Brinks armored car pulled onto the field and dumped $1 million in coins on the ground. Most of the coins were nickels and pennies, however, and the "lucky" fans, who got just two minutes to snatch up as much cash as possible, were fortunate to scamper away with more than five bucks in loose change.

Not so amusing was "Free Money on The Field Night" at El Paso. "Those people turned into animals," admitted El Paso Diablos owner Jim Paul. "They tore up the field." Paul did not repeat the event.

Diamonds are not always a girl's best friend; sometimes a little male companionship doesn't hurt. The Southern League's Orlando SunRays once carded a "Blind Date Night" in which single women were sold even-numbered seats and bachelors were assigned odd-numbered ones. Keeping with the theme, female patrons were provided with roses, and strolling violinists serenaded moonstruck fans. There is no confirmation as to whether heart-shaped nachos were sold by vendors.

A fairly recent addition to the minor league promotion bag-of-tricks has been what might be called "Revenge of the Mutant Fuzzy Dice." A pair of dice about three-feet square are rolled on the field with lucky fans winning the usual array of goodies. Fans may spastically toss the dice themselves or as at Syracuse—and this is a lot more fun to watch—see the dice tossed off the grandstand roof.

Back in May 1989, the South Atlantic League's Charleston Wheelers had been rained out nine straight times. In desperation, General Manager Dennis Bastien scheduled "Noah Night."

The concept was simple. "Anybody who came dressed as any kind of an ark animal and came two by two, we let in free," recalled Bastien. "And anybody who came dressed as Noah, we let in free. And anybody who brought along a toy boat, we let in for a dollar. We had a couple of hundred crazies come out with horns on. One guy wore a rhinoceros nose. Some came in with antlers they got off their father's gun rack. And, of course, it rained. In the fourth inning, it rained."

In 1993 the Fort Myers' Miracle came up with a particularly inventive special events schedule that included the following:

- •April 30: "Murder Most Foul," a murder mystery staged by the ballplayers
- •May 1: "Salute To Henry Wallace Night" in honor of FDR's left-wing vice president who he dumped from the ticket to make room for Harry Truman
- •August 16: "Two Dead Fat Guys Night"

I have no idea what the last event was about, but as Dave Barry would say: I'm not making this up.

Gaining in popularity (at least until the first lawsuit) is the practice of "bat races." No, this doesn't pit players against winged nocturnal mammals. It involves having two kids bend over a bat and spin around it 10 or 15 times until they are good and dizzy. *Then*, they have to race toward some person or object. Usually, one or both of the contestants pitches over several times before reaching their goal or is so disoriented they race right past it. Somehow I think this violates the prohibition on "cruel or unusual punishment," but the sight of a small child keeling over face first always gets its share of laughs.

Not all fan-related gimmicks are knee-slappers, however. One of the *least* exciting gimmicks may have been Zoom-Floom Dugout Golf, introduced by the 1994 Albany-Colonie Yankees. The idea is for some embarrassed fan to perch atop the Yankee dugout and attempt putting three balls (golf not baseball) into a bucket. For most of the fans in the park the action is invisible. Even for those who can see the trajectory of the ball, it's still a yawn.

Folks who took a chance on minor league ball when it was struggling—and kept at it—prospered. In 1980 a former minor league executive named Miles Wolff put together a bankroll of $2,500 and bought the Carolina League's Durham Bulls. The operation (helped, no doubt, by the publicity generated by the film *Bull Durham*) is now worth an estimated $9 million. Yet, Wolff cautions, "If you get in this game for fun, you've gotten in it for the wrong reason. It is not fun. It is 16 hours a day of hard work. If you don't put in the time, you'll be out of the business in two years."

Jim Paul has similarly done well for himself at El Paso. In fact, he was once named Texas' Small Business Person of the Year. Of course, that success did not come without *its* bumps. "At one point, we had a bad year and I had to sell my house to keep the team afloat," Paul, whose only source of income is from the Diablos, once admitted. "My wife wasn't too happy about that."

One of the Diablos' attractions is their public address announcer Paul "The Mouth" Strelzin. For a long stretch Strelzin maintained a bumptious public feud with the rival Jackson Mets. At one point an infuriated Jackson manager even charged up through the stands and attempted to throttle Strelzin.

Strelzin is an equal opportunity announcer, annoying not only rival managers but also umpires. He holds the honor of being perhaps the only public address announcer ejected from a game. Strelzin was amusing himself by playing Linda Ronstadt's "When Will I Be Loved." When he got to the line, "I've been cheated, been mistreated," the umpire had enough and tossed him. "It was an accident, I swear," said a not-very-convincing Strelzin.

Strelzin has also gained a reputation for a trademark routine involving Diablo fans. Whenever his team scores with two out, he shouts into the microphone: "How many outs are there?" The El Paso crowd roars back: "Two!" At which point Strelzin barks, "And who scores more runs with two outs than any team in baseball?" To which they respond with every-increasing gusto: "Diablos!"

Is El Paso's boast based on empirical data? "I have no idea," admits Strelzin. "But the crowd loves it."

Giving Strelzin some competition is St. Paul Saints public address major domo Al Frechtman. Frechtman maintains his own steady stream of witticisms, including his rather sardonic description of the Northern League club's "Coca Cola Family Section:" "Remember, there's no alcohol, no smoking, no fun, and you're not allowed to keep any foul balls you catch."

"In Baseball you don't die with every loss," El Paso's Jim Paul once observed regarding his basic philosophy. "The other night we had the biggest crowd in the history of El Paso, and we got beat, 14-1. But we had a great fireworks display afterward, and everyone went home happy."

Hagerstown and Frederick once participated in a unique three-team, three-city, three-league, one-state tripleheader, the "Maryland Marathon Baseball Day." On Saturday, June 6, 1992, a fan could take in a morning Eastern League contest starting at 11:05 A.M. at Hagerstown in western Maryland, dash eastward for an afternoon Carolina League game (2:35 start) at Frederick, and end up at Baltimore's then-brand new Camden Yards for the 7:05 P.M. nightcap.

An environmental trend oozing slowly across the minors is the appearance of tuxedoed garbage men usually known as "Mr. Trash"—although an occasional "Miss Trash" has been spotted. These folks patrol the stadium arayed in formal finery (usually donated by a clothing rental store and often emblazoned with their name). With hefty bag in hand they take "donations" of refuse from fans otherwise only too happy to toss their paper cups and half-eaten wieners under their seats.

"I saw the stadium being constructed and I figured it would be a good place to work," said Ryan Thornburg, the 1993 "Mr. Trash" at Rancho Cucamonga. "But I didn't want the usual job flippin' burgers and stuff like that. I like to try new things…

"Some people want to have their pictures taken with me. It absolutely blows my mind."

Bat days, cap days, senior citizen days, Drug Awareness Nights—all are part of a typical minor league schedule. So are appearances by a roster of travelling entertainers specializing in the minor league circuit.

Lanky, rubber-limbed Max Patkin has been doing his act for nearly half a century. The Famous Chicken is the grandfather of all team mascots. The Dynamite Lady seals herself in a crate at second base and blows herself up with—what else?—dynamite. An earlier version of this blowed-up-good style of routine featured an increasingly geriatric fellow known as "Captain Dynamite." The Hollywood Starlets theoretically play softball. But few males in the stands could later attest to their athletic abilities. Morganna, the top-heavy "Kissing Bandit," whose appearances have been sponsored by such entities as Frederick, Maryland's "Beneath It All Lingerie," doesn't even *pretend* to have ability.

Ted Giannoulas' Famous Chicken (then known as the San Diego Chicken) launched a new generation of *major* league mascots in June 1979. The Chicken, hired originally to promote a local radio station, hatched his idea in April 1974, the very night San Diego owner Ray Kroc threw his famous tantrum, apologizing to customers for his team's poor play. It was also the same night a streaker ran onto the field at Jack Murphy Stadium, and Kroc screamed into the public address system for police to arrest him.

"I was so frightened," said Giannoulas, "I literally ran out of the stadium because I thought he was going to say, 'Get that Chicken too,' thinking by mistake I was representing Kentucky Fried Chicken or something."

By 1984 the Chicken had fallen out of favor with Padres officials, particularly Manager Jack McKeon. Barred from using the *nom de plume* "San Diego Chicken," he changed monikers and took his act on the road. Occasionally, he would reappear at Jack Murphy Stadium in full costume. On at least one occasion, uniformed security guards escorted him off the premises. Amused San Diego fans assumed it was all part of the act.

It wasn't.

"He's a legend, a hero," boasts his promotional material. "He's become the most outrageous comic since his San Diego hatching. The Famous Chicken is a phenomenon for the funnybone. He's the one and only. Catch him in the act and have a fowl ball."

The Chicken has recently added a new wrinkle to his routine—the "Chicks." Five moppets are recruited out of the stands and are zipped into miniature Chicken outfits. The highlight of their act is when Chicken and Chicks give the first base umpire the "hydrant salute." I won't provide details.

"Yes, it gets warm and can get a little gamey," admitted one Chick, "but if you can't stand the heat, get out of the chicken—or something like that."

The Famous Chicken's appearances do not come "cheep," but they are worth a team's investment. Says minor league magnate Miles Wolff: "If we spend $5,000 to bring the…Chicken to our ballpark, we know we'll sell enough seats plus concessions and parking to make a profit on his appearance."

The same goes for the other attractions on the minor league vaudeville circuit. Columnist Jim Murray has written that "[Max] Patkin is 6'3"; 30% of that is neck. He looks like the world's biggest hunk of bubblegum." Lanky, rubber-limbed Patkin's minor league career ended with a sore arm after just three seasons. Hired in 1946 to do a comedy act during an exhibition game featuring the Class B Interstate League's Harrisburg Senators and the big league Cleveland Indians, he caught Bill Veeck's eye and worked for the flamboyant impressario at both Cleveland and St. Louis.

On the day Veeck brought midget Eddie Gaedel in to pinch hit, Patkin joined the Browns. "I always say, 'My nose weighed more than the midget'," recounts Patkin. In 1951 Veeck hired Rogers Hornsby—a man with *no* sense of humor as Browns manager. His first demand was that Patkin had to go. He returned to barnstorming and has amused up to 2 million fans a year. The act is hardly sophisticated, relying largely on slapstick and mugging. It changes little from year to year or even from decade to decade, but maybe that's part of its charm. "If I had class," Patkin admits, "there'd be no act. My act has no class. It's just a funny-looking act."

Seeing Patkin doing his version of Old Faithful or going through his contorted gyrations in the first-base coach's box gives one a link not only to the baseball of today but to all the baseball clowns of decades past—the Al Schachts, the Nick Altrocks, the Jackie Prices. When Patkin appeared in the film *Bull Durham*, its producers wanted him to expire in the film and have his ashes scattered over the mound at Durham Athletic Park. The scene got left on the cutting room floor.

It hasn't all been laughs for Patkin. The travel has definitely taken its toll. "Nobody knows the mental anguish I go through between bus stops and plane stops," he once confessed. "Nobody knows the mental anguish I go through in a hotel room by myself."

But after he slouches onto the field he puts the pain behind him. "Once I get on the coaching lines I forget about the whole world," says Patkin. "It's like the whole world stops. I go out there, I become another person."

Non-baseball attractions also regularly appear at minor league parks, forming part of baseball-show biz twin bills. The Beach Boys and Reba McIntyre have wowed 'em in Buffalo; the Oak Ridge Boys, Chubby Checker, and the Turtles drew huge crowds at Omaha.

A star attraction, however, does not always guarantee a turnout. "In 1969," Patkin once recalled, "I was in Great Falls, Montana, and there were four ---ing people in the stands. *Four ---ing people*! You know why? That was the day the man walked on the moon for the first time…"

When you can't import a colorful character, create your own. A good number of clubs now feature their own mascots, from Oklahoma City's "Robo 89er" to Wilmington's "Rocky Bluewinkle" to Harrisburg's "Senator Rudy the Reindeer" to Scranton-Wilkes-Barre's "The Grouch" to Buffalo's "Buster Bison."

These upholstered creatures range from the good to the bad to the ugly. Naturally, not all are beloved. Some are just dopey or lackluster, and one—who shall remain nameless to protect the guilty—was positively offensive. Traveling to a nearby rival ballpark, our mystery mascot "got drunk, went berserk, climbed the fence, and threatened the fans" according to his club's owner, "I got a two-page letter from the other owner and had to let him go. He was out of there."

Many a major and minor league franchise has had its own mascot. Many have bafflingly excited fan interest with "dot races" on their messageboards. But only one franchise was eccentric enough to combine the two. That outfit was the now-defunct Palm Springs Angels.

With game-time temperatures, even for night contests, hovering in excess of a 100 degrees, the Angels had to try everything. They even sprayed fans with a fine mist to keep them from passing out. One evening, they threw "Open House Night" and let everyone in for free. But it was a trio of racing dots which put Palm Springs on the map. Three giant colored disks, wearing sun glasses, provided a real-life version (I guess this is real-life, although come to think of it, it may been a mirage) of the electronic race that tromps across scoreboard after scoreboard.

Perhaps the most noteworthy mascot, however, is El Paso's "Henry the Puffy Taco." *USA Today Baseball Weekly* describes Henry as "a life-size conglomeration of lettuce, cheese, tomatoes, arms and legs. But the real treat is Henry's jalapeno-pepper feet. Each game, he races kids around the bases, but never wins." Whether Henry's tootsies were covered by "No Pepper" edicts was not revealed.

Then there are giveaways. Anyone can hand out bats and gloves and caps and seat cushions and baseball cards, but we're looking for a little more *imagination* in this chapter. El Paso once gave away bottles of soap bubbles. "Yeah, it's great to see 5,000 people blowing bubbles in the stands," said Jim Paul. "It's like Lawrence Welk." The Albuquerque Dukes provide fake funny noses and glasses on—what else?—"Funny Noses and Glasses Night." And the Eastern League's Pittsfield club distributed sunglasses at a *night* game. "I did that when we put new lights in the park," said then-GM Pat McKernan, tongue planted firmly in cheek, "you know, so the fans wouldn't become blind."

Used Car Night at Buffalo proved to be less than a roaring success. "We had a 19-year-old kid who really needed a car, and he won," admitted General Manager Mike Billoni. "But it wouldn't start. Literally, the engine blew right on the field. It cost us a fortune to get that car fixed."

Minor league clubs even have their own team fight songs. One of the more interesting is that of the Carolina League's Frederick Keys. The Keys (named after Francis Scott Key, who is buried right next to Frederick's Harry Grove Stadium) are one of the lower minors' major success stories. Harry Grove Stadium is a jewel of a facility, and the Keys regularly outdraw not only most Class A clubs but also a goodly number of Class AA franchises. Aiding *esprit de corps* is a theme song which has fans not only singing along but jangling their car keys during the seventh-inning stretch.

Penned by local songwriters Holly Garber and Lou Phrang, the song was originally about the *Florida* Keys, but with a few minor changes (like just about *all* the words), it fits the bill for the ballclub. It goes like this:

> We're the Frederick Keys
> Come on out and support the Team
> Baseball is Back in Town You Can Hear that Shaking Sound
> Bring the Family.
> We're the Frederick Keys
> We'll Park One In the Bleachers (Scream - *Go Keys!*)
> Come On Now Shake 'em with Me
> We're The Frederick Keys!!

"I'm a real fan," says Garber. "We put the song together before there was even a team." The song became so popular Holly and Lou (as they are known professionally) issued a single featuring the ditty.

Not as popular as Holly and Lou's *magnus opus*, was the fight song of the ill-fated Hamilton Red Birds, a departed New York-Penn league franchise. Based on the Washington Redskins fight song ("Hail to the Redskins!"), the Hamilton jingle ("Hail to the Red Birds!"), however, failed to excite local fans. "They hated it," admits former owner Joe Vellano.

Minor league owners and general managers have discovered that they can market their teams just like the big boys do, selling everything from cracked bats to fantasy camps. In 1992 the minors disposed of $12 to $15 million in licensed merchandise. In a field increasingly filled with competitors, teams now modestly bill themselves as having the "*Hottest* New Logo in Minor League Baseball" or the "Best Name & Logo in the Game." Thar's gold in them thar logos.

"I don't think it's a fad," contends Albuquerque Dukes General Manager Pat McKernan of the minors' resurgence. "I think it's something that people look forward to enjoying. It's a smaller game, but we don't want to portray it as a mom-and-pop operation. Rather, we want to make it a game that you can get close to, which is something you can't get in the major leagues."

41

JUDGE BRAMHAM:
Czar of the Minors

Baseball commissioners haven't been quite the same since Judge Landis was finally called up to meet his maker. Frick to Eckert to Vincent hardly competes with Tinkers to Evers to Chance.

But just as Kenesaw Mountain Landis' reputation towers over that of his successors, so does that of his contemporary, a fellow "Judge" whose memory is similarly revered.

The jurist in question, "Judge" William G. Bramham, ruled the minors as its strong-willed Czar from December 1932 until just before his death in July 1947. Unlike Landis, who presided over the Federal Judiciary's Northern District of Illinois, the North Carolina-bred Bramham was a judge in name only—so christened by law school classmates for his somber mien.

The jowly Bramham was born on July 12, 1874, in Hopkinsville, Kentucky, but relocated to Durham, North Carolina, in his youth. He studied law at the University of North Carolina (graduating with an L.L.B. in 1905), prospered in the practice of corporate law, and dabbled in Republican politics.

In his younger, more svelte days, he played semi-pro ball and umpired and managed in such circuits. His first involvement with organized baseball came in 1902 when he was named president of the Class D North Carolina League's Durham Bulls. Bramham's debut was hardly auspicious: the club folded in mid-season.

In 1920 the Tar Heel State had been without minor league ball since the North Carolina State League had folded in 1917. Bramham responded by founding the Class D Piedmont League, serving as its president until 1932. Within a year the circuit had advanced in status to Class C. By 1925, Bramham became president of two more leagues, the Class B South Atlantic ("Sally") and Virginia Leagues. In 1928, he founded the Class D Eastern Carolina League and became the first man to simultaneously rule over four separate circuits. He also held a seat on the Minors' National Board of Arbitration.

The Great Depression took its toll on baseball. Minor leagues dropped like flies, and National Association President Michael Sexton — with a tenure of 22 years — resigned in December 1931. A five-man executive committee (consisting of Bramham, Joe Carr, Warren Giles, J. Alvin Gardner, and Ross Harriott) took over. In late 1932, it unanimously chose Bramham as National Association president.

The minors had been on the ropes when Bramham assumed the reins. Only 15 circuits finished the 1932 season. And in December of that year only five leagues professed themselves ready to go for 1933. But by Opening Day 14 circuits had been rounded up and miraculously, in that worst year of the Great Depression—all 14 finished the season. In a single year Bramham had so turned things around that he was tendered a new five-year contract and a $2,500 raise.

"President Bramham's first year in office was marked by splendid progress and administration," noted *Spalding's Guide*. "Under his guidance numerous territorial liens were cleared up, routine work was systematized, and in general a better understanding was outlined of obligations to the public and the game."

One of the key elements in Bramham's success was his war on the practice of fly-by-night "shoestring" or "firecracker" leagues. Such circuits were loosely funded and organized and would often fold just after the Fourth of July.

Bramham saw that legislation was adopted, wrote National Association Secretary L. H. Addington in *Spalding's Guide*, making the " 'shoestring operators' future earnings from any source in base ball applicable to debts occurred in the past, regardless of location. This action it is believed will do more to strengthen public confidence in the game than any legislation enacted by the Association in recent years." Bramham also required that clubs provide salary deposits for players, an overdue reform that had been talked about for over two decades.

Bramham also dealt with the issue of liens against defunct franchises. Previously, there was a five-year ban against a club going into a territory in which liens still existed against a bankrupt franchise.

Bramham ended the ban, allowing the National Association's executive officers to permit baseball's return to such areas. But any new club was committed to setting aside a portion of its receipts to clear away its predecessor's debts. In an atmosphere where so many clubs had gone under, Bramham had swept away a troublesome roadblock to the minors' swift recovery.

Bramham also encouraged the new practice of night baseball (begun in force in the spring of 1930), although he was painfully aware it was a shock to the system of what he termed the "old guard which had watched and fostered the game under sunlight." He was more reluctant in his support of the so-called "Shaughnessy Playoffs," named after Montreal Royals executive Frank J. Shaughnessy. In order to preserve fan interest when pennant races were winding down, four-club post-season playoffs were scheduled in most minor circuits.

Bramham, however, was no fan at all of the ballyhoo that such practitioners as Joe Engel and Bill Veeck would employ to lure fans into minor league parks. "Damn the monkeyshines," he complained, but there was normally little he could do about it.

Aiding Bramham in saving minor league ball was a trusty assistant, Joe F. Carr. One of Bramham's first acts was to name Carr the National Association's promotional director. His job was twofold: to aid leagues in promoting their product and to help organize new leagues. The goal: "a membership that will match that of the Association's peak mark."

Carr was no amateur. In 1916 he was elected president of the Class D Ohio State League and in the mid-1920s helped organize the Tri-State League. Additionally, he served as president of the National Football League and as first president of the American Basketball League. As ABL leader Carr had cracked the whip, pledging rules "would be drastic regarding discipline, and fines and other penalties are provided for covering misconduct of any kind either by players, managers or spectators." He assisted Bramham at the National Association until his death in the late 1930s.

A controversy Bramham ruled on in 1935 involved convicted armed robber Edwin Collins "Alabama" Pitts. Pitts, a Sing Sing inmate, was offered a contract by the International League's Albany Senators on his release from prison. Bramham advised Albany management not to sign Pitts, feeling the move was a cheap, exploitative publicity stunt. "My decision is that ex-convicts will not be permitted to contract with the clubs of the National Association," said Bramham. The International League and the National Association's Executive Committee backed Bramham, but Albany appealed to Commissioner Landis who allowed Pitts to take his place in organized ball.

Bramham was an unwavering foe of on-field rowdyism, particularly violence against officials. For example, on September 16, 1942, Richmond Colts' player-manager Ben Chapman slugged Piedmont League umpire I. H. Case. Bramham banned the former American League outfielder from the game for an entire year. Oddly enough by 1944 Chapman was back in the majors—as a pitcher.

On September 2, 1941 Bramham suspended outfielder Frederick Shoemaker of the Class D Pennsylvania State Association's Oil City Oilers. His crime: spitting tobacco juice in the face of official scorer Joe Szarfaro, a sportswriter with the *Oil City Blizzard*.

Not that Bramham was in favor of violence *by* officials. Back in 1939, Texas League umpire William Wilson drew a knife when he was "menaced" by players during a San Antonio-Fort Worth game. Bramham handed Wilson a 90-day suspension for "conduct detrimental to baseball." Wilson appealed his sentence but was denied recourse.

The minors climbed back steadily under Bramham, from 14 leagues in 1933 to 20 in 1934, 21 in 1935, 26 in 1936, 37 in 1937-38, 41 in 1941, and 44 in 1940. In those years only two leagues failed to complete a season.

Bramham was given another five-year term on December 5, 1939, along with a $5,000 raise, thus bringing his annual salary to a hefty $25,000. In December 1944 he was again re-elected National Association czar but not without controversy. During the war most minor loops had folded, but these dormant leagues had each been given inactive status.

International League President Frank Shaughnessy challenged Bramham and had the support of five (the American Association, International, Pacific Coast, Piedmont, and PONY leagues) of the surviving nine leagues. Earlier Bramham ruled that the inactive circuits would have no vote. Now he reversed himself and allowed that the 15 dormant (but still dues-paying) leagues could cast ballots, citing Section 25 of the National Association Agreement: "membership and territorial rights shall terminate . . . unless renewed before Sept. 1."

Bramham posited that since each inactive club had sent in their renewal in the prescribed time-frame their membership — including voting rights — was intact.

"This gets down to a wrestling match as to who shall run the association, those in business or those on the sidelines," remarked Milwaukee's Bill Veeck, a Shaughnessy partisan. Syracuse's C. M. Schindler was so upset he stormed out of the session.

The handwriting was on the wall for the Shaughnessy forces, and they refused to place their candidate's name in nomination. Bramham won another five-year term (at a $25,000 annual salary) by a 18-0 vote, but those supporting Shaughnessy later appealed the entire procedure to Judge Landis. He refused to overrule Bramham.

Nonetheless, at Los Angeles in December 1946, at the National Association's annual meetings, a failing Bramham announced his resignation.

Bramham's final months as minor league czar were marked by rising concerns about gambling. At the session in which he announced his retirement he excoriated gamblers as "these 'roaches' who have become a menace to the game."

He continued: "For the first time in professional baseball since the so-called Black Sox scandal there has been strong circumstantial evidence this past season of players throwing games, betting against their clubs, and being in collusion with gamblers and bookmakers.

"In several cases it was found these gamblers were congregating in such numbers they were blocking the aisles in the grand stands and crying out their odds like auctioneers."

In August of 1946 he banned for life South Atlantic League outfielder Hooper Triplett, brother of Coaker Triplett. The right-handed batting Triplett, who hit .313 in 61 games for the pennant-winning Columbus Cardinals, had committed the near-ultimate baseball crime of betting against his own club. Triplett had said he had done it as a "joke," but it was no laughing matter to Bramham.

"The act of the player is a reflection on the game and his profession," noted Bramham, "but the greatest injury is to the player himself. If he remained in baseball, this act would relentlessly follow him. Though he might play his heart out to win, every excusable error he might make, every strikeout charged against him however hard he might try to hit, would find the cry, 'How much have you bet on the game?' ringing in his ears."

Even after Bramham's retirement (the National Association retained him for life as a $10,000-a-year consultant), he handled yet another major gambling case. It was not a pleasant episode in minor league history.

As the 1946 season ended, rumors swirled regarding events in the Class D Evangeline League. Seven players on two clubs were accused of throwing playoff contests. On January 18, 1947 Bramham banned five of them: right-handed pitcher William C. Thomas, center fielder Lanny Pecou, third baseman Alvin W. Kaiser, and first baseman Paul Fugit, all members of the Houma Indians; and catcher Don Vettorel of the fourth-place Abbeville Athletics.

Bramham wrote:

> Called upon to find as a fact that a game of baseball has been thrown, in the absence of a confession or most positive proof, is a precarious assignment. In the case of the investigation here dealt with, there are positive allegations and circumstantial evidence to support them. On the other hand each of the players enter [sic] a vigorous denial. I have a very definite personal opinion in the premises, but do not find it necessary to predicate any finding of guilt as to this allegation based upon that opinion. There is sufficient other conduct detrimental to baseball established by the record to justify the decision now rendered.

The 41-year-old Thomas (a 383-game winner in the minors) was particularly vehement in his protestations of innocence. In 1946 he had gone 35-7. With a 5-0 playoff record there was some logic behind his assertion of innocence. In August 1949 both Thomas and Pecou were reinstated by Bramham's successor George Trautman.

However, as Bramham took pains to note, it was not for throwing games that any of the five were banned. Thomas — much like the Black Sox' Buck Weaver — admitted to guilty knowledge of at least two attempts to fix contests. In 1945 Thomas' roommate, Babe Benning, introduced a man to Thomas who asked him to throw a game. A year later teammate Alvin Kaiser presented to him a bookie who offered Thomas a substantial amount of money if he threw three or four games. According to Thomas, he told the gambler: "You are not talking to me." More importantly, however, he did not inform anyone about either of these contacts.

"The failure to inform club and league officials," ruled Bramham, "of any attempt by any one to induce a player to throw a game or to do other than render one hundred per cent service to his club and duty to the public is most reprehensible contact and detrimental to the game."

Neither Kaiser nor Fugit bothered to appear before Bramham. Kaiser wrote to Bramham and admitted his part in a fixed race horse bet, but failed to see how this had anything to do with baseball. Thomas alleged Kaiser was employed by a bookie in the off-season and that both Kaiser and Lanny Pecou lived with that bookie for a period of time. Don Vettorel was accused of flashing around $600 and bragging he had earned it "manipulating games." He denied the charge and rebutted that he was being railroaded by "race track bookies" who had a personal animus toward him.

Bramham barely survived his ruling on this case. He died July 8, 1947, and his reputation as a forceful, honest dedicated leader of the minors was such that he was proposed for induction into baseball's Hall of Fame.

HOWARD GREEN:
Minor League Missionary

Except for the new independent leagues, bush league organization is largely cut-and-dried these days, governed pretty much by major league moneybags. But long ago, the minors were independent, not limited in size by how many working agreements would be doled out. One result was dedicated individuals who would spread the gospel from circuit to circuit like so many horsehide Johnny Appleseeds.

Specifics? From 1926 to 1932 former major league pitcher-out-fielder Dale Gear served for seven seasons (1926-32) simultaneously as president of both the Class A Western League and the Class C Western Association. In 1929-30, L.J. Wylie did the same with the Central and Three-I leagues. William Bramham led the Piedmont, Virginia, Sally, and Eastern North Carolina Leagues. Even earlier in the century colorful Alfred Lawson claimed to have founded 16 different circuits.

We won't see their like again, but we can still chat with Texas' Howard Green, who has similar credentials — president of four separate circuits; the Longhorn, Big-State, Gulf States, and Gulf Coast Leagues; club owner in the West-Texas-New Mexico League; and business manager in the Western League.

Well, unlike the old joke about Carnegie Hall, Howard didn't get there by practicing, he followed Bo Jackson's advise and "just did it."

Howard Green grew up in the west Texas town of Swenson in the 1920s and '30s. He was a baseball fan from the very beginning. "On the outskirts of Swenson in Uncle John Freeman's pasture, I was watching baseball at the age of three," says Green. "That's my first recollection. By 1929, I was eight and reading the sports pages with a religious fervor.

"Swenson had only three radios. One of them belonged to Guy Southern, the depot agent. When not impatiently waiting for the school bell to ring, I was at Guy's house on September and October afternoons listening to broadcasts of Dallas and Wichita Falls in the Texas League playoff, Dallas and Birmingham in the Dixie Series, and Joe McCarthy's Chicago Cubs and Connie Mack's A's in the World Series.

"Guy taught me how to keep a box score. Years later, as an official in the West Texas-New Mexico League, I didn't vary from his system."

Green grew older, played sandlot and semi-pro ball, and caught at McMurry College, where he obtained a degree in Business Administration. He moved to Abilene in 1936 and in 1939 got his first job in baseball, as assistant official scorer for the Class D Abilene Apaches. The Apaches bit the dust, however, on July 3, metamorphosing up into the Panhandle as the Borger Gassers. "Broke my heart," confessed Howard, who stayed in the game as the 20-year-old commissioner of a regional National Baseball Congress tournament.

In 1946, Green, then a 24-year-old former B-24 gunner and budding newspaperman, went after a club of his own.

"After the war, my dream was to own and operate a franchise in the West Texas-New Mexico League," recalls Green. "During a pair of 30-day furloughs from overseas duty, I convinced a couple of fellow veterans to join me in a bid for a franchise. We didn't have a park or a place to put it, and between the great wars, Abilene had failed three times at pro ball. We did have two big allies — desire and the total support of my employer, the *Abilene Reporter-News*."

The Class C Abilene Blue Sox were thus born, with Green and his two partners (George Steakley and a local dentist, Dr. Jimmy Bridges) putting up $2,500. Green had accumulated his nest egg in the service, but not in any traditional way — such as winning it in a crap game (George Steakley did that) — he did it by marketing a poem.

The epic was written by an associate and was titled *You Lucky Bastard*. Part of it went like this:

> Oh, hero of combat, pride of a nation
> Bemedaled receiver of high decoration,
> Object of womanhood's rapturous sighs,
> Battle-scarred veteran of war in the skies,

It mercifully ended:

> So go home to your women, your whiskey and jive,
> You are a lucky bastard to be alive.

Thanks in part to talent provided by the parent Dodgers, the Blue Sox were a roaring success. One reason Brooklyn was so generous was that the Bums had taken a liking to their young protégé, Green. In the spring Abilene had hired a manager, former major leaguer Alex Hooks, who arrived late and didn't even bother to suit up until the next day. Howard was upset and took the proverbial bull by the horns.

"John Reeves [of the Dodgers' Fort Worth farm club] called," recollects Green, "and said, 'Boy! You really made a hit with [Dodger scout] Wid Matthews. He got on the phone to Brooklyn, and he said, 'I saw a kid with guts!" he said, "He just walked up and fired him just like he's supposed to." ' "

As a result, the Dodgers took care of Abilene. Boasted Green: "We had better talent on our working-agreement club than the ownership-team at Santa Barbara in the California League that year and Meridian had in the Class B Southeastern League." He wasn't kidding. The Blue Sox, featuring first baseman Danny Ozark, third baseman Leo Thomas, and pitching prospect John Hall, had a .708 won-lost percentage (the best in baseball that year), and attracted over 100,000 fans — "which was unheard of for Abilene which was supposed to be a baseball graveyard."

Green's biggest legacy from his Abilene days was the hiring of legendary minor league statistician Bill Weiss as Blue Sox ticket manager. It was hardly a calculated move. Weiss had met Green while waiting for a bus at the minor leagues' meeting held at Columbus, Ohio.

"That was a summer I'll never forget," Weiss once recalled to journalist Mike Blake. "Blue Sox Stadium is a great name but slightly grandiose for the facility, which had a big sign on the press box on the top of the roof that said: DANGEROUS FOR OCCUPANCY BY MORE THAN SIX PERSONS. The offices of the Longhorn League and the Abilene Blue Sox were on the second floor of an old house, which was also where Howard and his wife lived. I had the spare bedroom, which also served as my office. It was also where the team stored the surplus bats and tickets. Since there were twin beds in the room, I got to share the room with stray ballplayers that came and went, usually for their first night in town before they got started.

"I don't think I'd trade that experience for anything. . . ."

One of Weiss' fondest recollections involved a 1947 game against the Lubbock Hubbers. Pitching for the Hubbers was football great Bobby Layne, and fan interest ran high.

Before the game, Dr. Bridges addressed the team, promising $5 for every hit they collected. "We still had people standing in line when the game started," recalls Weiss, "and I kept hearing Blue Sox after Blue Sox being announced by the PA. They were shelling Layne, batting around in the first inning, and Lubbock pulled him before a lot of people even got through the gate." The club pounded out 23 hits. But Bridges, sputtering all the way, paid out for each safety.

Early on, Green learned he should pay close attention to fan psychology. "In 1948," he recalled, "Manager Art Bowland of Abilene and I. B. Palmer of Lamesa got into a tussle over an alleged spiking at third base. I had planned to release Bowland as manager after that Sunday afternoon game, but because of his good showing in the fight he became such a hero to Abilene fans that I had to wait until the club had dropped five more in a row."

You'd think Green's Abilene success would satisfy the budding young impresario, but guess again. The following season he was out organizing an entirely new circuit, the Class D Longhorn League.

Recalled Green: "I was writing sports for the *Reporter-News*, and I went on a football trip with a college team, and I was reading a book on the way up, *The Detroit Tigers* by Fred Lieb.

"I read where Jack Zeller had been the youngest club owner in baseball history. I believe he operated the club when he was 21. Well, I thought I could become the youngest league president in baseball history if I organized a league."

It wasn't easy. "When he returned home, Green began writing to Chambers of Commerce and sports editors in West Texas," noted Fort Worth sportswriter Roy Edwards. The towns Green picked out — Big Spring, Midland, Ballinger, Sweetwater, Odessa, and Vernon — were real backwaters, lacking even facilities, but he was undaunted. "We built five parks and finished another one," says Green modestly.

In those days, there were some great rivalries in bush league cities across America, even in the oil country of the Longhorn League. For example, Odessa was where the "roughnecks" lived; Midland was home to the rigs' operators —"Odessa just hated Midland and vice-versa!"

"It was a kind of a silly thing for me to do business-wise," he now reflects, "because some of those towns had provided customers for Abilene, but I was such a crusader for baseball, I thought it was necessary."

The league first took shape at an organizational meeting at Sweetwater. Among those present were Amarillo's Bob Seeds, who had walloped seven straight homers for Newark in 1937, and Brownwood's Jack Knott, a former major league pitcher. Representing Odessa was a barber named Jim Payne. "About halfway through the meeting," recalled Green, "Payne exploded: 'We've got a kid here [Green] who knows nothing. We need to hold another meeting with someone who stands high with Bramham and has some experience.'

"At that point Seeds bounded to his feet: 'We've got the man in Green. He stands high already with Bramham and did something in Abilene that Alvin Gardner couldn't do, make a success of baseball in that church town.' " Gardner, long-time president of the Texas League, had lost $25,000 on a West Texas League franchise in that city in 1928.

That turned the tide. Two meetings later the Longhorn League was officially formed. Dodger scout Andy High snapped, "I'll give your league until the Fourth of July," but it lasted until Labor Day — of 1957.

As Longhorn League president Green was younger than any club president or manager. At one game he was introduced from the stands, prompting a female fan to exclaim, "Why he's just a child."

Green's 1947 season was marred by the death of Ballinger Cats outfielder James "Stormy" Davis. On July 3, Davis, just 20 years old, was struck in the head at Sweetwater in a Longhorn League contest against the local Sports. He died of a brain hemorrhage seven days later. Davis — whose Ballinger roommate was shortstop Roy McMillan — seemed to be a rising star, with a .303 average, 17 homers, and 64 RBI in just 48 games.

Nineteen forty-eight was far more pleasant. Outfielder Bob Crues tied the existing organized baseball record for homers in a single season when he collected 69 for the West Texas-New Mexico League's

Amarillo Gold Sox. Actually Crues hit 70, but the lighting system at Blue Sox Stadium was so horrid that the umpire blew a call that would have given Crues the record. "We had a center fielder, a young man from Sacramento named Gus Stathos," recalled Bill Weiss, "who had the nickname of 'Grandstand Gus, the Galloping Greek,' and Crues hit a ball out to center field. From the stands you couldn't pinpoint exactly where it hit. The umpire said it hit the fence and was in play, and Crues only got a double. After the game, Stathos said the ball had hit the bottom of the scoreboard. It should have been a home run."

Green operated the Abilene Blue Sox and ran the Longhorn League through the 1948 season, then resigned to take a job as business manager of the Western League's Pueblo Dodgers.

Pueblo attendance jumped from 116,000 to 141,000 under Green's tenure, but by 1950 he was back in Texas. That year John Reeves dispatched him to secure an Evangeline League franchise for the city of Monroe, Louisiana. Unable to purchase a team, Green went to work founding yet another new circuit, the Gulf Coast League, so Monroe could have a team. Oddly enough, Monroe never did see Gulf Coast League baseball. The Shreveport Sports' Bonneau Peters secured the Helena Seaporters' Evangeline League club and transferred it to Monroe. Undeterred by having his base of operations cut out from under him, Green doggedly continued putting the new circuit together.

Green had a hard sell in Crowley, Louisiana, population 13,500. But in those days, in those parts, all you had to convince was one man.

Green was "pouring his heart out" to a delegation of local pooh-bahs, when suddenly "a figure in the back got up. He said, 'Gentlemen, I think the fellow's got something.' And he walked out.

"A man named Schlicher was presiding. He said, 'Sit down, Green, we're in your league.' I said, 'I don't understand.' He says, 'Well, you don't know Crowley. That's Mr. Macon Freeman, and what he says in Crowley goes, and you have sold him so we will be in your league and we'll be a strong member . . .' "

That summer Green was at a local drugstore, chatting with the girl behind the soda fountain. A man came up and said, "You're Mr. Green, aren't you? You really did something for Crowley. This thing is the best thing to happen in a long time. Thank you."

It was Freeman himself.

"You really do rate," said the impressed native behind the counter. "He rarely ever speaks to anybody. What he says goes."

"He owned the rice mill in town," explains Green, "If you got to the right man in any of these towns, you had it made. That's the way things were in Louisiana ..."

The next year the Gulf Coast League reorganized, becoming a Class B circuit. That same season the now 29-year-old Green took over leadership of the Class B Big State League. In 1948 that league's president J. Walter Morris had fined Temple Eagles' General Manager O.W. "Bill" Hayes for replacing an injured ump with himself. Hayes was so incensed he led a palace revolt against Morris and ultimately replaced him with Green.

Green remained president of the Gulf Coast League through 1952 and of the Big State League through 1955. It was a time when minor league after minor league was folding. "Many an available pocketbook got flattened, and the end was inevitable," muses Green.

What did such aggravation pay? The Longhorn League gave Green $300 per month to be its major-domo; when he captained both the Longhorn and Big State circuits, he got $1,000 per month — "Which in 1951 wasn't too bad." Some years he put an estimated 75,000 miles on his car on league business.

Green found it was not always easy to recognize talent. "Bob Skinner tried to play outfield and first base for Waco in 1951," Green recalls. "Couldn't catch a thrown ball and had trouble corralling a fly. Made 35 errors in 94 games at first."

Developing umpiring — as opposed to playing — talent is a big chunk of any league president's job description. Green sent up such arbiters as Jimmy Odom, Bill Valentine, Al Smith, and Ken Burkhardt. Burkhardt had all the tools but wasn't winning any popularity contests.

The 1953 season began, and Green noticed that Burkhardt and his partner were working the Austin team 15 straight games, a situation that could only lead to trouble. From here on, we'll let Howard tell the story:

"I sent him a letter changing the schedule, and Burkhardt called me up on the phone, and he said, 'What the hell do you mean, changing my schedule like this?'

"Before he got any further, I said, 'Just a minute now. Am I working for you or are you working for me?'

" 'Well,' he said, 'I'm working for you.'

"I said, 'What's your problem?'

"And he said, 'Well, I put all my clothes in the cleaners, and I don't know what I'm going to do for a change.'

"I said, 'Why didn't you explain that to me before you flew off the handle. You're a real good umpire. You've got everything in your favor except that. I can understand the complaints that I've had from more than one club against you. Listen, you're in this league just to try to go to the majors. I don't care if it puts me in a bind. If I have the opportunity to send you up, you'll go. I'll recommend you, but with that kind of attitude I couldn't recommend you to anybody…"

Burkhardt got the message and within four months was sold to the higher-classification Western League.

In 1954 Green issued a controversial order to Big State League umpires: don't break up on-field donnybrooks. "When and if fights do start, the umpires are to stand by as spectators and not take on the duties of a referee," Green ordered. "We hope that the younger players who will be dotting league rosters will show a lot of spirit." National Association Proxy George Trautman hit the roof, but other Texas minor league executives thought it made sense. So did ABC radio commentator Bill Stern who supported Green on his national program.

Wrote Green to Trautman: "My experience has been that a good number of players pretend they want to fight and proceed to make a few threats, knowing full well that an umpire or a player will intervene to save them from harm. When they know nobody is likely to intervene, it is a genuine fight and creates a genuine rivalry between players and rival fans. I am of the opinion baseball needs more of the so-called old-time spirit than anything to restore its attendance. Too many pantywaists of today prefer verbal exchanges with the umpires in the form of alibis to honest-to-goodness combat with the opposition.

"It will mean an automatic fine in the Big State League this season for players of opposing clubs to display anything but hostility toward each other. Fraternizing is out from the time batting practice starts until the players have showered and dressed."

Of course, in those days, minor league ball had the enthusiastic support of community leaders, and they would pitch in to make it work. "Years ago," says Green, "farmers in places like Ballinger and Lamesa would pledge their crops for the team's survival. In Temple, a spot on the team's board of directors was more prestigious than a place on the city council. The baseball president outranked the mayor." However, Green ruefully adds: "But more than 20 years ago the remains of the Temple park were razed for industrial development."

Is there life after baseball? Howard Green has proved it. He entered Texas politics, serving as a state legislator, Tarrant County judge, and presiding officer of the County Court. But he's never forgotten his love of the national game, and helped lasso the Rangers for Texas, guiding the sale of Turnpike Stadium from Tarrant County to the City of Arlington. In 1975, Green helped organize — and, of course, became president of — the Gulf States League, a throw-back to the old days when most teams were independent. "I started out by going to Harlingen," Green explained. "I thought people might laugh at the idea, but they took it seriously." Green reasoned that hidden among the undrafted prospects out there were some players of real talent. "It's an accident," he observed, "that a guy like Mike Hargrove, taken 569th in the draft, really got a chance...A lot of fringe prospects would have an opportunity in a league like this."

Green put franchises in Baton Rouge, Seguin, Beeville, Corpus Christi, Victoria, and the Rio Grande Valley. Some were stronger than others. While the Baton Rouge Cougars folded in mid-August, the Corpus Christi Sea Gulls outdrew four out of eight franchises in the Class AA Texas League — and *every* team in the Class AA Eastern League.

Green's new circuit lasted for just two seasons, and was ahead of its time, given the rediscovered popularity of the bushes.

Since leaving baseball, Green has kept busy organizing the Dallas-Fort Worth Chapter of the Society for American Baseball Research (SABR). Looking back on his days in the game, he quotes Charles Ryder of the *Cincinnati Enquirer*, who in 1916 wrote: "Baseball must be the greatest of games in order to survive the people who run it."

AFTER PEARL HARBOR

Historians have by now pretty well chronicled major league baseball during World War II. But what about life in baseball's minors? War's travails hit the bushes far harder than the majors. The major leagues may have been forced to play retreads, graybeards, 4-Fs, and youngsters, but most minor circuits shut down entirely. Whatever baseball talent remained in the country seeped steadily upward, leaving the *real* bottom of the barrel in the minors. So if you think the worst baseball in history was represented by the 1944 St. Louis Browns, just imagine — just *try* to imagine — what the last-place Bradford Blue Wings of that year's Class D PONY League was like.

It wasn't for any lack of patriotism that a plague of woes befell the bushes. They tried. Minor league moguls renamed Indianapolis' Perry Stadium Victory Field; Syracuse's Municipal Stadium became MacArthur Stadium. And while the New Orleans Pelicans weren't about to rename their beloved Pelican Stadium, they did paint its grandstand seats red, white, and blue. War bond drives and scrap-iron drives filled minor league schedules, but the real scrap heaps were the ones players were recruited from.

Trouble had been brewing for the minors even before Pearl Harbor, starting with the first peacetime draft in U.S. history. By August 1941, 193 minor leaguers were in the service, still a small amount when one considered there were nearly 5,000 bush leaguers overall, but an ominous portend of things to come. The Snow Hill Billies of the Class D Coastal Plains League lost three players and disbanded after the 1940 season. In the Class B Interstate League, the Wilmington Blue Rocks' "Chugger" Rice, a .360 hitter, was a prominent loss. So was .328-hitting Tommy Flynn of the Ohio State League's champion Lima Pandas.

Going the other way, the first minor leaguer to be mustered *out* of the service was pitcher Johnnie Wilbourne of the South Atlantic League's Greenville Spinners. "Fort Jackson doctors discovered he was ruptured, so he's to be mustered out," noted *The Sporting News*.

Even Acts of God visited the minors. In spring 1941 an intense drought hit the southeastern United States. Precipitation decreased by half, and the Tennessee Valley Authority's reservoirs fell in volume by 60 percent. With the TVA providing so much of the region's electricity, officials demanded cutbacks in electrical usage. That was bad enough, but defense plants would have priority over what electricity was still being produced. Secretary of the Interior Harold Ickes ominously warned that night baseball might become one of the drought's first casualties.

Throughout the South minor leagues responded by reducing evening play. The Class B Southeastern League, featuring franchises in such places as Montgomery and Mobile, abandoned twi-night doubleheaders and arclit games on two weeknights. The Atlanta Crackers scrapped evening contests altogether. So did the Class D Georgia-Florida League's Albany Cardinals and Moultrie Packers.

The Alabama State and Appalachian Leagues took similar action. To save kilowatts, the *Birmingham News* proposed confining arguments with umpires to just 30 seconds during night games. "Most players can say too much in 30 seconds anyway," noted local sportswriter Zipp Newman. "Hustling to and from positions would save 15 minutes. Games have been lasting too long at night. The night games have been running from 15 to 35 minutes longer than the daylight games and no one yet has come up with a sound reason why this should be the case."

Soon the entire nation would be facing the question of whether night baseball was "essential." Leagues such as the Wisconsin State, West Texas-New Mexico, Texas, and Northern leagues expressed alarm, threatening to fold if they could not play at night.

International League President Frank Shaughnessy chimed in: "The majority of clubs allow ladies to attend night games free, and most of the ladies are accompanied by their husbands. This means that the homes are darkened during the ball games...I believe that if this factor is properly investigated it will prove that night baseball will not in any way hurt the defense program." Supporting Shaughnessy, *New York Daily News* sports editor Jimmy Powers quoted engineer

Herman Rosner, who found that "in practically every community throughout the nation, night baseball saves power."

Canadian-American League President Father Harold J. Martin vowed his league would continue, maintaining that the National Pastime was essential for the "spiritual" needs of America's defense workers.

Once war was declared, however, these problems seemed, well, "minor league." By 1943 only nine bush leagues featuring 62 clubs functioned, down from a total of 43 circuits and 314 franchises operating in 1940.

Staffing even the few surviving leagues wasn't easy. The PCL's Los Angeles Angels recruited 15-year-old Bill "The Angel Kid" Sarni from Los Angeles High School. He caught 33 games for them in 1943. The Columbus Red Birds featured a 17-year-old backstop, a more familiar name, Joe Garagiola, who hit a respectable .293 in 81 contests. And why not? The year before, the *16*-year-old Garagiola batted .254 for Springfield in the Western Association.

They weren't all callow youths. There were plenty of callow adults. Forty-nine-year-old righthander Herman Polycarp "Old Folks" Pillette hung on until 1945 with the PCL's Sacramento Solons. "Old Folks" had started his pro career back in 1917 with the Class B Central League's Richmond Quakers and pitched a record 23 seasons in one minor league, the Pacific Coast League.

In 1943 the Inter-State League's York White Roses signed a pair of aged ex-big leaguers: 56-year-old Thomas "Lefty" George and 43-year-old Charles "Dutch" Schesler. Schesler was a sergeant of the guard at a local steel mill. George, a grandfather who had two sons in the armed services, sold beer, keeping his day job and pitching only when the White Roses were at home. He began working relief, not having his first start until June 16. He took the loss — but helped stop Lancaster's George Kell's 32-game hitting streak.

Meanwhile, the Eastern League's Hartford Laurels bolstered their staff with a 44-year-old local druggist. Sam Hyman, hadn't pitched at the Class A level for 10 years, but late in 1942 Hartford faced a forfeit because of a lack of moundsmen. Hyman, who was sitting in the stands, informed manager Del Bissonette: "Del, if you're stuck for a pitcher, maybe I can help out."

The original plan was for Hyman to "hold 'em off" until a real pitcher arrived. Instead, he went nine innings, surrendering just eight hits and beating New Haven, 8-2.

Such stories were all too commonplace. The 1945 Buffalo Bisons featured a quartet of graybeards: pitcher Lloyd Brown (41), pitcher/outfielder Henry "Prince" Oana (37), and outfielders Ab Wright (39) and Ollie Carnegie (46). Colorful Babe Herman (41) remained with the Hollywood Stars until 1945. In 1943 44-year-old Hollywood pitcher-manager Charlie Root was the club's most dependable hurler (15-13). He remained with them in 1944 and might have still been pitching in 1945 except for the small matter of being fired as manager. In 1943 39-year-old Tony Lazzeri started at second base for the Eastern League's Wilkes-Barre Barons, batting .271 in 58 games. Fiftyish minor league manager Wally Schang filled in behind the plate for the 1942 Augusta Tigers and the 1943 Utica Braves.

Age wasn't the problem regarding a Durham Bulls' second baseman named Patterson. "When Patterson said he had played at Atlanta, I thought he meant Atlanta in the Southern Association," said Buzzie Bavasi. "It turned out he was just out of the pen at Atlanta."

And then there was Pete Gray. The famed one-armed Browns outfielder didn't start out as a one-armed Browns' outfielder. He started as a one-armed Trois Rivieres Royals' outfielder.

Gray lost his right arm as a boy, catching it in the spokes of a passing wagon. He learned how to throw left-handed and to field using a special glove. "You know, I had a shoemaker make that glove for me special," he once recalled. "He'd take out most of my padding, and I'd use it like a first baseman's glove, keeping my pinky inside. It helped me get rid of the glove quicker. I'd catch the ball, stick my glove under the stump, roll the ball across my chest, and throw it back in. No big deal. It was just grounders that gave me some trouble."

Before the war he played semi-pro ball at Trois Rivieres and for Max Rosner's fabled Brooklyn Bushwicks. By 1942, however, Trois Rivieres was in the Class C Canadian-American League and was short enough of talent to turn to Gray. "They signed me by telephone," Gray later recalled. "When I got up to Montreal, the manager [Justin Kennoy] met my train. I had a coat draped over my stump, and when I took it off, the guy almost passed out. But I figured I already had a contract, and he might as well give me a chance."

Despite the handicap of a broken collarbone, Gray batted .381 in 42 games. He might have played with Toronto in 1943 but offended manager Burleigh Grimes with some unflattering remarks overheard by Old Stubblebeard. Gray then caught on with the Southern Association's Memphis Chicks, where in 126 games he batted a respectable .289. Still with Memphis in 1944 he hit .333 and tied the league record of 68 stolen bases set 15 years earlier by Kiki Cuyler. Next stop: St. Louis.

In order to tap whatever talent might be lurking in draft-exempt war work, in 1943 organized baseball experimented with the Twin Ports League, history's only Class E circuit. It was a four-team operation with three of them in Duluth, Minnesota (the Marine Iron club, the Dukes, and the Heralds), and one in nearby Superior, Wisconsin. Most players worked at local war plants and shipyards, with eligibility restricted to players with no professional experience. Only four games per week were scheduled.

It might have worked, but it didn't. Crowds were slim, and the circuit, which began on May 30, was dead as a doornail by July 13.

Crowds were not sparse at ancient (built in 1888) Borchert Field, home of the American Association's Milwaukee Brewers. There young Bill Veeck was skillfully honing his promotional skills. One stunt saw Veeck present manager Jolly Cholly Grimm with a $1,000 war bond on his birthday. Grimm was suitably touched by such profligate generosity. "He knew we were practically broke," Veeck later wrote, "so he thought we were losing our minds until he discovered the bond was one which he himself had bought by payroll deductions."

Another Veeck promotion was his May 1943 scheduling of a 10 A.M. Borchert Field contest, accommodating second-and-third-shift war workers. Veeck helped pass out coffee, doughnuts, and cereal to the 3,500 fans in attendance. He also hired a seven-piece band (clad appropriately in night clothes and nightcaps) to serenade the crowd.

It turned out they needed some distraction. The visiting St. Paul Saints didn't show up until noon. Half the crowd had left by then (Veeck issued refunds), but those who stuck it out were rewarded with a 20-0 victory and the Brewers' 50 total bases, an American Association record.

Not only Veeck was concocting odd promotions. The Louisville Colonels collected 2,587 pounds of kitchen grease on "Waste Fat Night," and at Shreveport, Louisiana, Mrs. George Roby attended the local Sports' "Aluminum Night" where patrons donated that scarce metal to the war effort. When she returned to the parking lot, she found other public-spirited fans had patriotically donated her car's aluminum hubcaps.

Along both the East and West Coasts war created further restrictions on play. Military authorities prescribed "blackouts" to avoid aiding enemy planes or submarines. Most major league clubs were safely inland. In fact, only the Polo Grounds and Ebbets Field were actually hurt by such regulations (Braves Field, Fenway Park, and Yankee Stadium didn't yet have lights). But numerous minor league clubs were. The Class D Florida East Coast League's Miami Beach Flamingoes and Fort Pierce Bombers abandoned evening play until war's end and substituted starting times of 5:45 P.M. and 5:30 P.M. respectively. The Fort Lauderdale Tarpons and West Palm Beach Indians reacted similarly. The South Atlantic League's Jacksonville Tars and Savannah Indians were hit by Army regulations, requiring them to complete contests by no later than 9:15 P.M. Officials kept a nervous eye on the clock. Sally League President Dr. E. M. Wilder became so jittery he suggested night games be limited to just seven frames. That went over like a lead balloon, but 7:15 P.M. twilight starts were instituted. Games began in daylight, and lights could be switched on in mid-game — and remain on until visible in the dark of night.

Beyond that, regulations were adopted ensuring that games proceed speedily. Infielders no longer could toss the ball around after each out. Umpires hectored batters and pitchers to keep moving. Under such conditions, Savannah trounced Jacksonville, 12-3, on May 26, 1942, but it was still over by 8:59!

Legend holds that one Jacksonville game was halted when the blackout fell quite suddenly—just as the pitcher released the ball. No one was hurt. The catcher alleged it was a clear strike. The batter, on the other hand, thought it was a good foot outside. The umpire just called it a night and went home.

By 1943 the South Atlantic League was out of business.

It wasn't just along the coast that blackouts took place. One of the oddest occurred at Lancaster, Pennsylvania, in September 1943. In the midst of a blackout occurring during the Interstate League playoffs against York, a base was stolen. The theft was recorded not by playing personnel, however, but by a paying customer.

"Somebody," Lancaster Red Roses third baseman George Kell theorized, "came out of the stands, I think. When the lights came on, they had no second base. It created quite a stir until they found another bag."

Being in a higher classification did little to protect clubs from war's vicissitudes. The U.S. Army implemented regulations radically curbing outdoor illumination in the metropolitan New York area, and this affected both Newark and Jersey City. The military termed Jersey City's Roosevelt Stadium "the most flagrant spot" visible from the sea, and thus by enemy submarines, in the entire region. "The ranks of floodlights," one general noted, "threw countless brilliant lumens upward, downward, outward, all of them accumulating in a distinct glare...The total glow effect was startling."

Both clubs decided to substitute twilight play for night ball. In the bottom of the eighth of one June 1942 twilight contest at Jersey City, the local Giants (on Sid Gordon's four-bagger) pulled ahead of Montreal, 3-2. The Royals fought back, going ahead in the ninth, but Jersey City then went into a stall. If the Giants prolonged the inning, and it was not completed before the lights went out at 9:24 sharp (the contest started at 7:30 and lights were turned on in the fifth inning at 8:12), the action would not count. That meant the score would revert to what it was at the end of the eighth and the Giants would win. Even with each Royal batter swinging at any pitch within reach, Jersey City reliever Hugh East proceeded to walk four straight, and Montreal tallied eight runs. The Little Giants still came to bat, but with just one out, the clock struck 9:24, and like Cinderella it was *finis* for the Royals.

The contest was recorded as a Jersey City victory.

Well, *temporarily* recorded. International League President Frank Shaughnessy (a Montreal resident) hit the roof on learning of Jersey City's antics. He fined manager Frank Snyder $100 and ordered that when the Royals visited again in July the game would be resumed from the top of the ninth. An embarrassed Giants' farm director Bill Terry announced that Jersey City games would now start no later than 7:00 P.M. to avoid a repetition of the June 12 fiasco.

That was on the *East* Coast. The *West* Coast was far more nervous than that, fearing not just submarine attacks but an actual Japanese invasion. Officials adopted elaborate civil defense measures. Crowds exceeding 5,000 persons — for no matter what sort of gathering — were proscribed. Authorities actively considered banning *all* baseball, even day games. In response, the California State Assembly in January 1942 adopted a resolution urging the game's survival.

The Pacific Coast League scheduled evening contests for the coming season—but only if crowds did not exceed the 1941 average attendance (i.e., less than 5,000 per game). Regulations also directed that lights be easily squelched, that before each game patrons be warned on what to do in an emergency, that traffic lanes be kept open from parks, that loudspeakers be able to direct fans out of the stands, and that special police be on alert. So nervous were officials, that even with these restrictions, the threat remained that night ball would be banned at any moment. "The enemy situation," cautioned the Army, "cannot be forecast and what it will be on opening day, April 12, is entirely a matter of conjecture."

San Francisco President Charlie Graham announced fans could be issued "blackout checks" (in the same manner as "rain checks"). But even these precautions couldn't prevent night play from being banned along the entire Pacific Coast in August 1942. Not until after the close of the 1943 season would arclit games again be permitted.

Eventually 4,000 minor leaguers served in the armed services. The first professional player to give his life for his country was former Oakland Oaks second baseman/outfielder Billy Herbert, who had entered the military in January 1942 and was killed at Guadalcanal's Henderson Field that October.

The first pro player to enter the service, however, was outfielder Billy Southworth, Jr., son of Cardinals manager Billy Southworth, Sr. Prior to Pearl Harbor Southworth had been a terrific prospect, advancing as far as Toronto. In 1939, with the Rome Colonels, he had been Canadian-American League Most Valuable Player. One Rome teammate summed him up as follows: "A fabulous talent, what a great guy... He was the apple of his father's eye. He could run, throw, and hit. He was major league talent. He could do everything very well."

From being a *Rome* Colonel Southworth eventually became a *real* Lt. Colonel, piloting 25 bombing missions over Europe and winning the Air Medal and the Distinguished Service Cross. He was a true hero, strong, brave, athletic, and handsome, and it was only mildly surprising when Southworth — still in uniform — signed a 10-year movie contract with Hollywood producer Hunt Stromberg, a one-time *Sporting News'* correspondent.

In February 1945 all that changed. Now stationed at Mitchell Field (near the present site of Shea Stadium), Southworth was conducting a training mission when one of his engines conked out. He desperately attempted an emergency landing but overshot the runway. His plane ditched in Flushing Bay and exploded. Not until months later was the 27-year-old Southworth's body found. Ironically, the remains were identified only with the help of a Rome dentist who had once worked on Southworth's teeth and who would later become owner of the Rome franchise.

One of the least distinguished minor leaguers going *into* uniform was a first baseman-pitcher named Bert Shepard. On *leaving* the service he would display to all America what guts really were.

In 1940 the Indiana-born Shepard dropped out of high school intent on playing ball in far-off California. All he got was 10 days in the Amarillo jail for hopping a freight train. He did, however, briefly pitch for the White Sox' Class C East Texas League farm team, the Longview Texans. They quickly released him.

Shepard returned to high school but loved the game so much that on graduating he answered an ad to drive someone's car to Seattle so he could get even *that* close to major league spring training sites in California. He hitchhiked down the coast but failed a tryout with the A's, who, nonetheless, arranged for him to play with the California League's Anaheim Aces. Again he washed out, released because of control problems. He ended the year with the last-place Bisbee Bees of the Class C Arizona-Texas League. That he wasn't released at season's end was progress enough.

The league folded and Shepard was drafted into the Army. He applied for pilot training and in May 1944 was shot down in aerial combat over France, lost his right leg, and was captured by the Nazis.

The Germans fitted Shepard with a wooden limb, and he worked at playing ball while still a prisoner. Liberated from Stalag Luft IX-C in October 1944, he was taken to Walter Reed Hospital, where he met Under Secretary of War Robert Patterson. Shepard matter-of-factly informed Patterson he was going to play ball again professionally. Patterson, impressed by Shepard's positive attitude, told Washington owner Clark Griffith about the young man.

Griffith signed Shepard as a coach but gave him a chance to start against the Dodgers in a July 1945 war charity exhibition. Surprisingly, he allowed just five singles in four innings. On August 4 Shepard took the mound in a major league contest. With the bases loaded he entered a game against the Red Sox, striking out the first batter he faced, George "Catfish" Metkovich. Over $5\frac{1}{3}$ innings he allowed just three hits and one run, striking out three and walking just one.

Shepard hoped to stay with Washington in 1946 but with so many two-legged pitchers returning from the service he had little chance. Farmed to Chattanooga, he was soon felled by complications to the stump of his right leg. Five operations followed, and his career was finally over.

But Bert Shepard had showed everyone what determination could do.

Numerically, the minors hit bottom in 1943, fielding just nine circuits. In 1944 a new league (the Class D Ohio State League, which featured the Newark Moundsmens' young Ned Garver) brought their number back up to 10. In 1945 the Class C Carolina League and the Class D North Carolina State League increased the fold to an even dozen.

With the war ending in August 1945, the minors had not only survived. They were on the verge of an unprecedented prosperity.

THE MINORS'
SCREWIEST BALLPARKS

Charm — the minors have it in droves. Quite often the term is a definite euphemism for poor conditions, pitiful play, and Odyssey-like bus rides, but at other times the appellation fits.

Now, take ballparks.

Generally, they are cozy and intimate. Minor league diamonds, both past and present, have been as much an attraction as the game itself. Few astro-turf cookie-cutter diamonds clutter up the bush league scene. We're talking *character* in the minors, from death defying inclines to weirdly irregular dimensions to the most imaginative efforts at fan comfort.

Yet some parks have possessed what can only be described as *bizarre* phenomenon. Without further ado, let's cut to the chase for a sampling of the best — or worst — the bushes have offered:

ALBUQUERQUE

Sports Stadium claims the ultimate in Americana (in fact, it's a wonder it's not in California) — a drive-in. A 28-foot high, 20,000-square foot terrace formed from lava rock trucked in from a nearby volcano sits just beyond the outfield. The area serves 102 vehicles, and fans are provided with a mobile chuck-wagon and radio play-by-play to enhance their comfort level.

"It's kind of a natural," explained Jim Blaney, Albuquerque general manager. "The stadium was built by digging a big hole, then putting seats in one side. The first time I came out there was a big hole, and all you had to do was stand up there and say that this was a natural, that people could sit in their cars. I said, 'What are we going to do with this area here that has such an excellent view of the whole field?'...Those who come seem to feel they've added an extra dimension to viewing a game. They bring campers, school buses, anything. Whenever something happens, they honk horns instead of clapping."

Speaking of transportation, the city provides bus service *to* but not *from* the park. Once the Pacific Coast League Dukes have your money, you're on your own.

ATLANTA

Ponce de Leon Park was the home of the Atlanta Crackers from 1907 to 1964, housing franchises not only in the Southern Association and International League, but also in the Negro American League. In 1949 Crackers owner Earl Mann decided Ponce de Leon Park's left field was not an easy enough target for batters. He could have put up a fence — but *nooo!* that would have been too simple. Instead, Mann ordered a two-foot high hedge to run from the foul line to the opposite end of the park's elaborate scoreboard. The distance down the line was cut from 365 feet to 330. Fielders were not allowed to hop over the shrub to grab flies and were not even allowed to fall over it in making a grab.

Actually Mann *did* have a reason for the low barrier: so box seat holders would not have their view of the stadium scoreboard obscured.

There was plenty of room in center, as well. Not only room, but a handsome magnolia tree. Right field was relatively mundane, merely featuring a steep incline.

BALLINGER (TX)

After the 1949 season the Class D Longhorn League's Ballinger Cats moved from west Texas to New Mexico, becoming the Roswell Rockets. They took everything with them. "I mean everything," says statistician Bill Weiss. "They dismantled the ballpark, and put it on flatbed trucks and hauled it across west Texas, into New Mexico, and rebuilt it."

BIRMINGHAM

Mud from Delaware is now the standard for rubbing the gloss off of new baseballs, but this wasn't always the case. When Birmingham's Rickwood Park opened in 1910, umpires discovered that the dirt there was clay-like and particularly free of mica.

Birmingham's old park was known affectionately as the "Slag Pile." As most other Southern League ballyards, it had soil which contained a lot of mica. Rubbing the ball up with this mud made the ball even slicker. "Tobacco juice was mostly used for rubbing the balls," recalled umpire William B. Carpenter, "and umps who didn't chew had more or less trouble . . ."

Rickwood Park's unique clay was carried up to the International League in 1911 when Carpenter moved up from the Southern Association.

BUFFALO

Featured in Robert Redford's classic movie, *The Natural*, now-demolished War Memorial Stadium was hardly a natural for minor league or any league ball. With a capacity of over 40,000, and wildly inappropriate dimensions, this WPA structure was a cold, cavernous structure remembered more for its eccentricities than its positive aspects.

"Many long-time fans were upset about the sight lines in the so-called first base box seats;" notes Joe Overfield, the foremost expert on Buffalo baseball. "Others were vociferous in criticizing the toilet facilities. And traffic and parking in the area of the stadium were disasters."

Crime in the rapidly deteriorating neighborhood reached epic proportions in 1967, and all Bisons night games were moved a full county away to neighboring Niagara Falls. In 1969 War Memorial Stadium hit bottom when a knife-wielding gang invaded the home clubhouse during batting practice.

Officially the game was canceled due to "threatening weather."

COLORADO SPRINGS

I've heard of luxurious ballparks, but this is going too far. At Sky Sox Stadium, home to a PCL franchise since 1988, fans can watch the game from a private hot tub. The fee is $80 for a party of 10, and vendors will bring all the concessions you want to tubside.

Pass the tofu please.

EL PASO

Built in 1924 Dudley Field, lasted though the end of the 1990 season. It featured several unique features: the only park constructed of adobe brick, a levee in center field to prevent flooding from the Rio Grande, and giant venetian blinds on the grandstand to shield patrons from the blinding Texas sun.

All the comforts of home.

ELMIRA

Yet another WPA project, Dunn Field opened its doors in 1939. In years past, it featured a truly ecological groundskeeping system — goats — to keep turf down to size. Outfielders, however, complained of a certain side effect, and more conventional gardening means were implemented.

On August 16, 1951 Dodger farm hand Don Zimmer was married at Dunn Field's homeplate.

ERIE

Constructed in 1938 for the Class C Middle Atlantic League Erie Sailors, in the late 1980s and early 1990s Ainsworth Field "boasted" what many considered the worst playing surface in baseball. The Cards and Orioles were only too eager to yank working agreements from the city due to its horrid conditions.

Aside from its rutted field, Ainsworth Field also featured a bogus set of outfield dimensions. All of its measurements were off, with the right-field barrier being a mere 286.5 feet, instead of the posted 300 feet. The false numbers were a stratagem to keep the team's offensive stats from being pooh-poohed.

In 1994, after the New York-Penn League had finally abandoned the town altogether, the State of Pennsylvania finally authorized $8 million for a new downtown stadium.

HANNIBAL

Built in 1925 for the Hannibal Travellers of the Illinois-Missouri League, Clemens Field was named after local Samuel Langhorn Clemens (aka Mark Twain). It's last use for professional baseball was for the Western Association's Pilots in 1947. While it had a few interesting features in itself, its ancillary uses were exceedingly more noteworthy. During World War II, 200 German POWs were interned there and kept busy sorting shoes for wartime refugees. In April 1982 the city fathers authorized a KKK rally on the grounds, correctly thinking it was the safest place in town for such a controversial gathering.

HARRISBURG

No man is an island, but some parks are on them. The Eastern League's Harrisburg Senators, RiverSide Park, is one of them.

RiverSide is a strange — but very pleasing — mix of cold functionality and engaging whimsy. Situated just across from downtown Harrisburg, home of Pennsylvania's state capital, City Island is accessible via a conventional automobile bridge and by a steel-deck pedestrian bridge. The island features not just a ballpark (which is a little too heavy on steel bleachers), but a football stadium, buggy rides and stables, a paddlewheel steamboat, water taxis, a video arcade, a tidy riverwalk full of vendors, occasional chili cookoffs, and a kiddy-size railroad that can be seen chugging past the right-field fence. Once darkness falls, the pedestrian bridge, the arcade and the stable are outlined by strings of lights.

Pure charm — Eastern League style.

JOHNSTOWN (PA)

Point Stadium, at the confluence of where the Little Conemaugh Creek and the Stoney Creek meet and form the Conemaugh Creek, was built circa 1910, for the Johnstown Johns (or Jawns) of Class D Tri-State League. It featured portable fences "erected on large and heavy steel girders" which after a game were slid on rollers into two large barns. No kidding!

The reason for this oddity was to convert the field between games into "a children's playground." Seems like a lot of trouble to go to, but they must have had a good reason. Although frankly, it escapes me.

At an earlier local ballyard, a few years after the disastrous Johnstown Flood, an outfielder stumbled over something in the turf. Digging it up he found it was a human skull — a victim of the great deluge. But there was more. The rest of the poor fellow's skeleton was still attached.

MEMPHIS

After ancient Russwood Stadium burned to the ground in April 1960, the desperate Memphis Chicks moved into Hodges Field, a high school football facility. Although the right-field barrier was 40 feet high, it was only 204 feet from homeplate — the shortest distance in organized baseball since Chicago's old Lakefront Park. In a May 2, 1960 contest Birmingham and Memphis hit 11 homers. After that any ball hit over the right-field wall would count for only two bases.

The park's right-field dimension was nearly as cozy: 279 feet. Hodges Field was so unsatisfactory the Chicks moved out before season's end.

MILWAUKEE

Rickety old Borchert Field possessed not only abominable sight-lines from its first- and third-base grandstand, but also a cozy 266-foot right-field target. In 1942 flamboyant Brewers owner Bill Veeck rigged an electric motor to raise or lower a 60-foot right-field screen — depending, of course, on which side was batting. It was perfectly legal, but only for that first day.

NASHVILLE

First built in 1876, the Sulphur Dell qualified for immortality on two counts: aroma and topography. Built near the city dump it stunk to high heaven.

Beyond that, its right field was the ultimate in bizarre.

Wrote Phil Lowry in SABR's *Green Cathedrals*: "Sulphur Dell had the craziest right field in history. Right fielders were called mountain goats because they had to go up and down the irregular hills in right center and right. The incline in right rose 25 feet, beginning gradually behind first, then rising sharply at a 45 degree angle, then leveling off at a 10 foot wide shelf one third of the way up the incline, and then continuing at a 45 degree angle to the fence."

The Sulphur Dell (sometimes dubbed "Suffer Hell') hosted Nashville baseball until 1963.

NEWARK (NY)

From 1968 through 1979 and again from 1983 to 1987 Newark's tiny Colburn Park housed a New York-Penn League franchise. It wasn't much to look at and aside from Robin Yount getting his start there not much happened in the place — but maybe that's why it had to feature some high-tech entertainment. Bored younger fans could amuse themselves by tossing quarters into video games situated behind the stands.

PALM SPRINGS

Palm Springs' Angels Stadium is best known as the long-time spring training home of the California Angels, but it also doubled as a minor league site. Palm Springs is a terrific place in the winter, but in the summer its just terrifically *hot*. Temperatures typically hover over 100 at the start of night games. To entice paying customers, a misting system has been installed over the stands, lightly dousing fans with a fine spray. That mist has the effect of lowering the temperature 20 degrees. At just 80 or 90 degrees that's enough to make Palm Springs summer residents reach for their sweaters.

PAWTUCKET

Pawtucket's McCoy Stadium remains the smallest capacity park in Triple-A, but its grandstand is one of the highest. The WPA structure is so high that young fans (and greedy collectible types) resort to all sorts of inventiveness to garner autographs.

Unable to hand programs or balls to players for signing, fans hollow out two-liter plastic soda bottles (plastic bleach jugs work even better) and stow the items they want signed inside. Next step is to lower the contrivances down to field level via ropes, have them signed, and raise them back up.

All in a day's work, in the modern collectible market.

PENNINGTON GAP (VA)

Fences? We don't need no stinkin' fences. Pennington Gap's Leeman Park was the last of the unfenced parks. Distances, according to the 1938 *Minor League Digest*, were: LF - 900 feet, RF - 600 feet, and a whopping 1,200 feet to center!

PITTSFIELD (MA)

Stately old Wahconah Park has served Eastern, Canadian-American League, and New York-Penn League franchises, and all in all is a pretty good place to watch a ballgame.

There's just one small problem, though. Despite several renovations, the field faces the wrong way, and games can be interrupted by "sun delays." Recently discussed efforts to remedy the situation have ranged from hanging a mesh shroud from the light towers to installing a movie screen from a defunct drive-in to block King Sol's rays. Bring your sunglasses!

RANCHO CUCAMONGA

For a brand-spanking new ballpark in the middle of nowhere, Rancho Cucamonga's $11.5 million Epicenter (home of the California League's Quakes) certainly has a sense of history. Older fans may recall the environs of Cucamonga from the skit on Jack Benny's radio and television shows in which a train conductor would regularly bellow out his itinerary: "Anaheim, A-zu-sa, and Cuc-a-mon-ga!"

Rancho Cucamonga's civic leaders are no ingrates. They know what put them on the map. Accordingly, the Epicenter's grand entrance features a life-size statue of Benny. The stadium's address? Glad you asked. At the corner of Rochester and Jack Benny — where else?

ROME (NY)

Rome's turn-of-the-century New York State League diamond was cheek-by-jowl with the barns of the local fairgrounds. It was, to say the least, aromatic. Beyond that, it possessed some really incredible attributes, including a large cattle shed in right, which straddled both fair and foul territory.

Left field was no prize either. It abutted a race course and fielders would often run onto the course to corral flies. If they ran too far, however, they would pitch right over a steep cliff.

SACRAMENTO

When the Pacific Coast League returned to town in 1974, it discovered old Edmonds Field had become a shopping center. The Solons, (managed by Hall-of-Famer Bob Lemon) found a home in Hughes Field, your basic converted football stadium. Hughes Field, however, was less than basic. Since 1959 organized baseball rules have called for no fence to be less than 325 feet from home place (replacing the more tolerant 250 foot dimension that had previously existed). Sacramento's left-field barrier was a tad short of that, however. Ninety-four feet to be exact — just 231 feet down the line.

On August 6, 1974 the Solons and the Tacoma Twins each hit seven homers, setting a new PCL record. The Solons' Bill McNulty parked 55 homers that year; teammates Gorman Thomas and Sixto Lezcano delivered 51 and 34 respectively. Four hundred and ninety-one homers sailed out of sight in 1974, and the next year a Fenway-style barrier was erected.

SAN DIEGO

By now you've figured out that minor league parks are no strangers to somewhat irregular dimensions, but these usually involve outfield barriers. Lane Field (which literally met its end at the molars of chomping termites) served the PCL's Padres from 1936, when they moved down the coast from Hollywood, to 1958 when the club relocated to C. Arnholt Smith's Westgate Park. Lane Field did things one better in the dimensions department — a mere 87 feet from home to first.

SCHENECTADY (NY)

In 1946 the McNearney brothers, two local beer distributors, put their own money, nearly a quarter of a million dollars, into constructing McNearney Stadium. It was decades ahead of its time in hosting perhaps the minors' first full-service restaurant as well as a unique silver dollar-operated turnstile.

Although built for the Canadian-American League's Blue Jays, McNearney Stadium eventually was home to an Eastern League franchise. As minor league ball deteriorated in the late 1950s, Mc-Nearney Stadium was converted into the "Stadium Golf Course." Not torn down, but *converted*. The outside shell of the park remains to this day, and driving into its parking lot, one thinks he might be on the way to see nine innings instead of 18 holes. But once inside, *voila!* — a golf course.

TROY

Laureat Field, in the days of the old New York State League, was another island park, but with a difference. Left and right fields were extended by wooden planking and jutted out over the Hudson River. Outfielders charging over its boards were compared to "horses trotting over a rustic bridge." Whoa, Nellie!

Well, that's just a quick tour of bush league real estate. Although there have been some clinkers erected in recent years (the Eastern League's Albany-Colonie park comes rapidly to mind), with any luck the minors will be spared the blessings of symmetrically, one-dimensional facilities and will continue to sprout such idiosyncratic diamonds.

Or as Frenchie Bordaragay (or was it Wade Boggs?) might have remarked, *"Vive la Difference!"*

CRITTERS, FLORA, OCCUPATION:
Minor League Team Nicknames

In recent years, heady minor league operators have seen the cash value in a catchy name or logo. The results have been such commercially motivated team names as the Nashville Xpress, Carolina Mudcats, Trenton Thunder, Rancho Cucamonga Quakes, San Bernardino Spirit, Quad Cities River Bandits, Columbus Redstixx, and Fort Myers Miracle. Selling caps featuring, say, a sporty Mudcats logo, is actually *big* business.

But this trend is not something entirely new. Decades ago, before virtually every farm team was known by its parent club's nickname, local outfits were free to let their imaginations run wild, if not berserk. After all, it costs money for uniforms or buses or players, but a catchy nickname costs no more than a mundane one.

Basically, three broad species of *Nicknamus Baseballus* existed: critters, flora, and occupations, but it's possible to catalogue numerous other genuses, such as ethnics and sock colors and even theology.

Let's go first to the animal world. Who couldn't find a warm spot in their heart for the Galveston Sandcrabs, Evansville River Rats, Perth Blue Cats, Tarboro Serpents, Grand Rapids Wolverines, Yuma Panthers, Salina Cayotes, Denver Grizzlies, Kokomo Wildcats, Tupelo Wolves, Saginaw Krazy Kats, Kane County Cougars, Beaumont Golden Gators, Edinburg Bobcats, Santo Domingo Sharks, Anaconda Serpents, or the Aberdeen Black Cats?

There were less malevolent breeds in the minor league zoo, however: the Union City Greyhounds, Columbus Foxes, Ada Herefords, San Francisco Seals, Fond du Lac Webfeet, Carrollton Frogs, Lafayette Brahman Bulls, San Francisco Seals, Enid Buffaloes, Clinton Steers, Omaha Omahogs, Baker Badgers, Newark Bears, Dawson Stags, Montpelier Goldfish, Adrian Lions, Durham Bulls, Dyersburg Deers, Cairo Tadpoles, Thomasville Tomcats, Altoona Rams, Norfolk Clams, Hutchinson Elks, Roanoke Goats, Manhattan Elks, Madison Muskies, Kitchener Terriers, Zacatecas Gophers (or *Tuzos*, en espanol), Zanesville Swamp Foxes, Orlando Bulldogs, Billings Mustangs, Lincoln Ducklings, Bonham Jackrabbits, Memphis Turtles, Cedar Rapids Rabbits, Muscatine Camels, Victoria Mussels, and Smiths Falls Beavers. In a class by itself was Schenectady's "Frog Alley Bunch" of the 1902 New York State League.

Not exactly calculated to strike terror in the hearts of opponents, though, were the Elgin Kittens, Omaha Lambs, Tucson Baby Seals, or Cedar Rapids Bunnies.

The insect kingdom is hardly neglected. Starting with the rather generic Wilson Bugs, the list is filled out with such appellations as the Battle Creek Crickets, Bisbee Bees, Poughkeepsie Honey Bugs, Waycross Grasshoppers, Durango Scorpions, Burlington Spiders, Charlotte Hornets, Piedmont Drybugs, Berlin Busy Bees, Jersey City Skeeters, or Temple Boll Weevils.

And let's not forget our fine feathered friends. True, we today have the Cardinals, Orioles, and Blue Jays in our aviary, but there is nothing ordinary about the rest of our collection. Take the Leavenworth Woodpeckers for a starter. Follow them up with the Henryetta Hens, LaFeria Nighthawks, Northampton Meadowlarks, Port Arthur Sea Hawks, Hendersonville Skylarks, Saltillo Parrots (*Peroneros*), New Haven Prairie Hens, Opelika Opelicans, Portland Jay Birds, Greenville Robins, Neosho Night Hawks, Dominion Hawks, Jamestown Falcons, New Haven Black Crows, Dayton Ducks, Evansville Blackbirds, Grand Forks Flickertails, Aberdeen Pheasants, Sarasota Gulls, Fulton Chicks, Hartford Bluebirds, Sioux Falls Canaries, Waterloo White Hawks, Grand Rapids Bobolinks, Miami Beach Flamingos, Minot Mallards, Owls of the Two Laredos, Rio Grande Valley Whitewings, Newburgh Hummingbirds, Rock Hill Wrens, Fostoria Red Birds, New Orleans Pelicans, Abilene Eagles, Edmonton Gray Birds, Columbia Gamecocks, Rayne Rice Birds, and that quintessential minor league squad, the Toledo Mud Hens. Extra credit, however, goes only to the Rhode Island Reds.

Not admitted to the above company, for obvious reasons, are the Green Bay Duck Wallopers.

And dare we slight that old chlorophyll crowd, the plant kingdom, in favor of more mobile forms of life? (Mobile, did someone say Mobile? What about the Mobile Sea Gulls or the Mobile Bears? Or the Mobile Swamp Angels?) Opposition fans loved roasting the Idaho Falls Russets, but weren't above picking (on) the Suffolk Goobers, Selma Cloverleafs, Dubuque Shamrocks, Tacoma Daisies, Paris Red Peppers, Albany Nuts, Jacksonville Roses, Houston Magnolias, Hamilton Primroses, LaGrande Spuds, Hammond Berries, Spartanburg Peaches, Villahermosa Bananas, Danville Leafs, Little Rock Rose Buds, Hartford Laurels, Palatka Azaleas, Charleston Palmettos, Oakland Acorns, or Toronto Maple Leafs. And, for the historically minded, we present the York White Roses and the Lancaster Red Roses.

What gives more pride to a community (and a stranger name to a ballclub) than a local product or occupation? "We make stuff around here, and we're darn proud of it!" virtually screams from every uniform shirtfront.

Mull over the fine wares of the Amsterdam Rugmakers, Gloversville Mitten Makers, Kewanee Boilermakers, Oswego Starchmakers, Hastings Brickmakers, Cortland Wagonmakers, Troy Collar and Cuff Makers, Springfield Blanketmakers, Bristol Bellmakers, Bassett Furnituremakers, Lima Cigarmakers, Appleton Papermakers, Waverly Wagonmakers, Petersburg Trunkmakers, Gadsden Steel Makers, and Brockton Shoemakers.

But wait, we've just begun: The Pueblo Steel Workers, Gray's Harbor Loggers, Danbury Hatters, Kirksville Osteopaths, Cynthiana Cobblers, Anniston Moulders, Des Moines Undertakers, Ada Cementers, Lufkin Foresters, Lumberton Auctioneers, Durant Educators, Mayfield Clothiers, Edmonton Trappers, Waterbury Timers, Peoria Distillers, Greenville Spinners, Oil City Refiners, San Luis Potosi Tunamen, Alpine Cowboys, Borger Gassers, Adrian Fencevilles, Vancouver Horse Doctors, Elkin Blanketeers, Hannibal Pepsies, Baton Rouge Essos, Grand Rapids Woodworkers, St. Joseph Autos, Wausau Lumberjacks, Aguacalientes Railworkers, Findlay Natural Gassers, Norfolk Oystermen, Dubuque Packers, Crisfield

Crabbers, Asheville Moonshiners, Beatrice Milkskimmers, Cambridge Canners, Ilion Typewriters, Akron Rubbermen, Lexington Studebakers, Carmen Shrimpers, Cedar Rapids Pork Packers, Kannapolis Towelers, Charles City Tractorites (catchy name, comrade), New Bedford Whalers, Portsmouth Truckers, Superior Longshoremen, Marinette Lumber Shovers, Sharon Steels, Youngstown Puddlers, Erie Brewers, Newport News Shipbuilders, Concord Weavers, New Haven Profs, Connellsville Cokers, Marion Glass Blowers, Hutchinson Salt Packers, San Angelo Sheep Herders, Racine Malted Milks, Flint Vehicles, Tampico Dockworkers, Providence Clam Diggers, Muncie Fruit Jars, Douglas Smeltermen, and the Blackstone Barristers.

Ah, that old team of mine...the Welch Miners, Carlsbad Potashers, Bisbee Copper Kings, McAllister Diggers, Reading Coal Heavers, Virginia Ore Diggers, Morgantown Graniteers, Fort Dodge Gypsumeaters, Baker Goldiggers.

Those who till the earth come in for their share of glory: the Fresno Raisineaters, Morgantown Aggies, New London Planters, Easton Farmers, Moline Plowboys, New Iberia Sugar Boys, Larned Wheat Kings, Fargo-Morehead Graingrowers, San Jose Florists, Springfield Reapers, Villahermosa Banana Growers, Charleston Broom Corn Cutters, San Jose Gardeners, Lima Bean Eaters, Bradenton Growers, Hermosillo Orangepickers, Cordoba Coffeegrowers, and Gomez Palacio Cotton Growers.

And while no one can ever forget the Kalamazoo Celery Pickers, somehow one gets the feeling the Riverside Rubes and the Watsonville Hayseeds could have been accorded more respect.

The men and women in uniform also get their recognition: the Decatur Commodores, Danville Old Soldiers, Dayton Veterans, Greenville Majors, Mobile Red Warriors, Erie Sailors, Danville Warriors, Louisville Colonels, Elmira Gladiators, Hudson Marines, Fort Wayne Generals, Oakland Invaders, Rockford Rough Riders.

The races of mankind? Why not? We have many fine entries. Besides the overdone, and rather generic "Indians," consider the Dublin Irish, Terre Haute Hottentots, Fayetteville Scotties, Grand Rapids Boers, Memphis Egyptians ("Keep your eye on the ball and walk like an Egyptian!"), Canton Chinamen, Toronto Canucks, Lake Charles Creoles, Shenandoah Hungarian Rioters, London Cockneys, Harrisonburg Turks, Sulphur Springs Spartans, Fort William

Canadians, Shenendoah-Mahanoy City Huns, Baton Rouge Cajuns, Edmonton Eskimos, and Havana Cubans.

Getting back to our Native American friends, however, there are no shortage of chaps around beyond sundry "Indians," "Braves," and "Chiefs": the Pawhuska Osages, Lynn Papooses, Greenwood Choctaws, Syracuse Onondagas, Arkansas City Osages, Zanesville Kickapoos, Ottawa Modocs, Laredo Apaches, Auburn Cayugas, London Tecumsehs, Memphis Chicks (not named after cute little yellow birds but after the Chickasaw tribe), New Castle Nassannocks, Columbus Pawnees, Donalsonville Seminoles, Huntington Miamis, Lawton Medicine Men, and Waterbury Nattatucks.

But if you wish to go back a little farther than our current brethren, one can always jump back a few eons to the Lincoln Missing Links.

Theology? Ponder the Los Angeles Seraphs, Lufkin Angels, Charlotte Presbyterians, St. Paul Apostles, Palmyra Mormons, Natchez Pilgrims, Taylorville Christians, Battle Creek Adventists, Charleston Evangelists, Monterrey Gray Monks (*Monjes Grises*) Hazleton Quay-kers, and the St. Petersburg Saints.

And somehow I can't help but wonder if the Sandusky Fisheaters aren't a backhanded compliment to pre-Vatican II Catholics.

Just so you don't think the forces of light have the upper hand, however, consider the following: the Salem or Wichita Witches, Leon Red Devils, Frostburg Demons, Des Moines Devils, Graham Hijackers, New Castle Outlaws, Crookston Crooks, Bristol Tramps, Beaumont Roughnecks, Paris Parisites, Bartlesville Buccaneers, LaCrosse Outcasts, Macon Brigands, Ciudad Mante Smugglers (*Alijadores*), Joliet Convicts, Coalinga Savages, Longview Cannibals, Omaha Kidnappers, Corsicana Desperados, Davenport Prodigals, and the North Wilkesboro Flashers.

However, if things get too iffy for the good guys, expect the Hoquim Perfect Gentlemen to step in and save the day.

Tired of the merely mundane Red Sox and White Sox? Here's a veritable hosiery store of attire, including the Dublin Green Sox, Abilene Blue Sox, Amarillo Gold Sox, San Jose JoSox, Reno Silver Sox, Pasadena Silk Sox and the cryptically named Miami Sun Sox and the Colorado Springs Sky Sox. A team with a definite identity crisis was the Middlesboro Cubsox.

Think Charlie Finley was egotistical? All he ever named after himself was the A's mule. Consider the Omaha Roarkes, Auburn Boulies, Springfield Dunnmen, Duncan Uttmen, New Haven Weissmen (after Hall-of-Famer George Weiss, no less), and the Flint Halligans.

While just about every league has featured a squad named "Giants," few can match the lack of scale of the Des Moines Midgets. Except, of course, for fellow Iowans, the Waterloo Microbes.

Some teams just couldn't make up their mind as to what sort of athletes they were: the Hazleton Pugilists, Woonsocket Trotters, Haverhill Duffers, Jamestown Jockies, Headland Dixie Runners, and the Portsmouth Olympics.

If it's head-to-head matchups you want, consider these pairings:

- The Des Moines Prohibitionists vs. the Lafayette Wets
- The Iola Gasbags vs. the Waycross Blowhards
- The Mansfield Reformers vs. the Ottumwa Standpatters
- The Moose Jaw Robin Hoods vs. the Nashua Millionaires
- The Decatur Commies (aided by the LaCrosse Pinks) vs. the Kearney Kapitalists

And for those old enough to remember William Jennings Bryans' "Cross of Gold" Speech:

- The Meridien Silverites vs. the Grand Rapids Gold Bugs

And while we seem to be in a political mode, it's time now for our "politically incorrect" competition. As World War I deepened the Class D Middle Texas League's Brenham Kaisers certainly found themselves on the wrong side of history. They wisely became the Patriots. And had the Berlin (Ontario) Busy Bees — and the entire Class D Canadian League — not collapsed after the 1913 season, they too would have changed their name, but in an entirely different way. While there was nothing wrong with Busy Bees, there sure was with Berlin. The entire city changed its name to Kitchener.

But the all-time most politically incorrect monicker award goes to a team from the 1912 Class D Rocky Mountain League: the Canon City Swastikas. With a nickname like that it's no wonder the team vanished virtually without a trace.

Other names you might not see today are the Canton Chinks, the Fremont Freaks, Tarboro Tarbabies, Salem Fairies, and the Jacksonville Lunatics.

Standing above petty political concerns are the aristocracy of the minors: the Nazareth Barons, Mount Vernon Kings, Ottumwa Palace Kings, Victoria Sultans (*Sultanicos*), Paris Bourbons, San Jose Dukes, Pulaski Counts, Saskatoon Sheiks, and York Monarchs.

Of course, not just teams had nicknames. Whole leagues did: Pony (Pennsylvania-Ontario-New York), Kitty (Kentucky-Illinois-Tennessee), Sally (South Atlantic) and, my personal favorite, the Mink (the long-gone Missouri-Iowa-Nebraska-Kansas League).

Then there are the just plain inexplicable — the Regina Bonepilers, Yakima Pippins, Wilmington Blue Rocks, Newburgh Cobblestone Throwers, Newport Pear Diggers, Muscatine Pearl Finders, Orange Hoo-Hoos, Corsicana Gumbo Busters, Lowell Bingling Pans, Norfolk Mary Janes, Cairo Mud Wallopers, Nashua Rainmakers, Americus Pallbearers, Bay City Rice Eaters, Oakland Monday Models, Morgan City Oyster Shockers, Lincoln Treeplanters, Bloomington Suckers, Evansville Pocketeers, Minot Why-Nots, Americus Muckalees, Houston Babies, and Springfield Foot Trackers.

But the winner in the worst name of all time...drumroll, please... the never to be equalled Bluffton Dregs.

Boy, I'd love to see *that* logo.

PCL PARKS OF THE '50s:
Nostalgia Ain't What It Used to Be

Talk in the 1950s was that the Pacific Coast League — a circuit so strong that it was granted a special title "Open Classification" — would gradually evolve into a major league.

Certainly, looking back at what did happen — big league clubs supplanting PCL franchises in San Francisco, Oakland, Hollywood, Los Angeles, San Diego, and Seattle it would almost appear that the old PCL *did* go major.

Back in the '40s and '50s the caliber of play on the coast, — and the level of compensation — was so strong that occasionally a player preferred *not* to graduate to the bigs. For example, San Francisco Seals owner Paul I. Fagan had a $5,000 minimum wage, roughly equal to that of the majors'. Both Ferris Fain in 1945 and Bill Werle in 1947 were unhappy to be promoted respectively to the A's and Pirates because they earned more with San Francisco. Seals manager Lefty O'Doul drew a princely $45,000-$50,000.

Yet the era's PCL parks were hardly of a uniformly impressive caliber. From Seattle to San Diego stadia were often beset by problems ranging from termites to beer-soaked infields to lack of parking to poor lighting. Nostalgia has a habit of clouding the warts on the faces of our old acquaintances. Believe me, that phenomenon applies to the PCL's parks of the 1950s.

Let's take a look at what these fields were like, say, in 1952. Said Charley Dressen, 1949-50 Oakland Oaks manager, "I know of Class

A, and even B, circuits that wouldn't tolerate some of the Coast League layouts."

SEATTLE

A Fourth of July 1933 fireworks display ignited a blaze which leveled old, wooden Dugdale Park. The Indians quickly sought shelter at Civic Field, a windblown high school diamond with a skin infield. "The outfielders pounded the turf of Civic Field and received more than their share of sore legs and charley horses," noted *The Sporting News*. "Infielders have taken many a bump from ricocheting balls and the fans endured the inconvenience of view-obstructing light poles and the chill winds of Puget Sound...Civic Field was never meant for pro ball."

It was not until 1938, however, when a new owner, prosperous local brewer, Emil Sicks, constructed namesake Sicks' Stadium. Compared to Civic Field and many contemporary PCL facilities it was a positive paradise (save for low water pressure which could be a problem when large crowds attended), reasonably accessible by all forms of transportation and with perhaps the best parking in the circuit. Sicks' Stadium lived to be a major league venue, hosting the expansion Pilots in 1969.

PORTLAND

Not only was Vaughn Street Park's (aka Lucky Beavers Stadium) parking substandard, but its lighting was reportedly the league's worst. Dating back to 1901, it was largely unchanged since 1912 and by far the circuit's oldest facility. Ownership mulled significant improvements as far back as the 1920s, but they never took place. Its wooden grandstands were in the habit of catching fire, and in 1947 the left-field bleachers burned to the ground. A local fire marshall periodically threatened condemnation of the grandstand unless a sprinkler system was installed.

Jimmy Dykes, who had managed the Hollywood Stars from 1946 to 1948, categorized its locker rooms (as well as San Diego's) as "worse than can be found in some Class C parks."

Located next door to the Electric Steel Foundry, it reeked of unchecked industrial pollution. The *Portland Oregonian's* L. H. Gregory waxed poetically of "a feeling of intimacy with the players. . . . Vaughn Street grew in the simple days when wood stands were good enough; it gives way to a complex era of steel and concrete, of formality in design and in living," but *The Sporting News* less romantically described it as "an eyesore to fans, players and scribes alike."

SACRAMENTO

The Solons' Edmonds Field, named after *Sacramento Union* sports editor Dick Edmonds, was known as Moreing Field when it was first built in 1930. On July 12, 1948 it was destroyed by fire but was rebuilt by the following Opening Day. Its capacity was a mere 10,800, but was capable of expansion.

OAKLAND

Once a minor league source of pride, Emeryville or Oaks Ball Park had degenerated into "Splendid Splinter Emporium." The name was based on harsh truth. Towards the end of the park's history (it was torn down in 1957) whenever a liner or fly hit the left-field barrier, it literally sent splinters flying from the fences' rotting boards. Only a minimal roof covered its long, low grandstand. On the positive side Emeryville featured perhaps the best lighting in the circuit.

SAN FRANCISCO

Built in 1931 for $600,000, Seals Stadium, nonetheless, had no roof over its grandstand. Fans chattered and froze (shades of Candlestick!) as there was nothing overhead to keep whatever heat existed from escaping straight into the ozone. With damp ocean fogs blanketing the place and chilling winds of 15 to 20 MPH blowing from left to right field, Seals Stadium fans needed all the help they could get, but didn't get *any*.

The 23,000-seat park hosted both the San Francisco Seals and Missions for several years. After the 1937 season the Missions moved South, becoming the Hollywood Stars. Located next to a brewery, Seals Stadium featured a unique beer-sodden infield. Steam escaping from the brewery would be condensed by cold air and precipitate onto the diamond!

Other problems included no warning track, poor parking, and a lack of police protection, causing chaos both within and without the stadium.

To compensate for these frailties, in 1950 owner Paul Fagan provided Seals Stadium with a significant face-lift. The game's first glass backstop went up. A spotting tower to pinpoint fights and drunks was erected. Ladies rest rooms were upgraded to such an extent that females often spent a good part of the game in them (perhaps they were seeking shelter from the freezing cold); radio accounts of the game were even piped into them.

The Seals' home clubhouse was unusually luxurious, boasting a barber chair, a shoe-shine stand, a soda fountain, and beer on tap. A Scottish golf course groundskeeper was imported to manicure the diamond, and Fagan banned all advertising from outfield fences, a decision costing him $20,000 a year in revenue.

HOLLYWOOD

The Stars rented wooden, 12,987-seat Gilmore Stadium from oil baron Earl Gilmore, but when the lease ran out in 1958, CBS held an option on all of the land under the park (except right and center fields, that is) and eyed the site for a new studio. Although the Stars were backed by such real-life stars as George Burns, Gracie Allen, George Raft, Barbara Stanwyck, William Powell, Gene Autry, William Frawley, Gary Cooper, Walt Disney, Bing Crosby, and directors Cecil B. DeMille and George Stevens, they faced financial difficulties on several fronts. The rival Los Angeles Angels held all territorial rights to the City of Angels and got a cut of five cents for every Stars ticket sold. Earl Gilmore received all revenue from Gilmore Field parking and even partial control over Stars radio and TV rights.

It was an unusually snug park ("Friendly Gilmore Field" is how it was often advertised), but that was in part due to violation of design rules. Instead of the standard 60 feet from homeplate to the backstop, Gilmore Field measured 34 feet. From first and third base to the stands, distances were a minuscule 24 feet. In fairness, however, parking was unusually good.

LOS ANGELES

Wrigley Field was a terrific park. Built in 1925 for $1.1 million it featured a nine-story tower, ivy-covered walls in left (yes, it was owned by *those* Wrigleys), and could accommodate 23,000 fans and 700 cars. In freeway-dependent Los Angeles that spelled problems.

While Hollywood's Gilmore Field was the haunt of Tinseltown's elite, Wrigley Field did a little starring of its own, such as in the film version of *Damn Yankees* (empty shots only — by this time the PCL had left town) and Ray Milland's 1948 opus *It Happens Every Spring*. A decade later the popular (at least it was popular among the younger set) television series *Home Run Derby* was shot there. Because of its relatively small capacity and the lack of parking, the Dodgers chose not to use it when they moved west in 1958. Wrigley Field had its last hurrah in 1961 when it hosted the expansion American League Angels. Because of Wrigley Field's cozy power alleys (345 feet), home runs were plentiful.

If any stadium in Coast League history looked big league, it was Wrigley Field. Doubled-decked and roofed the entire length of its grandstand, Wrigley Field was a minor league showplace and *should* have been considering its cost. Situated on filled land above a long-forgotten creek bed, Wrigley Field required substantial foundation work, resulting in what was then the highest per-seat cost of any park in the country.

SAN DIEGO

Built as a WPA project in 1936 and thus one of the PCL's younger parks, Lane Field nonetheless had multiple problems —proving perhaps once again the inefficiency of government projects. Owned by the U.S. Navy it was only 12 feet from homeplate to the backstop. And if you think that's bad, only 87 feet from homeplate to first.

By the way, about that 12-foot distance from homeplate. When the Padres first occupied Lane Field, it was only partially completed. There was no roof and, as there was no roof, there was no easy way to fashion a screen to protect patrons. A rash of injured fans with sore jaws and broken noses resulted.

There was limited parking, poor lighting, and more termites than you could safely shake a wooden bat at. In the early 1950s, 1,200 bleacher seats were condemned due to termite infestation.

Aside from that, it was great.

PCL PARKS 1952

City	Park	Capacity	LF	CF	RF
Hollywood	Gilmore Field	12,987	335	400	335
Los Angeles	Wrigley Field	23,500	340	412	339
Oakland	Oak Park	12,352	335	407	329
Portland	Lucky Beaver Stadium	13,352	331	368	315
Sacramento	Edmonds Field	10,800	326	463	326
San Diego	Lane Field	8,800	390	500	350
San Francisco	Seals Stadium	23,000	360	400	365
Seattle	Sicks' Stadium	15,000	305	405	345

ALABAMA PITTS

One in a Million. That's what ex-convict Ron LeFlore called himself in his autobiography, reflecting on his remarkable rise from prison cell to batter's box.

With a better sense of history, the fleet-footed Tiger star might have titled it "Two in a Million," because decades earlier there had been another man with a checkered past who longed to break into pro ball.

That player was Edwin Collins "Alabama" Pitts, who in 1935 sent shock waves across baseball as he attempted to leap directly from Sing Sing to the very highest level of the minors.

As a 19-year-old, the Alabama native was one of two men convicted of holding up a New York City grocery store at gunpoint, getting $72.50 from the cash register. He was arrested and sentenced to not less than eight, nor more than 16, years behind prison bars.

At Sing Sing the former Navy enlisted man seemed to find himself. Uniformly described as a "model prisoner," Pitts outshone all in athletic competition. Pitts stood six feet tall, weighed in at a trim 170 pounds, and reportedly did not "smoke or chew." Progressive Sing Sing Warden Lewis E. Lawes encouraged him in his activities. At whatever sport Pitts attempted, he was described as the finest Sing Sing had ever witnessed. Besides his diamond activity, he starred in the backfield of the prison 11 and at track and field.

During his five years at Sing Sing he paced his club in batting, homers, triples, doubles, RBI, and stolen bases. In 1935 as he approached parole, Pitts, who threw and batted right, hit better than .500 in 21 games, with 41 hits and 78 total bases, including eight home runs. He was termed, with justification, "an excellent fielder."

The International League's Albany Senators were keeping an eye on Pitts — as were several other clubs. The barnstorming House of David, the Class C Middle Atlantic League's Dayton Ducks, and supposedly two big league teams were interested. Albany Senators' General Manager Johnny Evers offered Pitts a $200-per-month contract, and, in April 1935, Warden Lawes advised Pitts to take it.

On April 25 Evers wrote to Judge William G. Bramham, president of the National Association, inquiring if there were any rules barring the signing of a fellow such as Pitts. Two days later Bramham indicated his feeling was that it was not a good idea. Warden Lawes then wrote to Bramham begging him to give Pitts a chance. On May 22 Bramham met privately with the National Association's Executive Committee to discuss the case. It was thumbs down for Pitts, but Bramham did not respond until June 3.

On that date Bramham requested Albany to refrain from offering Pitts a contract, but Evers wired back that one had already been signed on May 29. On June 5, Bramham officially ruled that Albany could not sign Pitts. "We are of the opinion," wrote Bramham, "that the interests of baseball generally and the interests of players in our association will best be served by not admitting players who have been considered by society a much greater offense than offenses for which our own association permanently disqualify a player."

Motivating Bramham, in part, was a fear that Pitts was being manipulated by major league forces. "He was tipped off," his assistant, L. H. Addington, later wrote, "by what he termed a reliable source that a National League club was the prime mover in behalf of Pitts, and the Minors were simply being used as a guinea pig. If Pitts 'got by' and drew big crowds in the Minors, then the idea was that he would be called in for a swing around the circuit by his original promoters. Bramham literally 'burned up' at that."

That same day Syracuse Chiefs President Jack Corbett dismissed the Pitts signing as a cheap publicity stunt, saying if the outfielder was signed at all he should have played under "another name." Additionally, Corbett failed to see how a player of Pitts' meager experience could make the grade at the minors' highest level — a legitimate point that was soon to be lost in the controversy that enveloped the case.

At 10 A.M. on June 6 Pitts was paroled. As the prison gates swung open, more than a hundred reporters, photographers, and curiosity seekers greeted him. The storm of media and public attention was just gathering steam.

Public support reached out to Pitts. Two hundred fans greeted him at Albany's Union Station. A Manhattan radio station offered him a job as a sports announcer. A semi-pro club in Utica, New York, tendered him a contract. So did the football Brooklyn Dodgers. Arthur Swartz, chairman of the NYS Assembly's Codes Committee, denounced Bramham's ruling as a black mark against baseball, in his view fully as serious as the Black Sox scandal. A petition signed by over 100 Allentown (PA) fans threatened to "retaliate in like manner against the game itself" if Pitts was not allowed to play. Similar petitions circulated in other cities.

Even Philadelphia Phils manager Jimmie Wilson said he'd be happy to have a fellow like Pitts on his squad: "I need a good hard-hitting extra man. If Pitts can fill the bill, there's a suit waiting for him at the clubhouse. I don't care what he did. He's paid his debt to society and that is finished. He should not have to pay any interest until he dies." Dizzy Dean, Kiki Cuyler, and Pepper Martin voiced similar sentiments.

Not every one was so enthused. Frederick A. Moran, executive director of the NYS Parole Board, issued a public statement not exactly supportive of Pitts' crusade. "The Division of Parole," he noted, "is not out to throw cold water on what baseball may have in store for Pitts. However, he has a position awaiting his acceptance in the midwest, one that points to a good future in business." He commented he "would rather see" Pitts choose that option.

The Albany Senators appealed to the National Association's Executive Committee to overturn Bramham's ruling. Future National League president Warren Giles, then the president of the Rochester Red Wings, personally brought their decision to Pitts. It was not positive.

"We thought," explained Giles, "and still think that the fans and players would not desire persons with prison records in the game. If we're wrong and baseball is hurt, we're to blame, not the Albany club."

"Well, Mr. Giles," said Pitts, who had literally burst into tears on hearing the news, "are you trying to make an example of me? You're telling me I cannot earn my living at the best thing I know. Baseball is the thing I do best and the thing I want to do most!"

Giles seemed uncomfortable with his ruling. "I could have wired you the result of my poll," he told Evers, "but I wanted to avoid being accused of ducking. I did not intend to come here with the Rochester club, but I made the trip purposely in order to give the decision in person and face the music."

Johnny Evers was outraged, threatening, "I will retire from baseball if Pitts is not allowed to play. I know this is a broad assertion, but I will make good on it."

"I guess this ends it," said a downcast and shaken Pitts. "It looks like I never will get to play."

The Albany club wasted no time in taking their case to baseball's ultimate arbiter, Judge Kenesaw Mountain Landis. While the flinty commissioner pondered the case, the nation's sympathy went out to Pitts. Comedy legend Hal Roach offered him a Hollywood contract, although it was hardly of blockbuster proportions — $50 to $75 per week to act in Roach's comedies. Pitts appeared on NBC's "Briggs Sports Review" and even on the "Kate Smith Show." Charles Evans Hughes, Jr., son of the Supreme Court justice and a prominent Washington attorney in his own right, wired the Senators: "Courage. Stay with your decision. Anyone opposed to Pitts is un-American." Clarence Darrow dismissed Bramham's ruling in just one word, "Rotten." The East Side Ministers' Council of Buffalo pled that Pitts should be extended "a fair chance to establish himself as a law-abiding member of society."

Commented Warden Lawes, "It is not only Alabama Pitts who is on trial, but the whole American people as to whether they wish to destroy the rehabilitation of men sent to prison."

And even the man Pitts robbed, John Costello, came to his defense. Costello wired the Senators: "If the parole commissioner thinks it safe to send Pitts out it ought to be safe for baseball players. My sympathies are entirely with Alabama in this controversy."

What the nation's fans did not know, was that Bramham had first conferred with Landis before issuing his controversial decision. He thought he had Landis' backing. "I wanted to get the commissioner's viewpoint before making any decision, and thought I was expressing it when I ruled against Pitts," he later revealed to close friends.

But public pressure favoring Pitts had reached floodgate levels. Letters and telegrams poured into the commissioner's Chicago office. Newspapermen badgered him for comment, and he took to ducking them altogether. Finally, one reporter cornered Landis and showed him the proofs of a forthcoming *Saturday Evening Post* editorial. It assumed that Landis had ruled in favor of Bramham, and blasted

Landis mercilessly. That was it; Landis would rule in favor of Pitts. "The sentiment for Pitts was so strong, and those wishing to give him a chance in baseball were so unanimous, that no one could resist this tide," the commissioner supposedly confided to Bramham. Landis' decision came on June 17. He ruled that the flyhawk could play for Albany — but with one significant stipulation. In order to defuse concerns that the Senators were signing Pitts just to capitalize on the publicity, Landis decreed that Alabama could not appear in any Senators exhibitions in 1935.

Landis was no bleeding-heart, however. He took pains to spell out that, despite press accounts to the contrary, Pitts was no choir boy, explaining that he was armed while his accomplice merely acted as lookout on the fateful night of the Costello robbery, that he had been "involved in at least five other similar robberies," and that despite subsequent sympathetic media reports there was nothing in the record to indicate extenuating circumstances such as that he was "drunk" or "hungry."

"In the course of the considerable publicity in this case there have been created erroneous impressions which require correction," wrote Landis. "It has been represented that the offense committed, which is the basis of the National Association ruling, grew out of an 'escapade' wherein Pitts, 'drunk' and 'hungry,' was misled into accompanying 'an older man' (or 'a tough guy') into a store, only to discover that his companion's purpose was robbery, which the companion accomplished by using a gun, while Pitts, unarmed and merely obeying his companions orders, took '$5 or $10' from the cash register; that this was the only offense in which Pitts ever was involved; and that Pitts pleaded guilty out of consideration for his companion's wife and children and to lessen his companion's punishment by 'taking the rap' for him.

"The official record, certified by the court which sentenced Pitts, establishes that it was Pitts who entered the store, held up the clerk with his loaded revolver, and took $76.25 from the cash register. (The amount is not important — it depended upon what the cash register contents happened to be — but $5 or $10 is more consistent with the 'drunk' and 'hungry' and 'escapade' representations.) Pitts' accomplice (one year older than Pitts) acted as 'lookout' and was unarmed."

Landis also took pains to quote from Morris Koenig, the judge who sentenced Pitts to prison. Koenig had written: "There is no evidence before me that he [the lookout] was in any other robbery than this, while Pitts has been in at least five other robberies…

"I should think Pitts was very fortunate that he was not compelled to plead guilty to robbery in the first degree, where the mandatory sentence would have been 20 years."

In his conclusion, Landis revealed sympathy for Bramham and basically admitted that it was only the force of public pressure that forced him reverse his fellow czar: "As originally presented to the President and Executive Committee of the National Association, this case involved only a general question [involving the hiring of felons], which they decided properly, as their duty required, and as the Commissioner would have been obliged to rule. Since then, however, a new situation has arisen. Conditions have been created as the result of which there can not be much doubt as to the destructive effect, upon Pitts' effort toward rehabilitation, of not permitting him to enter baseball employment. This was not contemplated by, nor is it due to, the ruling of the President of the National Association. And in this situation, reputable people have expressed to me their belief that there has been a complete reformation in Pitts' character, and their confidence in his earnest intent to regain an honorable position in society. Solely for these reasons, Pitts will be allowed to play…"

Not surprisingly, the blond flyhawk was overjoyed. He itched to get in a game. But the Albany club maintained the suspense, waiting until their next home day game, on Sunday, May 23, 1935, before pencilling him into the lineup. Eight thousand ecstatic fans thronged Hawkins Stadium as Pitts went 2 for 5, drove in one run, scored another, and flawlessly handled four chances in center. Making it all sweeter was that it came against Jack Corbett's Syracuse Chiefs. "It felt great," beamed Pitts.

It was so much like a dream, but Pitts' wake-up call rang early. International League pitching proved to be too much for him, and, while he could chase down a ball with the best of them, his throwing arm was definitely substandard. Adding injury to insult, he was hobbled by a bruised shoulder, a sprained finger, and blood poisoning from a spiking. At season's end, Alabama Pitts had batted just .233 in 43 games, with no homers or triples and just three doubles and three stolen bases.

Senators owner Joe Cambria reassured him: "I am more than pleased with the progress you are making. I am confident you will hit close to .300 next year." In the off-season, Pitts signed with the Philadelphia Eagles but washed out after two regular season NFL contests.

Despite Cambria's optimism the following season Pitts was reassigned to the Class A New York-Pennsylvania (now the Eastern) League's York White Roses — also owned by Cambria — where he continued to flounder, batting a puny .224 with two homers and 11 RBI in 41 games. He was let go in June. The next stop was with the hapless Winston-Salem Twins in the Class B Piedmont League. There Pitts hit .278, but appeared in just 23 contests. After that, it was off to the Charlotte and Valdese clubs in a North Carolina "outlaw" circuit. In 1940 he turned up with the Hickory (NC) Rebels of the Class D Tar Heel League, where he hit a respectable .302 with 39 RBI (but with no homers) in 64 games.

In 1937 Pitts had married a Miss Mary Walker, a fellow textile mill worker, and settled down in North Carolina. They had a daughter. Then, on June 7, 1941, Pitts hied himself to what has been described as "a combination filling station, tavern and swimming pool" in Valdese. A dance was going on, and Pitts attempted to cut in on one couple. He picked the wrong one. Newland LeFevres of nearby Morgantown took offense. He knifed Pitts, severing an artery in his shoulder. In a few hours Edwin Collins "Alabama" Pitts was dead.

"I'm deeply distressed to learn of his death," said Warden Lawes. "Pitts had an excellent record here — as he had in the Navy before he came to Sing Sing. The boys who knew him will feel bad."

BUSH LEAGUE
SCRAPBOOK: Part I

As brevity is the soul of wit, not all baseball tales merit a chapter of their own but are still well worth telling. Without further ado, here are some items of more than passing interest from the bush league scrapbook:

BEANBALL

Ray Chapman is the only big leaguer to die from an on-field mishap, when he died from a Carl Mays' pitch. But at least six minor leaguers have met similar fates at the plate.

The first unfortunate was the New England League's Lynn Shoemakers' Tom Burke, who was beaned on August 9, 1906, by Fall River's Joe Yaeger. Two days later, Burke was dead. Yaeger attended his funeral, and when he took the mound two days after that, he was charged with manslaughter. He was released a few days later.

Other batters who met similar fates were Dayton second baseman "Cupid" Pinkney in 1909, Mobile infielder Johnny Dodge in 1916, Springfield third baseman Jesse Batterson in 1933, Ballinger outfielder Stormy Davis in 1947, and the Dothan Browns' Ottis Johnson in 1951.

The 24-year-old Johnson was leading the league with a .393 mark and had a 23-game hitting streak going when he was killed by a pitch thrown by Headland Dixie Runners southpaw Harry "Jack" Clifton. Even before the beaning, a Dothan sportswriter had warned: "Jack Clifton is a dangerous man as long as he is in uniform." In Clifton's next start he no-hit the petrified Panama City Fliers, 19-2. The Panama City, Dothan, Ozark, and Enterprise clubs demanded Clifton —

and manager James "Bubba" Bell — be banned from the league. When Headland ownership refused, the protesting teams shut the league down. A compromise was reached in which Clifton (22-6 with a league leading 245 strikeouts) agreed to play only in the outfield for the rest of the year, but he later returned to the mound.

THEY DIDN'T HAVE A KLU...

Memphis Chicks slugger Ted Kluszewski had a whole week's worth of hitting on the afternoon of July 27, 1946. Against the visiting New Orleans Pelicans, he started out slowly, with a pop-up, but then there was no holding him. He homered to right, tripled, flied out, and singled in regulation time. In the 13th he tripled again to nail down a victory.

In the nightcap, Klu tripled again in the first frame, doubled in the third, singled in the fourth, and just missed another homer to right again in the sixth, when the ball hooked foul by a few inches. At that point pitcher Tom Sunkel just gave up and walked Ted intentionally.

On July 28 of the same season Kluszewski set an Southern Association record with 23 putouts in a 14-inning game versus the Mobile Bears.

ROUND ONE

In the 1931 Texas League, Dallas Steers catcher Al Todd and Houston Buffaloes pitcher Dizzy Dean went at it in one of baseball's most memorable fights. It's said that Todd won his chance at the majors thanks to the pugilistic skills he exhibited that day. With perhaps that battle as an inspiration, in 1953 Shreveport outfielder Joe Szekeley and Beaumont third baseman Jim Williams traded punches for a full half-hour, stopping only due to "sheer exhaustion."

BOY WONDER

Perhaps the youngest manager in baseball history was 22-year-old Eddie Malone, appointed in 1942 as skipper of the Class C Northern League's Duluth Dukes. Catcher Malone had been in pro ball since 1938, signing as a 17-year-old with Albuquerque. Malone set no other records as a manager, however. The Dukes, a largely inexperienced team, finished a mere sixth (56-69). Malone, though, continued with his backstopping duties, hitting a respectable .309 in 123 games.

DON'T GO OUT AFTER DARK

In June 1942 Vancouver Capilanos pitcher-manager Don Osborn notched an unusual record — 31 consecutive victories in the daylight. The 30-year-old began his streak in June 1940, winning 13 Saturday afternoon contests that year, 15 in 1941, and his first three in 1942 (he was 5-1 in night contests). Class B Western International League sportswriters dubbed the sinkerball pitcher "Death in the Afternoon."

"It's a tough job being pitcher and manager at the same time," noted Osborn. "But I like it. After all, nobody knows better than the chucker himself how he's going, and I won't hesitate to yank myself out of there if I haven't got the stuff."

FAME IS FLEETING DEPARTMENT

The modern season strikeout record was long thought to be held by a fellow named Bill "Lefty" Kennedy, who back in 1946 K'ed 456 batters for the Coastal Plains League's Rocky Mount Rocks, averaging 14.7 whiffs per nine innings. Just back from the service, Kennedy also compiled a sparkling 1.03 ERA in going 28-3, surrendering only 149 hits in 280 frames. The Carnesville, Georgia, native went on to hurl for the Indians, Browns, White Sox, Red Sox, and Reds, but never won more than eight games in a single big league campaign.

However, in 1992 truth-seeking Society for American Baseball Research (SABR) member Ray Nemec burst Kennedy's bubble when he pieced together statistics from the 1907 Class D Eastern Illinois League. He discovered that the *actual* record is held by right-hander Grover Cleveland "Slim" Lowdermilk, who fanned 465 batters for that year's pennant-winning Mattoon Comers. Lowdermilk (23-29 in the majors) won 33 games and posted a miniscule league-best ERA of 0.93.

AND DON'T COME BACK

Perhaps the shortest managerial career on record was that of former 30-game winner Gus Weyring, who hurled in the National League from 1887 to 1901. Back in 1910 he was given his first managing post, piloting the Class D Western Association's Tulsa Oilers. After losing the season opener, Weyring was canned and never managed again. He concluded the season by pitching a handful of games for the Texas League's Galveston Sandcrabs.

THIS TOWN *IS* BIG ENOUGH . . .

The American Association's Toledo Mudhens were bizarre pawns in the Federal League War of 1914-15. The team had been controlled by Cleveland Indians owner Charles Somers for several years prior to hostilities and, to keep the Feds out of Cleveland, he moved the Mud Hens to Cleveland's League Park in a "continuous ball" scheme.

His idea worked in that the Federal outlaws never invaded Cleveland, but local residents never exhibited any interest in watching American Association action. Back in Toledo a Class C Southern Michigan League franchise set up shop at Swayne Field, but again fans were not satisfied with a lower quality of ball. By the season's second half, the Southern Michigan League club was playing all its games on the road; by 1916 it was out of business.

When the real Mud Hens (managed by Roger Bresnahan) returned home in 1916, they drew 16,005 fans on Opening Day, the largest crowd in Toledo baseball history.

BANKING ON BANKHEAD

The first black manager in organized baseball was Sam Bankhead who in 1951 piloted the Farnham (Quebec) Pirates, a Pirates farm team in the Class C Provincial League. The team, which was well integrated, featured pitcher Humberto Robinson, outfielders Al Pinkston and Joe Taylor, pitcher-outfielder Bob Trice, and third-sacker Josh Gibson, Jr., but was not exactly a roaring success. The club finished 21 games back, and Bankhead, brother of pitcher Dan Bankhead, was relieved of his duties.

EXCUSE ME

One of the biggest foul-ups in baseball history occurred in

Rochester on August 8, 1903. The Eastern (International) League game between the Rochester Broncos and the visiting Providence Grays went into the 10th inning before umpire Tom Kelly realized that Providence had actually won the contest, 1-0, in regulation time. A lackadaisical scoreboard boy had failed to tally Providence's lone run in the fifth inning. The Providence bench obviously wasn't paying much attention either. Kelly refused to heed protests from the crowd, thinking them some sort of a ruse. Rochester had even scored a run in the bottom of the 10th, before Kelly finally realized what had happened. He yielded to reality only when shown the official scorebook.

BUT *WHO* STRUCK HIM OUT?

Joe Sewell was justifiably renowned as a man who could put the bat on the ball, once striking out just four times in an entire big league season, but he had nothing on Knoxville Smokies catcher Lee Head who fanned just once in 402 plate appearances in the 1935 Southern Association season. The righty batter hit .281 for the season.

WHAT'S *BIG* FALLS LIKE?

The 1987 Little Falls Mets of the short-season Class A New York-Penn League featured some of the tallest players in professional baseball history — 6'6" first baseman Bob Olah, 6'9" pitcher Terry Bross, and 6'8" southpaw Eric Hillman. Both Hillman and Bross eventually reached the majors.

KEY TO SUCCESS

One of the worst teams in organized baseball annals had to be the International League's 1926 Reading Keys. The Lauer's Park denizens went 31-129 for a .194 won-lost percentage, finishing a staggering 75 games in back of Dan Howley's Toronto Maple Leafs. This pathetic outfit was managed by none other than Frank Shaughnessy and "Hooks" Wiltse and featured two 20-game losers —southpaw Charles Swaney at 10-29 and righty Jim Marquis (8-23). Lefthander Jim Beard chipped in with a 4-15 mark and a stratospheric 7.26 ERA. Pat Shea went 2-12 as the Keys were last in International League pitching, hitting, *and* fielding. Against Toronto the Keys went 2-22 for the year.

THE HIGHLANDERS WIN THE PENNANT!
THE HIGHLANDERS WIN THE PENNANT!

Talk about exciting pennant races. The 1910 Class D East Carolina League championship went down to the final day of the season with the Fayetteville Highlanders and the Rocky Mount Railroaders in a flat-footed tie. The two teams met head-to-head, and the race wasn't wrapped up until Fayetteville turned in a ninth inning triple play to nail down the game (and the flag) by a 2-1 score.

NOW, THAT'S A NO-HITTER...

Pitcher Fred Toney is best known for the double-no-hitter he and Hippo Vaughn matched up for on May 2, 1917, but it wasn't his first noteworthy no-hitter. Back on May 10, 1909, hurling for the Class D Blue Grass League's Winchester Hustlers, Fred threw 17 hitless frames before subduing the Lexington Colts, 1-0.

THAT WONDERFUL YEAR...

Nineteen fifty-two saw some strange incidents in the bushes. Here are some of the more bizarre:

At Longview, Texas' Legion Field on April 21, caretaker Sam Neal was lowering Old Glory after the local Cherokees had been obliterated by the Wichita Falls Spudders, 12-2. The 50-year-old Neal was positioned on the soggy turf when a gust of wind blew the chain on which the flag was held against a high voltage power line. An emergency squad worked on him for a full hour and a half, but he was dead on arrival when he reached the hospital.

The minors that year were reeling under the competition of that still new-fangled device, television. A couple of teams that showed no fear, however, were the Pacific Coast League's Los Angeles Angels and the Hollywood Stars. Both televised every contest in their respective home schedules as KHJ-TV paid each club $75,000 for the rights to telecast 90 games per team.

More primitive means of communication were being used to

report on a May 1952 California League exhibition. The Ventura Braves and the Fresno Cardinals were playing at Ontario, California. A hundred miles away, Ventura radio station KVEN was interested in broadcasting the contest. Re-creations were still a pretty standard way of covering away games in the bushes, but using the telegraph was out due to a telegraphers' strike. For some reason the decision was made to use carrier pigeons. The winged messengers were to be dispatched after each inning. Seven hours after the game started the first bird arrived at KVEN. Unfortunately, he was reporting on the *second* frame. At this point, a decision was finally decided to just pick up a phone to get game play-by-play. After a while, accounts of the first and fourth innings flapped in, but by that time they were too late.

By the way, Ventura won, 9-3.

NOT BAD, KID

Detroit's Virgil "Fire" Trucks may be best known for his major league no-hitters (both pitched in 1952), but those were hardly his only no-hitters. During his five-year minor league career he tossed four such gems, including a $9\frac{2}{3}$ inning losing effort for the Buffalo Bisons against Montreal on May 31, 1941.

In 1938 the 19-year-old Trucks was 25-6 for the Andalusia Bulldogs, leading the Class D Alabama-Florida League with a microscopic 1.25 ERA, establishing the league strikeout record with 418 in just 273 innings. On Opening Day he struck out 20.

That year he pitched two no-hitters. The first was on May 18, 1938 when he defeated the Evergreen Greenies' Francis Manheim, 1-0. Manheim surrendered just one hit, which Trucks collected in the ninth inning, enabling him to score the game's only tally.

His second no-hitter that season came on June 4 when he defeated the Dothan Browns, 6-0, fanning 15.

PACKING 'EM IN

One of the biggest and most enthusiastic of minor league crowds greeted hurler Satchel Paige when he took the mound for the International League's Miami Marlins on August 7, 1956. Legendary showman Bill Veeck was running the club and announced he wished to shatter the old bush league attendance mark (56,391) set by the Jersey City Giants in 1941.

To do so, Veeck booked the Marlins into the cavernous Orange Bowl. He billed the contest as "The Baseball Party To End All Baseball Parties" and engaged Cab Calloway and Margaret Whiting to help put on the show. But the big attraction was the ageless wonder Paige. A throng of 51,713 (the flexible Veeck claimed this as the record anyway since most of the Jersey Cityites were no-shows) saw Satch depart with a 4-0 lead against the visiting Columbus Jets.

REVENGE

Releasing hurler Lee Fairbanks certainly came back to haunt the Utica Utes of the 1907 Class B New York State League. The rival Albany Senators picked up Fairbanks and he pitched two key games for manager Michael Doherty. On September 12 Fairbanks vanquished Utica, 4-0, in 16 frames, and allowed just two hits and two walks while he fanned 16. Just one week later he pitched 10 more scoreless innings versus his former mates — although he didn't record a decision as the game was called on account of rain.

Albany took the pennant by winning nine of their last 10 games, in what the *Spalding Guide* termed "one of the most brilliant and stubbornly contested battles on the diamond that had ever been seen."

A MIGHTY OAK

Babe Ruth and Mickey Mantle certainly hit some shots, but none can compare to the 618-foot blast walloped by Oakland Oaks flyhawk Roy "Dizzy" Carlyle on the Fourth of July 1929. The four-bagger sailed over the right-center field barrier at Oaks Park in Emeryville, continued on over Watts Street, landing in the gutter in front of 1212 Park Avenue. The 28-year-old Carlyle had compiled a .318 American League batting average with the Nats, Red Sox, and Yankees in 1925-26. The San Francisco Seals' Ernie Nevers, who gave up the blow, later starred in pro football.

ALL BY HIMSELF

The first unassisted 20th Century triple play was *not* shortstop Neal Ball's in 1907. A journeyman former major league first baseman named Harry P. "Hal" O'Hagan holds that honor. In August 1902 he was named player-manager of the International League's Rochester Broncos. On Monday, August 18, he joined his new team at Jersey City's new Skeeters Park, then considered "the finest in the league, beyond question."

With none out, Jersey City runners Mack Dooley and George Shoch held first and second base respectively. Skeeters batter, catcher Johnnie Butler, attempted to sacrifice but bunted the ball up in the air. O'Hagan made a diving catch, scrambled to his feet, and stepped on first to double up Dooley. Shoch, oblivious to events, was racing towards home. O'Hagan alertly scampered toward second to "triple" him up.

Rochester went on to win, 10-6.

BUSH LEAGUE
SCRAPBOOK: Part II

For those of you who thrived on the assorted trivia found in our earlier installment of Bush League Scrapbook we offer the following morsels:

TAX TIME

Keeping the wolf from the door is an old minor league necessity, but the first club to be auctioned off by IRS officials (the auction took place right on the diamond) was the International League's Richmond Virginians on November 14, 1955 to satisfy tax liens of $79,218.68. Franchises, equipment, and player contracts fetched just $20,000.

Of course, the Virginians were doing better than the Norwich Reds of the Class B Connecticut State League. On December 4, 1906 the pennant-winning Reds were sold at sheriff's auction. The price: $25.

ROW, ROW, ROW YOUR BOAT

When hurler Lon "The Arkansas Hummingbird" Warneke was scouted by a Cleveland bird dog while performing in the Class D Cotton States League in the late 1920s, he didn't exactly create a marvelous first impression. During a rainout, Warneke plopped down at second base and "rowed" a make-believe boat. The scouting report read huffily: "He's a screwball. Forget him."

CAREER YEAR?

It-would-be-interesting-to-know-what-he-did-the next-year department: "Dod" Clark of the Jamestown club of the New York and Pennsylvania League went 51-16 in 1892 with 22 wins in succession.

MURDERERS' ROW

I can think of a few big league clubs who wouldn't mind having the outfield of the 1927 San Francisco Seals. The Pacific Coast League franchise boasted Smead Jolley, who hit .397 to pace the circuit, in right; Earl Averill, a future Hall-of-Famer, in center; and Lefty O'Doul, a lifetime major league .349 hitter, in left. All three had career *big league* averages in excess of .300. The following year the 6 foot 3 inch, 202 pound Jolley hit .404, and won the PCL Triple Crown.

SAY IT AIN'T SO!

Shades of the Black Sox! Who recalls the Southern Association gambling scandal of 1959? Chattanooga first baseman Jess Levan and shortstop Waldo Gonzalez were suspended indefinitely on July 3 by association president Charles A. Hurth of New Orleans for failure to report a bribery attempt. After further investigation, Hurth barred the 31-year-old Levan for life while the 24-year-old Gonzalez was given a one-year ban. Levan was batting .331 at the time in 75 games, while Gonzalez was swatting a mere .179.

At season's end further controversy hit the club when National Association's George Trautman banned former American League backstop Joe Piton from the minors. His crime? Back in 1957 he had received two payments for purposely hitting foul balls.

WHEN IT RAINS...

Besides torrential rain, poor attendance, and the first Sunday night game in Birmingham history, the 1958 Dixie Series — the next to last — had more than its share of controversy.

The Birmingham Barons, champions of the Southern Association, were scheduled to play the winner of the Texas League Playoffs, either the Corpus Christi Giants or the Austin Senators. However, a Birmingham city ordinance prohibited athletic events featuring mixed-race competition and both Corpus Christi and Austin featured several black players. Corpus Christi (with blacks Cal Dorsey, Bo Bossard and Jim Miller) defeated Austin in a seven-game series and won the championship, but National Association President Trautman refused to either challenge the Birmingham statute or allow substitutions for the black trio.

But injuries to Bossard and Miller did allow two white substitutes — the Fort Worth Cats' Joe Macko and the Dallas Eagles' Art Dunham — to play for the Giants.

That didn't help Corpus Christi (a New York Giants' farm club that featured pitchers Frank Funk and Eddie Fisher), as they fell to the Barons in six games — the sixth contest being a historic Sunday night event that, nonetheless, drew a paltry 766 customers.

BIG BOPPER

The Class B West Texas-New Mexico League saw its share of sluggers, such as Amarillo's Bob Crues (69 homers, 254 RBI, and 185 runs scored in 1948), Lamesa's Glenn Burns (197 RBI in 1951), and Lubbock's Virgil Richardson (196 RBI in 1948), but even they never had a day like Plainview Ponies manager Jodie Beeler enjoyed at Amarillo's Gold Sox Field on August 21, 1955. It was a doubleheader — a pair of seven-inning contests — and Beeler smote two homers in the first game as his club went down to defeat, 8-6.

He picked up steam in the nightcap, walloping four more round-trippers — good for six RBI — as he powered his club to a 18-13 triumph.

It was the sixth time in league history that a player had crashed four dingers in a single game — and one of three occurrences that campaign. Pampa's Sonny Tims and Amarillo's Paul Mohr were the other two. Mohr drove 11 runs across the plate that game.

EAST IS EAST...

While that's impressive for *West* Texas, what about *East* Texas? The East Texas League operated off-and-on (and under a variety names such as Lone Star, Dixie, and West Dixie Leagues) from 1916 to 1950. League records for that circuit include:

Batting Average — Tom Osborne (Mt. Pleasant), 1924, .432
Home Runs   — Moose Clabaugh (Tyler), 1926, 62

RBI   — John Stone (Henderson), 1947, 185
Stolen Bases   — Tom Tatum (Henderson), 1939, 60
Victories   — Red Lynn (Jacksonville), 1937, 32
Won-Loss Pct.   — Ralph Pate (Longview), 1948, .885 (23-3)
Innings Pitched — Red Lynn (Jacksonvile), 1937, 340
Strikeouts   — Walter Schafer (Jacksonville), 1937, 274

PUT ME IN, COACH

Roy Hobbs. Joe Hardy. Joe Carolan.

Joe Carolan?

Yes, just like a fictional character, 21-year-old Joe Carolan's dreams came true in dramatic fashion. The Detroit native had to literally buy his way into the ballpark, Columbus, Georgia's Golden Park (situated, as you will no doubt recall, hard by the banks of the famed Chattahoochee River) on April 24, 1954.

Carolan proceeded to purchase a scorecard — so as to learn the name of Redbird General Manager Jim Grieves, who he then asked for a tryout. The weak-hitting club gave him one, and in batting practice Joe clubbed three balls out of the park.

Manager George Kissel promptly inserted him into the outfield. In the second inning, Carolan stepped to the plate for the first time. The sacks were loaded. Columbus was down, 3-0, and Joe swung hard at Macon lefthander Calvin Howe's offering. The ball sailed out of sight — a grandslam in his first at-bat!

The rest of the story is not so inspiring. The 230-pound Carolan smashed only three more homers in 33 Class A South Atlantic League games that year, finishing with a puny .231 average.

BIG TRAIN

It's not usually remembered but Hall-of-Famer Walter Johnson managed in the bush leagues — with the 1928 International League's Newark Bears. New owner Paul Block gave The Big Train a talented roster to work with, but nothing went right. Johnson fell ill before Opening Day, and despite a pitching staff that featured Al Mamaux, Jim Bagby, Jack Bentley, and Hub Pruett, and hitters such as Jacques Fournier and Merwyn "Baby Doll" Jacobson, the club finished a poor seventh — although the club ended up just nine and a half games back of Billy Southworth's pennant-winning Rochester Red Wings.

Nonetheless, perhaps thanks to Johnson's popularity, the Bears paced the league in attendance, drawing 300,000. Johnson wasn't back in 1929 — he was replaced by none other than Tris Speaker. Despite hitting .368 — and having the help of former Yankee Wally Pipp — Speaker got the Bears only as high as sixth.

CRASS COMMERCIALISM

The Rochester Hop Bitters of the 1877 International Association (generally recognized as baseball's first minor league — although a strong case is made by former SABR president Lloyd Johnson that it should be recognized as a major league) were not only named after a popular brand of patent medicine, but team owner Asa T. Soule, president of the Hop Bitters Manufacturing Company, forced each player to take a sip of the restorative prior to each contest. The Hop Bitters finished third, with a 10-8 record.

WHO'S ON THIRD?

In the majors, he was known as a catcher, but in the bush leagues, Bobby Bragan was a pretty fair infielder. For the 1939 Class B Southeastern League champion Pensacola Pilots he went 43 consecutive games without a miscue.

CRIME PAYS

Bill Martin — no, not *that* guy — was a real speedster. On July 4, 1947, he swiped nine — count 'em — bases in a two-city doubleheader.

The Montgomery Rebels center fielder pilfered four sacks in a day contest versus the Selma Cloverleafs at Montgomery's Cramton Bowl, then moved over to Selma's cozy Rowell Field where he stole five more. The speedy outfielder lead the Class B Southeastern League that year with 79 steals, while hitting .320 and driving in 80 runs in 131 games.

EVEN-STEPHEN

The first month of the 1928 Class B New York-Pennsylvania League saw unusually balanced action. On May 5, all eight clubs —

the Harrisburg Senators, Binghamton Triplets, Wilkes-Barre Indians, Williamsport Grays, York White Roses, Syracuse Stars, Scranton Miners, and Elmira Colonels — had a .500 record.

DANGER ZONE

A fellow named Higgins of the Detroit Wolverines of the 1890 International League was a chap you didn't want to get in the way of. On May 14, 1890, he lined a ball off the forearm ("midway between the wrist and elbow") of a Toronto Canucks' pitcher named Serad. Serad threw Higgins out at first, and, in intense pain, summoned a doctor who diagnosed a broken arm.

The year before a liner off Higgins' bat broke the hurling arm of Toledo Black Pirates lefthander Ed Cushman. Players then were made of stern stuff. Cushman came back in 1890 to no-hit the Rochester Jingoes.

DOUBLE TROUBLE

August 20, 1914 was a red-letter day for the Class C Southern Michigan Association. Mount Clemens Bathers pitcher Bravenor (12-16) no-hit the Battle Creek Crickets while hurler Robbins (20-16) of second-half champion Saginaw Ducks did the same versus the rival Jackson Chiefs.

SHARE THE WEALTH

Those pushing revenue-sharing by major league clubs might lift a page from the books of the old Class D Nebraska State League. Back in 1928 these folks took the idea to extremes. Each club — the McCook Generals, Lincoln Browns, Beatrice Blues, North Platte Buffaloes, York Dukes, Norfolk Drummers, Grand Island Champions (who despite their grandiose name finished seventh), and Fairbury Jeffersons — was incorporated in the amount of $40,000. The circuit itself was incorporated at $18,000. The salary limit per club was $1,400 per month, with each manager paid $150. Each manager was given two seven-passenger cars to transport his club —"and as the roads are graveled or paved there is no trouble to make the circuit."

"The league president," commented James Beltzer, who held that title, "takes charge of all the money that the league receives, including sales of players, gate receipts, advertising, and so on. He pays all the bills for the entire league. The ballplayers receive their checks from the league office…With this plan all clubs are financially equal, the losing club is just as strong financially as the leading club, and no club will suspend operations or leave the league."

THE FAMILY PLAN

When Jimmy Piersall signed his first minor league contract with the Red Sox, it included not just $4,000 a year for three seasons but a trip to the Leahy Clinic for his father, who had suffered a debilitating heart attack while watching his son have his jaw dislocated in a Connecticut schoolboy tournament.

HIS BIG CHANCE

In the 1950 Class D Sooner State League, McAllister Rockets infielder Whitey Herzog learned the value of not counting your chickens before they hatch. After garnering six doubles in a doubleheader and raising his season average to .446, he was summoned to manager Vern Hoscheit's room.

Thoughts of promotion to a higher classification danced in his head.

Recalled Herzog: "But all he did was flip me the keys to the bus and say, 'Drive the boys into town tonight. I've got a social engagement.' "

KEEP YOUR EYE ON THE BALL

While Travis "Stonewall" Jackson was with the Arkansas Travellers in the early 1920s he once collided with great force with the club's center fielder. Jackson suffered a deep gash to his head. The center fielder lost an eye.

FIRST IN WAR…

Nap Rucker met some interesting folks in his minor league career. It was Grantland Rice who recommended him to Atlanta manager Abner Powell — and got the Georgia-born lefthander his first job in pro ball.

Wildness plagued Rucker at Atlanta, and Powell shipped him off to the Augusta Tourists in the Class C Sally League. There he roomed with young Ty Cobb.

After a game Cobb invariably would arrive at his room before Rucker. One day the southpaw got knocked out of a contest and arrived home before the Georgia Peach. Cobb found Rucker taking a bath, and, with his temper raging out of control, burst into the bathroom — and proceeded to strangle the startled pitcher.

Rucker knocked Cobb back and asked, "Are you crazy, Ty?"

"You don't understand, Nap," said a visibly unnerved Cobb. "I've just got to be first — all the time."

BAT-HER UP

In right field for the Class D Arkansas-Missouri League's Fayetteville Bears on September 7, 1936 was Sonny Dunlap, who was making *her* pro debut. Dunlap, formerly an AAU basketball player with the Tulsa Stenos, went hitless in three trips to the plate. She was the last woman to play in the minors. Fayetteville beat the Cassville Blues, 5-1.

BACK-TO-BACK

Oh sure, you've heard of minor league flash Ron Necciai. But what about his teammate Bud Bell? With the Bristol Twins in May 1952 Bell pitched back-to-back no-hitters. The Twins, by the way, had nothing to do with any future Minnesota Twins. The Twins represented both Bristol, Virginia, and Bristol, Tennessee.

THANKS FOR THE HONOR . . .

Democracy in the workplace is nothing new. Back in August 1952 the floundering St. Petersburg Saints got to elect their own manager. On a suggestion from Class B Florida International League President Johnny Burroughs, they went to the ballot box to select their fourth pilot of the year. The virtually unanimous winner was right fielder Roxie Huberson.

Despite the turmoil, the Saints finished a respectable fourth. The last place Fort Lauderdale Braves, on the other hand, were guided all season long by just one pilot, Barney Lutz — but had their franchise taken over by the league in June. Transferred to Key West, they became the Conches.

THEY PRACTICED IT IN SPRING TRAINING

On August 21, 1917 in a Salt Lake City-San Francisco PCL contest, the bases were loaded and Red McKee of the Seals attempted to steal the already occupied third base. His strategy succeeded as the startled opposing pitcher balked everyone up a free base.

DEJA VU ALL OVER AGAIN

On July 15, 1952, while pitching for the second-division Tulsa Oilers of the Texas League, Johnny Vander Meer did it again, tossing yet another gem, no-hitting the pennant-winning Shreveport Sports, 12-0. Vander Meer, then 37, was 11-10 for Tulsa with a 2.30 ERA.

IT'S-TOUGH-TO-GET-GOOD-HELP DEPARTMENT

Former major league pitcher Charles Sweeney in June 1898 officiated in a California State League contest between the San Francisco Olympics and the San Jose Florists. Sweeney had just been released from California's San Quentin Prison, where he was doing time for manslaughter.

BUGGING THE OPPOSITION

Johnny Vander Who? On July 4, 1905, past and present major leaguer (and major drunk) Arthur "Bugs" Raymond, while with the Class C South Atlantic League's Charleston Sea Gulls, no-hit opponents in *both* games of a morning-afternoon doubleheader.

I SUPPOSE IT COULD HAVE BEEN WORSE

One Wednesday October 8, 1905 game between the Portland Beavers and Oakland Oaks at Oakland was attended by just a solitary paying customer. In announcing the lineups, the umpire began, "Dear Sir . . ."

MR. OCTOBER

In 1947 Bill Serena, a future Chicago Cub infielder, blasted 70 homers for the Lubbock Hubbers of the Class C West Texas-New Mexico League. That total included 57 regular-season dingers and 13 more in the playoffs.

THEY ALSO SERVE

Most minor league home run kings never make the majors. That wasn't the case with first baseman Joe Macko, although Joe — with the same big league club for over two decades — never actually *played* in the majors.

In the minors with the Indians' and Cubs' systems from 1948 to 1970, Macko collected 306 homers, including seven 20-homer seasons.

He saw duty as a player-manager and manager in the Cubs' system and as general manager of the Texas League's Dallas-Fort Worth Spurs before the Washington Senators moved to the Lone Star State. In 1972 Macko served as Rangers business manager and since 1973 has been Texas' equipment manager and home clubhouse manager.

His late son, infielder Steve Macko, played for the Cubs in 1979-80.

DOUBLE TROUBLE

One of the most impressive — yet for some reason obscure — minor league records is for doubles in a single season. In 1924 for Jack Lelivelt's Tulsa Oilers, outfielder Lyman Lamb collected 100 two-base hits. That year Lamb batted .373 in 168 Western League games, while hitting 19 homers, four triples and a league-leading 261 hits. Tulsa in 1924 led the Class A Western League with a .326 team batting average.

In 1922 Lamb had a league-leading 68 doubles; in 1923, he led the circuit with 71. In 1925 he dropped off to just 24. The secret of his success was the short left-field dimensions of Tulsa's McNulty Park. The right-handed Lamb readily admitted that every time he came to bat at Tulsa he consciously tried to pull the ball over third and into the left-field corner. For the Oilers, Lamb had 289 doubles in 731 contests. In his overall minor league career he collected 608.

FRANK SHAUGHNESSY:
He Saved the Minors

On the Notre Dame campus Francis Joseph "Shag" Shaughnessy helped place his school firmly on the gridiron map, but his most lasting achievement in the sports world — and there were many — was to introduce the post-season playoff system to baseball, an innovation that without question helped save bush league play. Shaughnessy did it in the minors in 1933 and traditionalists screamed — but in the mid-1990s we saw a variation of his scheme introduced in the *majors*.

The "Shaughnessy Playoffs" were widely credited with saving minor league baseball in the depths of the depression. With attendance plummeting and leagues dropping like flies, Shaughnessy, then general manager of the International League's Montreal Royals, took an old hockey idea and put it to work for minor league baseball. His proposal, noted author Bob Obojski, is "generally acknowledged to have saved the minors from total financial ruin in the depression-ridden 1930s."

Shaughnessy was born on April 8, 1883, at Amboy, Illinois, the youngest of seven children. His father worked on the Illinois Central Railway and, to help make ends meet for his large Irish immigrant family, Frank, while still attending high school, worked virtually full-time at a local pharmacy.

Somehow he found the time for athletics and won a partial baseball scholarship to Notre Dame, when, as he said, "it was little more than a farm and the nuns made our meals and washed our clothes."

In 1904 Shaughnessy graduated from Notre Dame with a degree in pharmacy, earning a law degree two years later. It was not his academics, however, which distinguished him. While at South Bend, he excelled in baseball, track, and particularly football.

Shaughnessy's mother didn't want him playing "that terrible game," but that didn't stop him. While still a freshman, he went out for the team and was first assigned the task of running back kickoffs. "I quickly learned the art of feigning, of letting the tackler make the first move, and of stiff-arming," said the then reed-like (6'0" and 155 pounds) Shaughnessy.

Just a few weeks later "Shag" Shaughnessy (he received his nickname from two previous Shaughnessys who had matriculated at Notre Dame) was quarterbacking his teammates, who, like he, were often seriously outweighed by their opponents.

"My mother spent Saturday afternoons in church lighting candles so that I would not get hurt," Shaughnessy later recalled. "In the days of the flying wedge, injuries were frequent. Her prayers must have been heard because I escaped with only four broken collarbones."

When Shaughnessy said "only" a broken collarbone he meant it. After one fracture he stayed in the game and ran 107 yards for a touchdown against Kansas. Shaughnessy ultimately became team captain, and in 1903 the Fighting Irish were unscored on all season.

Shaughnessy kept busy off the athletic field as well. "It seems like I can't remember a time when I wasn't working hard," he explained. "While I was at Notre Dame, I also ran the campus newspaper, a confectionery concession, and was the correspondent for several Chicago newspapers."

Of course, in Shaughnessy's case, writing for those papers had one significant drawback: "I couldn't say anything about my own feats."

In 1905-06 the Catholic Shaughnessy served as a pigskin coach at the Baptist-founded Welch Neck High School in Hartsville, South Carolina. Among Welch Neck's opponents was The Citadel. In 1907-08 he coached both baseball and football at Clemson.

But aside from boxing, about the only place for an active athlete to earn *decent* money was baseball. So even before graduating, Shaughnessy (like so many of his contemporaries) took to playing ball in the league under an assumed name, "Shannon." Before long he was using his own name with the Iowa-South Dakota League Sioux City Soos and the Kitty League's Cairo Champions.

He batted .483 with Cairo, and in 1905 the Washington Senators acquired Shaughnessy. He trained with the club at Charlottesville, Virginia, and lasted with them until June.

"It wasn't easy in those days, believe me," said Shaughnessy. "Regulars would actually chase a rookie with a bat if he attempted to take a turn hitting. A regular held his job until somebody drove him out, and every youngster was regarded as a menace. I got into one game with the Senators and then was sent to Montgomery."

In that one brief foray in the majors Shaughnessy was 0-for-3.

Shaughnessy played more minor league ball with the Montgomery Black Sox, but didn't enjoy the experience: "Heat and mosquitoes soon drove me north again." So did a .115 batting average. He headed for Montpelier-Barre in the Vermont-based semi-pro Northern League. In August that circuit folded, and Shaughnessy returned to his old stomping grounds of South Bend. Playing under the name of "Shag" with the Class B Central League's South Bend Greens, he hit .333 in 16 games.

Shaughnessy appeared with the Pacific Coast League's San Francisco Seals in 1907, hitting just .237. He started 1908 with Al Lawson's abortive third major league, the disastrous Union League. Shaughnessy, who played under former National League infielder Art Irwin at Washington, was actually one of the bigger "names" in this pathetic circuit which folded ignominiously in early June.

Nothing is known of Shaughnessy's statistics in the Union League, but his performance was good enough to win him a return to the majors with Connie Mack's Philadelphia Athletics. His first game with the A's promised great things. On June 8 at St. Louis' Sportsman's Park, he went 3-for-4 against the great Rube Waddell. Shaughnessy didn't last long. In fact, he didn't play one game at Philadelphia's Columbia Park, being soon injured and then traded at season's end to the Class B Tri-State League's Reading Pretzels for future Hall-of-Fame third baseman "Home Run" Baker.

"I thought I had a good chance with the A's," said Shaughnessy. "I was hitting .310 after eight games and was feeling pretty proud of myself. Then one cold day in Chicago, I had to make a hard throw to the plate and something snapped in my arm. I couldn't throw overhanded for a year and Connie Mack traded me to Reading for Frank (Home Run) Baker.

"That was a pretty good deal for the Athletics. I guess I wasn't much of a player."

That was Shaughnessy's last shot as a major leaguer, but two significant events would soon take his career in entirely new directions.

In the fall of 1908 he married Katherine Quinn of Ottawa. This shifted Shag's base of operations permanently northward to Canada. The second was he became player-manager of the Roanoke Tigers in the Class C Virginia League. At just 24, he was the youngest manager in organized baseball.

"My first move then was to buy a share of the ball club at Roanoke..." said Shaughnessy. "In the fall I made plans to coach freshman football at Washington and Lee University. While in Roanoke, I got one of the first automobile agencies in the country and bought a substantial interest in two cigar stores." If he didn't have enough on his platter, he also opened a law office in the Virginia city.

But it wasn't all business for Shaughnessy. In 1909 he led the Virginia League with five (count 'em) homers and took the club to the pennant. Roanoke finished second in both 1910 and 1911. In 1911 he led the Virginia League in both runs (93) and hits (160).

The following year Shag became player-manager of the Fort Wayne Railroaders in the 12-team Central League. In a climax to a wild four-club race, the Railroaders won the pennant with a torrid second-half finish, coming from last place on July 1. At both Fort Wayne and Ottawa he was aided greatly by his relationship with Tigers owner Frank Navin, who regularly supplied him with players. At Ottawa he developed righthander Urban Shocker and, in gratitude to Navin, offered him to Detroit. Navin wired back: "Mr. Jennings [Hughie Jennings, the Tiger manager] does not like spitball pitchers."

Shaughnessy was to be sold to the Pacific Coast League for 1913, but as he had already been involved in the formation of a Canadian League franchise back in Ottawa (where he had lived since the winter of 1911), he bought his release and became that club's manager. Winning Canadian League pennants in 1913, 1914, and 1915, he ended up owning the club.

The First World War, however, ended the Canadian League, and Shaughnessy managed in the rickety Class D Inter-State League in 1916, before joining the 207th Battalion of the Canadian infantry. There he coached baseball and football for the troops. Before war's end he shifted over to the artillery, earning the rank of captain and seeing service with the Allied expeditionary forces in Bolshevik Russia.

"I just missed going in an earlier draft to Siberia with Colonel [Raymond] Massey [the future actor]," recalled Shaughnessy. "I hear that's where he got his first practice as a thespian."

Mustered out of the service, in 1919 Shaughnessy managed the

Michigan-Ontario League's Hamilton Tigers to a second-place finish. That same year he moved to Montreal, where he would live for the rest of his life. In 1920 he was out of baseball, but by June 1921 was hired to pilot the International League's Syracuse Stars, beginning a 40-year relationship with that circuit. At Syracuse, he helped feed some of the first players into the Cardinals farm system: Sunny Jim Bottomley, Wild Bill Hallahan, Watty Holm, Chick Hafey, Art Reinhart, and Les Bell.

It was at Syracuse that Shaughnessy encountered a man who would be one of the greatest influences on his baseball career: Branch Rickey. "That was one of the best breaks I ever received. . . .," said Shaughnessy. "I started learning from him the first time I met him. That was at spring training in Orange, Texas, in 1922.

"Rickey was the greatest baseball man I ever met. I learned more from him than anyone else. He had wonderful ideas. I guess he wasn't too successful as a manager because he was too smart. His players couldn't think with him and he expected too much."

Shaughnessy lasted in the Salt City until May 1925, when after nothing but second-division finishes, he was unceremoniously relieved of his duties. A week later he found employment with the Eastern League's Providence franchise. In 1926 he started the season managing the International League's Reading Keys, but after a shabby 1-8 start was again let go. Firing Shaughnessy did little to improve a wretched club. The Keys finished the year at 31-129 for a miserable .194 won-lost percentage.

In all these years, Shaughnessy hardly confined himself to baseball. Aside from coaching football in the States at William and Mary and at Clemson, he guided McGill University's football Redmen for 23 years, bringing them Dominion championships in both 1912 and 1931. He was particularly instrumental in introducing the American style of play to Canada, with forward passing and laterals factoring in the strategy.

Shaughnessy scouted and coached for the Tigers before leaving baseball in 1929 to enter a Montreal mining brokerage. In 1932 the lure of the game proved too strong, however, and he replaced Walt Hapgood as Montreal general manager.

That year, though, the powerful Newark Bears ran away and hid from International League competition, winning the pennant by 16 games. Combined with the effects of the Great Depression, that spelled

gallons of red ink for the league. With a growing family (eight sons —
all of whom called him "sir" — and one daughter) to support, Shaughnessy wasn't about to sanguinely accept financial disaster. His response was the Shaughnessy Playoff System, in which the league's top
four clubs would meet in post-season play. He had borrowed the idea
from his hockey experiences (for a brief while he had managed the
Ottawa Senators in the old National Hockey League).

"It was in 1933 when I was business manager of the Montreal
club that I came up with the idea," he explained. "Most of the teams
in the International League were losing money. One of the clubs was
way out in front and the fans were losing interest.

"The other clubs started to get panicky. They began selling all of
their good players and the others began losing interest. We had to find
some way to make it worthwhile for the players to put out and to have
the teams fighting for four places instead of just for the pennant."

The concept was first implemented at the end of that 1933 season
not only by the International League, but also by the Texas League.
Despite the opposition of certain traditionalists, it was an immediate
success.

"The fans are given better baseball," contended Shaughnessy,
"for the players hustle to the end of the season and club owners, instead of weakening their teams by sales, try to strengthen them, thus
assuring keen competition throughout the closing month, whereas in
the past, both interest and competition waned."

Minor league czar "Judge" William G. Bramham tried to halt the
playoffs. He based his attempt on a technicality. The bonuses paid to
players who participated in the playoffs violated a section of the standard minor league player contract. That was quickly corrected. Panicky owners, who saw their franchises going down the drain, hurried-
ly called for a mail ballot, and changed the rules.

In just a few years virtually every league had adopted the
"Shaughnessy Playoffs," but Shaughnessy's days in the Montreal
front office were numbered. In 1935 he was, as he complained, "sad-
dled ... with a field management job" for that franchise. But he responded by capturing that club's first pennant in 37 years. In appreci-
ation for his achievement, he received a rare honor — a trophy from
the Canadian prime minister, the Right Honorable Richard Bedford
Bennett. It read in part: "To Francis Joseph Shaughnessy from the
Prime Minister of Canada in recognition of his keen sportsmanship

and especially of his honest efforts throughout his career to inspire the youth of Canada toward clean living and sportsmanship."

Every silver lining has a cloud. The Royals could not fully savor their triumph; ironically, they lost the playoffs to the second-place Syracuse Chiefs.

The Royals' talent supply, however, was seriously depleted the following year, and a frustrated Shaughnessy quit his post in August 1936.

He was not out of the game for long. In October 1936 the International League unanimously elected Shaughnessy its president, replacing former Rochester executive Warren Giles who was promoted to run the Cincinnati Reds. Shaughnessy would remain in that post for 24 years. During his tenure, Jackie Robinson entered the International League, thus breaking baseball's color barrier. Under Shaughnessy's leadership, from 1937 through 1949, the International League enjoyed unusual stability, avoiding even one franchise shift. From that point on, however, Shaughnessy had to fend off the challenges of radio, television, increasing interference by major league operators, and the territorial threat from a proposed third major league, the Continental League.

Shaughnessy, a member of the Veterans Committee of the Hall of Fame, retired in 1961 with a $10,000-a-year pension, but in June 1963 — at age 80 — on the death of National Association President George M. Trautman, returned to service as temporary head of the minors.

Shag enjoyed relatively good health until March 1967 when he was hospitalized with a circulatory ailment and had his right leg amputated above the knee. "The doctors told me," Shaughnessy growled to Montreal sportswriter Elmer Ferguson, "that it was my leg or my life. A poor choice, but I took it, and when I get my wooden leg or some such other artificial contraption, I'll be out there again playing some golf."

Frank Shaughnessy lived to see his adopted hometown of Montreal gain major league status in 1969. "This is great," he marvelled. But later he was stricken with a massive aneurism and was rushed to Montreal General Hospital. Said his grandson, Frank III: "I was the last person to see him and right at the end he was giving the nurses a dressing down."

Shaughnessy, who was elected to the Canadian Baseball Hall of Fame in 1983, died on May 15, 1969. *The Sporting News* called him "one of the great figures in minor league history." Few would dispute their judgment.

FRANK SHAUGHNESSY'S PLAYING RECORD

Year	Club	League	G	AB	R	H	2B	3B	HR	SB	RBI	B.A.
1903	Sioux City	IA-SD	34	137	18	29	-	-	-	12	-	.212
1904	Cairo	Kitty	-	-	-	-	-	-	-	-	-	.483
1905	Washington	AL	1	3	0	0	0	0	0	0	0	.000
1905	Montgomery	SA	7	26	7	3	0	0	0	2	-	.115
1906	Mont.-Barre	Northern	-	-	-	-	-	-	-	-	-	-
1906	South Bend	Central	18	66	7	22	3	1	0	2	-	.333
1907	San Fran.	PCL	77	295	33	70	13	1	1	22	-	.237
1908	Reading	Tri-State	67	233	27	63	7	4	1	18	-	.270
1908	Phil.	AL	8	29	2	9	0	0	0	3	1	.310
1908	Washington	Union	-	-	-	-	-	-	-	-	-	-
1909	Roanoke	VA	125	477	54	136	14	5	5	31	-	.285
1910	Roanoke	VA	115	414	58	103	13	2	0	43	-	.248
1911	Roanoke	VA	123	489	-	160	-	-	-	57	-	.327
1912	Ft. Wayne	Central	121	470	77	143	33	6	1	34	-	.304
1913	Ottawa	Canadian	102	385	79	131	21	7	2	37	-	.340
1914	Ottawa	Canadian	119	446	61	129	22	4	6	37	-	.289
1915	Ottawa	Canadian	101	380	55	112	10	3	3	30	-	.292
1916	Wells-Bradford-Warren	Interstate	76	299	35	90	18	7	0	19	-	.301
1917		Military Service										
1918		Military Service										
1919	Hamilton	MI-Ontario	109	380	35	119	20		11	1 9	-	.313
1920	Hamilton	MI-Ontario	93	290	89	76	13		2	31	25	.262
1921	Syracuse	IL	29	62	4	16	3		0	1	-	.258
1922	Syracuse	IL	12	17	1	4	1		1	1	-	.258
1923	Syracuse	IL	1	0	0	0	0		0	0	0	.000
1924	Syracuse	IL	1	1	0	0	0		0	0	0	.000

FRANK SHAUGHNESSY'S MANAGERIAL RECORD

Year	Club	League	Standing	Won	Lost
1909	Roanoke	VA	1	73	49
1910	Roanoke	VA	2	68	52
1911	Roanoke	VA	3	63	56
1912	Ft. Wayne	Central	1	77	52
1913	Ottawa	Canadian	1	66	39
1914	Ottawa	Canadian	1	77	45
1915	Ottawa	Canadian	1	76	39
1916	Wells-Bradford-Warren	Interstate	4	41	37
1919	Hamilton	MI-Ontario	2	75	36
1920	Hamilton	MI-Ontario	2	71	46
1921	Syracuse	IL	-	29	38
1922	Syracuse	IL	7	64	102
1923	Syracuse	IL	6	73	92
1924	Syracuse	IL	6	79	83
1925	Syracuse	IL	-	9	29
1925	Providence	IL	-	49	69
1926	Reading	IL	-	1	8
1934	Montreal	IL	-	15	18
1935	Montreal	IL	1	92	62
Total				1,098	952

BEFORE YOU CAN SAY
JACK ROBINSON:
Pro Baseball's Black Pioneers

Jackie Robinson certainly earned his stripes in 1947 as the man who broke the major league's color barrier, but he was not professional baseball's first black player—not by a long shot, or even by several decades.

In the early mists of diamond history, a handful of African-Americans had been gingerly allowed inside the game's sacred portals. They were not always welcomed eagerly, but from 1878 to 1898 blacks appeared with some frequency in professional ranks, often earning comparison to the best white talent baseball had to offer.

Cooperstown-native (born in nearby Fort Plain, he moved to the "Birthplace of Baseball" at age one) John W. "Bud" Fowler (real name: John W. Jackson) was the first African-American to play professionally. That was in 1872, when he performed for an otherwise all-white independent club in New Castle, Pennsylvania. In 1878 he became the first black to appear in organized league play when he pitched briefly for the International Association's Lynn Live Oaks and the New England League's Worcester Brown Stockings. Primarily a second baseman, Fowler could handle any position with skill. Yet due to the mores of the time, few teams would employ him. He may have played a part in his own troubles. "He was not docile when threatened and had several confrontations with other players and management in the course of his career," noted Society for American Baseball Research (SABR) founder L. Robert Davids. "It is accurate to say he was a contributing factor in the collapse of several clubs and even the disruption of leagues, but he continued to play with white teams as long as he could."

While he was the first black pro player, he was not, however, the initial black to perform in an official major league game. That honor goes to catcher Moses Fleetwood Walker. Like Jackie Robinson, Walker was college-educated—the son of a physician—who attended (but did not graduate from) Oberlin College and Ann Arbor. At both schools he distinguished himself as a catcher, impressive enough to earn a berth with the Toledo Bluestockings of the 1883 Northwestern League, where he batted a modest .251 in 60 games.

Prior to a Toledo exhibition with Cap Anson's Chicago White Stockings, Anson threatened to walk off the field rather than compete with a Negro. Bluestockings manager Charlie Morton called Anson's bluff and the game went forward—with Walker behind the plate. "The joke of the affair," noted *Sporting Life*, "was that up to the time…the Toledo people had no intention of catching Walker, who was laid up with a sore hand, but when Anson said he wouldn't play with Walker, the Toledo people made up their minds that Walker would catch or there wouldn't be a game."

The next year Toledo advanced to the major league American Association and Walker became the first African-American big leaguer. Again he hit .251. Although reputedly an excellent backstop, not every teammate appreciated his presence. "Walker," said star Toledo pitcher Tony Mullane, "was the best catcher I ever worked with, but I disliked a Negro and whenever I had to pitch to him I used to pitch anything I wanted without looking at his signals."

Joining Fleet later that season was his younger brother Weldy, an outfielder who hit .222 in five games. Meanwhile at Stillwater in the Northwestern League, Bud Fowler returned to organized baseball ranks, pitching this dreadful club to its first victory of the year after 15 defeats, earning a bonus of $10 and a suit of clothes in the bargain. The money came in handy in July when he was fined for an errant throw that let in two runs.

In 1885 Fleet Walker and Bud Fowler were the only blacks in organized baseball—Walker first with Cleveland (Western League) and later with Waterbury (Southern New England League); Fowler with Keokuk (Western League) and then with Pueblo (Colorado League).

In 1886 Bud Fowler remained in organized baseball with the Western League's Topeka Athletics, while Fleet Walker continued with Waterbury. They were joined by two very noteworthy newcomers—George Washington Stovey and Frank Grant.

Lefthander George Stovey, who pitched for Jersey City of the International League, has been described as "the first great Negro pitcher." Opposing batters hit a measly .167 against him in 1886. He still holds the International League single-season record for victories, based on his 33-14 mark in 1887. It was rumored that Jim Mutries' New York Giants would have signed him but for his color.

Frank Grant, described in SABR's *Nineteenth Century Stars* as "the greatest Negro baseball player of the 19th century," appeared for Meriden of the Eastern League. Born in Pittsfield, Massachusetts, circa 1865, the compact (5'7½", 155 pounds) second baseman tore that circuit apart, hitting .316, and was promoted to Buffalo in mid-season.

As a fielder, Grant was dubbed the "Black Dunlap," a reference to nonpareil National League second baseman Fred "Sure Shot" Dunlap. Grant continued in organized ball with Buffalo through 1888, with Trenton in the Mid-State League (1889), Harrisburg of the Eastern League and the Atlantic Association (1890), and Ansonia of the Connecticut State League (1891). As racial attitudes hardened, he met increasing resistance from both opponents and teammates alike. He—like Bud Fowler—was forced to fashion wooden shinguards to protect himself from sharpened spikes. Reputedly, in both in 1886 and 1888, his white teammates refused to pose for team photos due to his presence.

Eighteen eighty-seven was a turning point as far as integration was concerned. More blacks than ever were performing creditably on the field, particularly in the International League. Frank Grant hit .366 with Buffalo, leading the circuit with eight homers. Bud Fowler (who hit .350) and pitcher William Renfro were at Binghamton. Harry Stovey was, of course, 33-14 at Jersey City. Fleet Walker batted a modest .263 for Newark. Robert Higgins went 20-7 for Syracuse. On Fowler's recommendation second baseman Randolph Jackson was signed by the IL's ill-fated Oswego club.

In the Ohio State League, several blacks appeared. Third baseman Sol White (most famous for authorship of *Sol White's Official Baseball Guide*, an invaluable history of black baseball to past the turn of the century) hit .381 (second in the league) for the Wheeling Green Stockings, while catcher Richard Johnson batted .294 for Zanesville. Welday Walker was at Akron and another catcher named "N. Higgins" appeared for Columbus.

Yet the screws were steadily turning in the opposite direction, and soon they would firmly seal the door shut on the Negro in organized baseball. For example, the press oddly reported: "Complaint is being made that Grant…is being used as a star player by Manager [John C.] Chapman of Buffalo. This accounts for the amount of ground he is allowed to cover…and no attention is paid to such a thing as another man's territory."

In June, two members of the Syracuse Stars refused to pose for a team portrait because of the presence of Robert Higgins. On July 14, the International League met in Buffalo to mull "the question of black players. Several representatives declared that many of the best players in the League were anxious to leave on account of the colored element, and the board finally directed Secretary White to approve no more contracts with colored men." On June 19, Cap Anson refused to have his White Stockings play the Newark Little Giants if Stovey or Walker was on the field. Stovey feigned illness to avoid controversy. In July, the Binghamton Bingoes released Fowler and Renfro on condition that no other International League club sign them. The other clubs agreed, and Fowler drifted over to the Cuban Giants while Renfro headed for Topeka, where he hoped to catch on with the Western League. At season's end, Newark released Stovey—despite his having the circuit's second best won-lost record. The Ohio State League passed a resolution banning Negro players but later rescinded that edict, and Richard Johnson returned to Zanesville in 1888.

It was of this legislation that Weldy Walker, in a letter to the league president, so eloquently complained: "The law is a disgrace to the present age, and reflects very much upon the intelligence of your last meeting, and casts derision at the laws of Ohio—the voice of the people—that says all men are equal. I would suggest that your honorable body in case that black law is not repealed, pass one making it criminal for a colored man or woman to be found in a ball ground.

"There is now the same accommodation made for the colored patron of the game as the white, and the same provision and dispensation is made for the money of them both, that finds its way into the coffers of the various clubs."

The following year saw colored ranks thinned to just Grant, Robert Higgins (who jumped Syracuse in mid-season), and Fleetwood Walker—all in the Eastern (International) League, Richard Johnson at Zanesville, and Bud Fowler, who had stints with Crawfordsville-Terre Haute in the Central Interstate League.

In 1889 blacks were represented by Bud Fowler at Greenville in the Michigan State League, Fleet Walker still with Syracuse, first baseman Richard A. (Charles) Kelley at Danville in the Illinois-Indiana League, and Richard Johnson, now with Springfield in the Central Interstate League. But there was a significant new development—two all black teams in the Middle States League. The Cuban Giants, a successful independent club since their organization in Babylon, New York in 1885, and the Gorham Giants, a survivor of an abortive all Negro league in 1887. The Giants represented Trenton, New Jersey, and were anchored by none other than Frank Grant, who hit a solid .313.

In 1890, the Middle States League was renamed the Eastern Interstate League. The Gorhams dropped out, but the Cuban Giants remained, now representing York, Pennsylvania, and renamed as the York Monarchs. They won the pennant under manager J. M. Bright with a roster featuring: Sol White, George Williams, William Selden, Arthur Thomas, Jack Frye, Andrew Jackson, Billy Whyte, Abe Harrison, Ben Boyd, William Jackson, Oscar Jackson, William Malone, and W.W. Terrill. Not every black in the league was with York, however. Frank Grant and third baseman-catcher Clarence Williams played with rival Harrisburg, although it took a lawsuit to pry them away from the Monarchs.

Meanwhile, Fleet Walker was ending up his career with a brief trial with the Western International League's Terre Haute Hottentots, and Richard Kelley was with Jamestown of the New York-Penn League. Frank Grant starred with Harrisburg of the Eastern Interstate League, where he hit .333. A model of consistency, after that team transferred to the Atlantic Association, he hit .332.

Eighteen ninety-one saw a new all black club in organized ball—the "Big Gorhams" representing Ansonia in the Connecticut State League. On board were the by-now familiar faces of Stovey, Grant, and Clarence Williams. "A. Davis, proprietor of the Gorhams, signed every man of the York Monarchs," wrote Sol White. "In addition he signed C. Williams, F. Grant and George Stovey. This tea ... was without a doubt one of the strongest teams ever gotten together, white or black. Their ages ranging from 22 to 32; every man placed where he was strongest, pitchers and catchers strong in field and at bat, every man a student of the game and experienced, they were a hard team for any club to beat. Their lineup was as follows: Arthur Thomas and Clarence Williams, catchers; George Stovey, William Seiden and W. Malone pitchers; George Williams, first base; Sol White, second base; A. Jackson, third base; F. Grant, short stop; O. Jackson, centre field, and pitchers or catchers in left and right fields."

Nonetheless, *Sporting Life* reported, "They are making themselves unpopular by misbehavior and may be fired from the league." Sol White himself jumped to Harrisburg of the Eastern Interstate League. Others may have followed (the multi-racial team was derided in the local press as the "Polka-Dots"); the Connecticut State League collapsed in mid-season. Meanwhile, Richard Kelley was now at Jamestown where his race appeared to create little stir.

From 1892-94 blacks disappeared from organized baseball, but in 1895 Sol White was back with the Western Inter-State League's Fort Wayne Warriors, and Bud Fowler organized a new black club, the Page Fence Giants, which he headquartered in Adrian, Michigan, home of the Page Fence company—inventors of barbed wire. The Page Fence Giants were not part of organized baseball, but in mid-season the local Michigan State League franchise hired six of Fowler's club players (Fowler, catchers Pete Burns and Vasco Graham, third baseman William Binga, and pitcher-outfielders Joe Miller and George H. Wilson) to assist them in a key series versus the rival Lansing Senators.

After 1895, blacks again vanished from organized baseball but returned in 1898 when another all black team emerged—the Acme Colored Giants, representing tiny Celeron, New York, in the Iron and Oil League. Organized by a white promoter named Harry Curtis, who promised "we will have the strongest colored club in America, if we are the youngest," the Celerons were not the stuff of legends. Going 8-41 before folding on July 7, the Acme Colored Giants were the end of the line for blacks in organized baseball.

The door had slammed shut, yet at least one other black player would sneak into baseball's ranks. That was Jimmie Claxton.

Claxton was of mixed ancestry. His mother was Irish and English; his father black, French, and American Indian. Considering that mix, a surviving photo (found on a Zeenut candy trading card) reveals surprisingly dark features. Nonetheless, in May 1916 the Pacific Coast League's Oakland Oaks attempted to pass Claxton off as "from an Indian reservation in Minnesota"—although a later version of his resume had him producing "an affidavit signed before a notary showing him to be from one of the reservations in North Dakota." A "part-Indian from Oklahoma" named Hastings had been scouting the Oakland Giants games. He hooked Claxton up with Herm McFarlin, business manager of the Oaks, lying to McFarlin that Claxton was "a fellow tribesman."

On May 28, Oakland pitched Claxton in both ends of a double-header against the Los Angeles Angels. In neither appearance was he scored upon. It's believed that shortly thereafter, Oaks manager "Rowdy" Elliot was tipped off to Claxton's true background. On June 3 he handed the pitcher his walking papers. "No reason was given," recalled Claxton, "but I knew. They tried to get out of paying me, but I had my contract and the notice of release. They had to come through with the money."

What is remarkable is not that Claxton momentarily gained entrance into organized baseball. Numerous others have been rumored to have done likewise. It is that Claxton was *not* an unknown. He had been playing for prominent black teams for some time: the Cuban Stars, the Chicago Giants, and even the local Oakland Giants.

The doors would not swing freely open again until Branch Rickey and Jackie Robinson forced them open in 1946.

STEVE DALKOWSKI:
The Tragic Fireballer

Kevin Costner's *Bull Durham* certainly brought the romance of minor league ball home to America's collective heart. No doubt about that, just check the attendance — er, box office — figures. But the film's most engaging character, at least in my humble opinion, wasn't the Cooperesque Costner's "Crash Davis" nor even Susan Sarandon's seductive "Annie Savoy" — but was instead the amazingly wild, blindingly fast phenom, "Nuke LaLoosh."

The creator of all these characters was former Oriole farmhand Ron Shelton. It's no accident that an old Baltimore chattel concocted a characterization such as Mr. LaLoosh, because decades ago a real live "Nuke" existed in their system, and he was much more incredible, far more fabulous, than any fictional personage could ever hope to be.

Meet Steven Louis Dalkowski.

Dalkowski never made the majors and hasn't thrown a pitch since 1966. His nine-year career occurred in metropoli like Kingsport and Aberdeen and Pensacola and Kennewick. He reached Triple-A for a mere dozen games. Yet his name still evokes awe — deep, deeper, deepest awe. His statistics, well, they're astonishing all right, but it's the individual episodes in Steve's career which comprise the real Dalkowski saga.

After all, his career record was only 46-80 with a rather sad 5.59 ERA. But Steve Dalkowski was *fast*, probably the hardest thrower in baseball history. Unfortunately, he was also the wildest. The southpaw struck out an astonishing 1,396 batters in 995 career innings — but walked an equally stupifying 1,354. As an 18-year-old, he whiffed 121 Appalachian League batters in just 62 innings.

One Dalkowski fastball literally ripped the earlobe off an opposing batter. He broke umpire Doug Harvey's mask in three places and propelled him back 18 feet. A Dalkowski wild pitch smashed through a minor league backstop, and fans wisely refused to sit behind home-plate when he pitched. He once plunked a batter *in the on-deck circle.* He threw six wild pitches in a row. In Rochester, Dalkowski's pitches were strong enough to smash a split-log outfield fence.

"I remember one night in Kingsport," says former Baltimore minor league executive Harry Dalton, "when he hit a batter in the head and the ball came back over his head and almost wound up at second base."

And it wasn't just velocity: Steve Dalkowski could throw for distance as well. "We walked out of the bullpen," recalled catcher Frank Zupo, "and some of the guys bet Steve he couldn't throw the ball far enough to reach the clubhouse — over 410 feet away. Without even warming up, he let loose and bounced the ball off the top of the clubhouse. He was an amazing athlete."

In 1959 the Orioles took Steve to the Aberdeen Proving Grounds to measure his heater. The results were impressive — 93.5 miles per hour. Now, that's fast, although it is hardly the stuff of legends. A certain explanation is in order. First, Dalkowski was not pitching off a mound — that would have added 5-8 MPH to his delivery. Second, he had started a game just the day before. Third, with his usual lack of control it was not until the 80th pitch that he actually hit his target. By this time he was one tired farmhand. "If they measured Dalkowski today," claimed Cal Ripken, Sr., "I'm sure they'd get him at 120."

"Hearing him warm up on the sideline was like hearing a gun go off," marvelled Dalton Jones. "I kept thinking: if this guy ever hits me, he'll kill me. I batted against Nolan Ryan and 'Sudden Sam' McDowell, but Dalkowski was noticeably faster."

Then there's the Ted Williams story. Dalkowski once went to spring training with the Orioles and the Hall-of-Famer stepped in to face his offerings. Dalkowski throws just one pitch. Teddy Ballgame lets it go by. He pauses, drops his bat, and simply walks away.

This great hitter, who reputedly could tell you what side of the ball he had hit it on, confessed he had never even *seen* Dalkowski's offering. And he was *not* about to try again either.

"I don't know who that kid is," marveled Williams to nearby reporters, "but he is the fastest pitcher I've ever seen, and I'll be damned if I'll ever face him again if there's any way I can help it."

Against the Reds, Dalkowski fanned the side on 12 pitches. Cincinnati manager Birdy Tebbetts threatened his men with a $100 fine if any one of them stood close enough to the strike zone to swing.

"I got them this far," confessed a relieved Tebbetts, "I want to open the season with them."

Dalkowski had signed out of New Britain (CT) High School with the O's. He wasn't big, just a 5'10", 160-pound lefthander who could throw a pork chop past a wolf. And he could throw a football as hard as a baseball. In 1956 he quarterbacked his school to a Connecticut state championship. In 1957 he captured high school All-American honors. "He could throw it 70 yards flatfooted," remembered Frank Zupo. "When he wound up, he could throw it 100 yards."

In Dalkowski's senior year he recorded two no-hitters. In one he struck out 18 — and walked 18. In another game he fanned 24. In American Legion ball Dalkowski threw three no-hitters, three one-hitters, and a two-hitter. He whiffed an average of two batters per inning. "It was easy then," he once fondly recalled. "If I didn't strike out 18 in a game, it was a bad day."

But he wasn't nearly as cocky as that statement makes him sound. "He was a shy, introverted kid with absolutely no confidence," contends the scout who signed him, Frank McGowan. "Even in high school he walked everybody."

In those days signing bonuses were limited to just $4,000, but top prospects like Dalkowski could get a little more. "There was a lot of money on the table," recalled Steve years later, "I got $45,000 to sign and $1,000 a month…" On another occasion his story had him getting a more modest 10 grand plus a shiny new Pontiac.

His rookie season was remarkable. In 62 innings Dalkowski struck out 121 batters and surrendered just 22 hits. But he walked 128, lost eight and won just one, posting an astronomic 8.13 ERA. On August 17, 1957, he walked 21 and uncorked six wild pitches in losing a contest, 9-7. On August 31 he struck out 24 but issued 18 free passes in defeating the rival Bluefield Dodgers, 7-5. "They yanked me," says Dalkowski, "and put me in the outfield. Then they brought me back in and I struck out the last batter. Then I went out and drank some beer."

Some contend it was in Dalko's rookie season that his troubles began —when he nearly killed a batter with a pitch. "He hit him in the side of the head with a fastball and the boy never played ball again," revealed Frank McGowan.

The Orioles tried all manner of stratagems to get Dalkowski's pitches over — or at least, *near* — the plate. They would have him throw for an hour before a game, theorizing that if he were sufficiently tired, he'd throw with some control. They made him pitch from 30 feet and work his way back to the regulation distance. They put two batters at homeplate while he warmed up. They had him aim at wooden targets. He smashed them to bits — but he still couldn't throw strikes in a game.

Dalkowski's sophomore year was nearly as interesting as his first. With Aberdeen in the Northern League he lost a one-hitter, 9-8. Yes. Nine-to-eight. He struck out 15 batters but walked 17. On May 17, 1959 — still with Aberdeen — he no-hit Grand Forks, 6-0, striking out 21.

In 1960 Dalkowski set a California League record when he walked 262 batters in just 170 innings. In one game he struck out the first nine batters and was leading 2-0. "The tenth guy up," recalled umpire Doug Harvey, "Dalkowski's first pitch hit 40 feet up the backstop.

"After that, he never got the ball back over the plate. When they came to take him out, the score was tied, 2-2, and the bases were loaded and he still hadn't given up a hit."

In 1961 he added the Northwest League base on balls record to his resume when he issued 196 free passes in 103 innings.

Steve lacked control in more ways than one. His drinking was also the stuff of legends, and being a teammate of Bo Belinsky did not help matters any, either.

He had met Bo in Knoxville in 1958. "They told me if I ever roomed with Belinsky they'd get rid of me," said Dalkowski. Yet he kept running into the playboy southpaw. When Steve washed out with the Smokies, he was demoted to Aberdeen where Belinsky was already there waiting for him. "He looked like he owns the whole town," marvelled the impressionable Dalkowski.

Baltimore kept putting temptation in the path of their prize lefthander. "We sent [Dalkowski] to Pensacola to play under Lou Fitzgerald, an easy going old-timer," recalled Frank McGowan. "And who do you think Steve hooked up with down there? Bo Belinsky and Steve Barber."

"I don't think there were ever three flakier guys on one team," admitted Harry Dalton. "The manager, Lou Fitzgerald, had a heart attack in the middle of the season."

"Poor Stevie," says Billy DeMars, his manager at Aberdeen, "he never could say no to anyone. I would try to tell him that the only reason the guys thought he was funny was because they were laughing at him, not with him. It got to the point that nobody in the organization wanted to take him because of the problems he was causing off the field, and the fact that most managers felt they couldn't win with him *on* the field."

"Most of the guys would have two or three beers after a game," Dalkowski confessed. "Me, it seems, I had to close up the bar."

In spring training 1961 Dalkowski teamed once more with Belinsky and Barber. They were staying at Miami's McAllister Hotel. Belinsky was assigned to room 812, and in the very next room was the current Miss Universe, a native of Colombia (that's Belinsky's version; others say she was merely Miss Ecuador). Jealously guarding her was her mother, a woman of grim determination, who was not to be trifled with.

Belinsky was unconcerned. "There were so many pretty girls in Miami that it didn't matter to me," he recalled. "I really didn't care. But to Dalkowski, it was a different matter." When Steve set eyes upon this beauty queen, he instantly hatched a scheme.

He raced down into the hotel basement and purloined a drill from the maintenance shop. Then he drilled approximately 20 holes in the wall separating Belinsky's room from Miss Universe's.

Dalkowski got quite an eyeful, and wasn't about to keep his good fortune a secret. The next evening about a dozen fellow players gathered for the show. Their voyeurism might have gone undetected, had not one Oriole brought a flashlight with him.

Recalled Belinsky: "She creeps into bed, turns out the light and rolls over. This one guy flashes the light into the room. He's moving it around as she rolls over toward our side. When the light hits her, she lets out a scream. Now we know we are in trouble."

The distraught beauty queen summoned the hotel security force, who secured entrance into Belinsky's room and discovered Dalkowski's holes.

First Dalkowski, then Barber and Belinsky, were ordered to report to manager Paul Richard's room. Hotel security was already there. Belinsky denied drilling any holes. Then Richards turned to Dalkowski.

"Uhh, yes, I think maybe I did," he sort of admitted, but he adamantly wouldn't confess to looking through them.

"Why in hell would you drill holes in a wall into a girl's room if you didn't intend to look through them?" stormed the exasperated Richards.

"Oh, I don't know, Skip," blandly remarked Dalkowski. "I just like to drill holes."

Belinsky was shipped out to Little Rock; Dalkowski all the way down to Kennewick where he led the Northwest League in walks and posted a horrific 8.39 ERA.

By the time Steve reached Elmira in 1962 he was finally able to walk fewer batters than innings pitched (114 versus 160). He also recorded a quite reasonable 3.04 ERA. His manager was Earl Weaver.

"When Steve joined the team, there was nothing I could tell him," Weaver explained. "Hell, he had gotten every piece of advice, tried everything, and had the best pitching coaches in the world talk to him. What was I going to say? So I didn't say anything. Just let him pitch...

"He was the fastest pitcher I ever saw."

At Elmira, Weaver administered a Stanford-Binet intelligence test to his charges. Dalkowski finished in the first percentile. "That means that if you taught 100 guys something, Steve would be the last to learn," said a frustrated Weaver.

However, Weaver did admire Dalkowski's work ethic. "He was a hard liver and a hard worker," admitted Earl, "He had to be put to bed at 3 A.M. Saturday night and then had to be told to stop his wind sprints Sunday morning."

For his part Dalkowski couldn't stand Weaver: "I met Weaver for the first time in Macon, Georgia. He's one guy I never got along with. In fact, I hated Earl. . . .

"When I got [to Elmira] guess who I run into? Weaver. He said, 'What the hell are you doing here?' I asked him the same thing. We didn't talk much the rest of the season."

It finally looked, however, like Dalkowski was on his way to the big leagues. In spring training of 1963 he pitched two shutout innings against the Dodgers, striking out five and walking *none*. Then, disaster struck. While fielding a bunt by the Yankees' pitcher Jim Bouton, Steve felt something pop in his elbow. His fabled arm was never quite the same.

Steve Dalkowski's last game in the Orioles system was in 1965 for the Northwest League's Tri-Cities (Kennewick) Atoms. Dalkowski spent the road trip downing a six-pack, then continued guzzling in the hotel bar until just two and a half hours before game time. He vomited in the clubhouse showers. Yet once on the mound, he threw as hard as he had in years. In the opposing lineup was Dodger $104,000 bonus-baby Rick Monday. Monday, who had so much promise, the sort of promise Dalkowski had largely squandered, seemed to infuriate Dalkowski.

Dalkowski fanned Monday four times, twice to end an inning, each time screaming curses and epitaphs ("$104,000, my ass!") at the youngster.

This graceless triumph provided yet another excuse to hoist a few. By evening's end, Dalkowski had been slapped by a local female, just barely escaped a donnybrook, and put his hand through a bar's plate glass window.

"The police had Steve cold," said teammate Tim Sommer. "Fortunately, the bar owners wouldn't press charges if someone paid for the window — $21. I paid them off and got Steve back to the hotel."

The police did contact manager Cal Ripken, Sr. Rip was under orders to convey such news back to Baltimore, and, suddenly, Steve Dalkowski was no longer an Oriole.

"Steve took it calmly," remembered Sommers, "When we got home, he came in to clean out his locker, say goodbye to everyone, and repay all the money he'd borrowed. Steve was incredibly honest."

He caught on with San Jose in the Angels' system, but was released the following spring. He later threw some winter ball in Mexico, but basically that was it.

The years have not been kind to Steve Dalkowski. After retiring, he returned to Stockton, married a school teacher, and obtained a job in his mother-in-law's pet store. He continued drinking heavily, and the marriage was over in two years. He drifted deeper and deeper into alcoholism, drunk tanks, DT's, hallucinations, and back-breaking work as a migrant farm laborer. He would struggle to stay on the wagon but would invariably topple off with a crash.

"Don't be a hero," one local cop once warned. "Don't try to help him, he's getting by. Some woman fell for him again, is trying to clean him up. It won't work, never has, every five years some decent broad tries to clean him up. Fails. Leave it to the broads. Nothin' can be done."

Hopefully, he's doing better now.

And did Ron Shelton really base "Nuke" LaLoosh on Steve? Well, a couple of years later he *did* pen a chapter on him in the book *Cult Baseball Players*.

You be the judge.

STEVE DALKOWSKI

Year	Club	League	G	GS	CG	SHO	IP	H	W	L	Pct.	SO	BB	ERA
1957	Kingsport	Appal.	15	10	2	1	62	22	1	8	.111	121	129	8.13
1958	Knoxville	SAL	11	10	0	0	42	17	1	4	.200	82	95	7.93
1958	Wilson	Carol.	8	0	0	0	14	7	0	1	.000	29	38	12.21
1958	Aberdeen	North.	11	10	3	1	62	29	3	5	.375	121	112	6.39
1959	Aberdeen	North.	12	10	3	1	59	30	4	3	.572	99	110	5.64
1959	Pensacola	AL-FL	7	6	0	0	25	11	0	4	.000	43	80	12.96
1960	Stockton	CA	32	31	7	1	170	105	7	15	.318	262	262	5.14
1961	Kennewick	NW	31	22	1	1	103	75	3	12	.200	150	196	8.39
1962	Elmira	EL	31	19	8	6	160	117	7	10	.412	192	114	3.04
1963	Elmira	EL	13	2	0	0	29	20	2	2	.500	28	26	2.79
1963	Rochester	IL	12	0	0	0	12	7	0	2	.000	8	14	6.00
1964	Elmira	EL	8	2	1	0	15	17	0	1	.000	16	19	6.00
1964	Stockton	CA	20	13	7	1	108	91	8	4	.667	141	62	2.83
1964	Columbus	IL	3	2	0	0	12	15	2	1	.667	9	11	8.25
1965	Kennewick	NW	16	15	4	1	84	52	6	5	.545	62	52	5.14
1965	San Jose	CA	6	6	2	1	38	35	2	3	.400	33	34	4.74
	Total		236	158	38	14	995	782	46	80	.317	1396	1354	5.59

TOMMY LASORDA:
Minor League Veteran

He's been at Dodger Stadium so long now we think he was born there, but it took Tommy LaSorda a long, long time to make it to the big leagues. For a seemingly interminable amount of time, the now famous Tommy was an unheralded toiler in the humble minors.

Born in Norristown, Pennsylvania, on September 22, 1927, Tommy was just 17 years old when he impressed Phillies scout Jocko Collins at a February 1945 tryout. Collins offered him $100 a month. "If you'd waited five minutes more, I would've offered *you* $200 a month to let me play professional baseball," Tommy informed Collins *after* he signed.

LaSorda never got to Utica — and that spring he didn't even make it to Florida. The Phillies trained at not exactly balmy Wilmington, Delaware. They dispatched the lefthander to Concord of the Class D North Carolina State League where the fiery LaSorda lost his first game when a groundball scooted through his shortstop's legs. LaSorda responded by jumping on top of him in the clubhouse and wailing the tar out of him. Manager John "Pappy" Lehman, a veteran minor leaguer, warned him, "You can't go around fighting with your own teammates... Lemme tell you something — you win as a team and you lose as a team, and you better learn that quick if you want to stay in baseball."

LaSorda thinks that's the most important lesson he ever learned in baseball.

The following season, LaSorda found himself serving in the United States Army. In the Army he supplemented his income playing for local semi-pro teams, getting $75 a game pitching for Goldville and

$100 pitching for Camden. LaSorda was discharged in 1947, but received an offer so lucrative from Camden that he begged off reporting to a Class C League for a measly $200 per month.

A RECORD PERFORMANCE

In 1948 LaSorda thought it wise to return to pro ball. The Phils assigned him to the Class C Canadian-American League's Schenectady Blue Jays. Tommy's manager was Lee Riley, another veteran busher, whose son Pat grew up to coach the Los Angeles Lakers and New York Knicks. Competition in the circuit included the likes of Jim Lemon and Billy Hunter. Against the Amsterdam Rugmakers (a Yankee farm team) on Monday evening, May 31, 1948, LaSorda had one of the finest games any pitcher ever had, striking out 25 in a 15-inning contest. Rugmaker leftfielder George Morehouse fanned six times against Tommy.

As icing on the cake, when LaSorda came to bat with two on and two out in the 15th, he singled to left, driving in the winning run.

However, LaSorda also walked 12 in the historic game and committed two miscues. Poor control plagued LaSorda that year as it would his entire career. He led the circuit in wild pitches with 20 and while he stuck out 195 (an impressive average of 9.14 per nine innings) he issued 153 bases on balls (an average of seven per game).

He also filled in at first and in the outfield. In 143 at-bats he hit .211. On Saturday night, May 15, 1948, he pinch-hit in extra innings and walloped the ball out of the park at the 355-foot sign in right field.

"Tommy would fight at the drop of a hat," recollects Blue Jays Travelling Secretary Guy Barbieri. "He wouldn't take any guff from anybody. If there was players fighting, he'd be the first one in the scuffle. He'd be the first one in anything."

"Tommy was a real dummy when he was here," recalls former Blue Jay hurler Charley Baker, "He didn't know enough to come out of the rain, but he sure knows now. He was a good pitcher. He had a curveball that would drop right off the table, but he was 'smart' and a wise guy. One of those types. He and [pitcher] Duke Markell teamed up together, and, boy, they were something else! Nobody liked them."

THE ONE ABOUT THE CAB

"In fact, probably the biggest story about [Tommy] was that he missed the bus going to Quebec, and so he got into a Yellow Cab and told him to charge it to [Blue Jays owner Pete] McNearney and rode all the way to Quebec, and McNearney almost died when he got the bill, you know. He was cheap anyway. It was more money than La-Sorda's monthly pay, I guess. McNearney almost died . . .

"Tommy was flamboyant, cocky and aggravating. You name it."

Yet, Tommy made one heck of an impression even then. Schenectady once seriously considered erecting a statue of LaSorda at the site of old McNearney Stadium. The main issue was whether to depict the pre- or post-Slim Fast Tommy.

THE CLAY BRYANT FAN CLUB

At season's end LaSorda was drafted by the Dodger organization (Branch Rickey himself visited Schenectady that season; but he didn't see LaSorda pitch; Charley Baker did the honors). The follow-ing season he found himself with the Greenville Spinners of the Class A South Atlantic League, managed by Clay Bryant. Back in the 1930s Bryant had pitched six seasons for the Chicago Cubs, enjoying just one good year — 1938, when he won 19 games and paced the cir-cuit in both strikeouts and walks. The Virginia-born Bryant was not exactly the Great Communicator. "He never tried to teach us any-thing, or encourage us, or boost our confidence," LaSorda ruefully noted in his autobiography, "he just ruled by fear. Before a game we weren't allowed to talk with anyone in the stands, including our fam-ilies. During a game his idea of a discussion on the pitcher's mound was to grab the ball and say 'Get out.' And if we lost a game, after-wards he'd make us sit in front of our lockers, staring at the floor, until he was ready to take a shower — maybe half an hour after a game...Even off the field, if he met one of his players in an elevator, he wouldn't say hello."

Not quite a role model for future managers.

PARLEZ-VOUS FRANÇAIS?

Despite Bryant's baleful influence, LaSorda went 7-7 with a spar-kling 2.93 ERA, and the next season earned a promotion all the way up to the Montreal Royals. The Royals were the jewel of the Interna-tional League. From 1945 to 1955 they never finished lower than third — and that happened only once. Five times they made the Junior World Series. Four times Royals won the IL MVP Award —shortstop Bob Morgan (1949), shortstop Junior Gilliam (1952), and first sacker Rocky Nelson (1953 and 1955). There LaSorda met Walter Alston, who was a big improvement over Bryant. "He was the perfect manager for the Montreal club because he knew how to win and how to teach young players how to win," thought LaSorda. Tommy went 9-4, displayed his usual control problems, and began a 10-year playing career at the Triple-A level.

LaSorda had cups of coffee with the Dodgers (he claimed it took Sandy Koufax to keep him off the Brooklyn roster, and technically that was true) and Athletics and shifted over to the American Association's Denver Bears and the PCL's Los Angeles Angels, but as a minor leaguer, Montreal was home, and in 1958 LaSorda returned to the Royals. It was a mixed blessing. True, he was going "home" in one sense — and beyond that he was put on the roster as a pitcher-coach, which at this stage of the game was vitally important to Tommy's future. He knew the arm was not going to last forever. The bad news was his manager was the ever-popular Clay Bryant. Despite Bryant, it was a great year: LaSorda was honored by a "Day" at Delorimier Downs on August 23, 1958, was International League Pitcher of the Year, and lead the circuit in victories, frames pitched, and complete games.

He went 12-8 in 1959 and was still pitching effectively when the end came suddenly for him on July 9, 1960. A disagreement with Bryant led the parent club to brand LaSorda as a Royal Pain in the Butt and to release him as both pitcher and coach. His career seemed finished. LaSorda was crushed. Then came a heartwarming reversal of fortune. Every Royals player but one signed a petition backing LaSorda. Dodgers executive Buzzie Bavasi realized a mistake had been made and rehired Tommy — not as a Royal, but as a scout.

A NEW CAREER

It was not until 1965 that Tommy returned to minor league ranks, having been named manager of Los Angeles' Pioneer League farm club at Pocatello, Idaho. Bavasi provided him with one word of *strong* advice: ease up on the fighting. Tommy told him no problem, but on the night of his managerial debut a gigantic brawl erupted with Idaho Falls. LaSorda's career hung by a thread, but the big club decided once again to stick with him. Pocatello finished second that year and the following year it and Lasorda transferred to Ogden, Utah. Conditions at that level were pretty primitive. Steve Garvey, who started his career under Tommy at Ogden, remembers stretching meal money by dining at a place "called Chuck-o-Rama or Chuck Wagon Buffet, where you could get all you could eat for $1.99. Salisbury steak, chicken, pork chops. It was a pre-game ritual. Everybody went, including LaSorda."

Facilities were equally primitive. "We had nothing," remembers Garvey. "LaSorda's standard reply when some new kid would ask directions to the whirlpool was to tell him to stick his foot in the toilet and flush it."

Yet his players respected him. "In many ways," says Garvey, "LaSorda was the perfect manager for us. He was a big, good-natured uncle. He knew baseball and he taught baseball, but he also understood the situation. Maybe that was even more important."

"The very first thing I did when I arrived in Ogden was have stadium club cards printed," LaSorda wrote in his autobiography. "I sent them to all the people at Dodger Stadium, telling them if they visited Ogden, we'd have dinner at the stadium club and I'd have their names posted on the message board at the park. Fortunately, few people took me up on it. We really didn't have a message board at the stadium. In fact, we didn't even have a stadium club."

Despite that, Ogden captured three straight pennants — with won-lost percentages of .591, .621, and .609. After that, the Dodgers gave LaSorda a giant promotion to Spokane of the Pacific Coast League.

HE HAD THE HORSES

Again LaSorda finished second in his first season (1969) with a new club, but on Opening Day 1970 the ever-confident Lasorda, boldly announced over the Indians' Stadium PA system: "Ladies and Gentlemen, I would like to introduce to you the 1970 Pacific Coast League champions, the Spokane Indians. . ." He was as good as his word. The club won the PCL's Northern Division by an astounding 26 games, featuring such talent as Steve Garvey, Bobby Valentine, Bill Buckner, Bill Russell, Davey Lopes, Charlie Hough, Doyle Alexander, Von Joshua, Tom Paciorek, Jerry Stephenson, and Jose Pena. It would have been tough for LaSorda *not* to win the pennant. To top it off, he captured the playoffs in four straight. And he did it all by out-generalling some pretty stiff competition: Chuck Tanner at Hawaii, Charlie Fox at Phoenix, Don Zimmer at Salt Lake City, and Whitey Lockman at Tacoma. *The Sporting News* named LaSorda Minor League Manager of the Year.

In 1972 the club shifted to Albuquerque. Again LaSorda captured pennant and playoffs, aided by such talent as Paciorek, Lopes, Joshua, Ron Cey, Larry Hisle, Jose Pena, Doug Rau, and Geoff Zahn. With horses like that, the powers-that-be decided that LaSorda didn't deserve any awards, but the Dodgers gave him one anyway, a promotion to the big club's coaching ranks.

The rest, as they say, is history . . .

TOMMY LASORDA'S MINOR LEAGUE PLAYING RECORD

Year	Club	League	G	IP	W	L	Pct.	H	SO	BB	R	ER	ERA
1945	Concord	NC St.	27	121	3	12	.200	115	91	100	84	55	4.09
1948	Schenectady	Can-Am	32	192	9	12	.489	180	195	153	122	99	4.64
1949	Greenville	Sally	45	178	7	7	.500	141	151	138	81	58	2.93
1950	Montreal	IL	31	146	9	4	.692	136	85	82	73	60	3.70
1951	Montreal	IL	31	165	12	8	.600	145	80	87	75	64	3.49
1952	Montreal	IL	33	182	14	5	.737	156	77	93	90	74	3.66
1953	Montreal	IL	36	208	17	8	.680	171	122	94	77	65	2.81
1954	Montreal	IL	23	154	14	5	.737	142	75	79	66	60	3.51
1955	Montreal	IL	22	143	9	8	.529	125	92	62	58	52	3.27
1956	Denver	AA	16	83	0	4	.429	94	54	34	54	46	4.99
1957	Denver	AA	6	17	3	4	.000	29	8	6	25	23	12.18
1957	Los Angeles	PCL	29	132	7	10	.412	134	72	59	73	57	3.89
1958	Montreal	IL	34	230	18	6	.750	191	126	76	77	64	2.50
1959	Montreal	IL	29	188	12	8	.600	192	64	77	93	80	3.83
1960	Montreal	IL	12	45	2	5	.286	79	17	24	48	41	8.20
Total			406	2,184	136	106	.560	2,030	1,309	1,220	1,096	898	3.70

FATHER MARTIN RAN
A MINOR LEAGUE

Picture a player on a hardscrabble baseball diamond years ago, when semi-pro leagues still flourished. Now visualize a servant of God, caring for a flock of parishioners, aiding the destitute, even rushing into a raging fire to minister to those in danger of death.

The stuff of movies? Or, more likely, of two separate and wildly different films? No, not at all. Once there was a priest, Father Harold J. Martin. Known as the "Baseball Priest," his life revolved around both God and the diamond. A simple parish cleric, his career was written up in *The New York Times* and in nationally syndicated columns.

"Judy" Martin, born in South Boston in 1895, graduated from South Boston High School, Boston College, and Fordham University. At each school he excelled not only in the classroom but also as a star pitcher.

And he was playing in some pretty fast company. Two of his Fordham teammates went on to the majors — infielder Al LeFevre and Hall-of-Famer Frankie Frisch. Martin was also talented, yet he was, well, *different*. First, he could come at you with either arm. "He could throw both ways," recalled Frisch, "and he did. He was truly ambidextrous."

"He was a pretty good hitter from both sides of the plate, too," added LeFevre, "though he wasn't very big — about five-seven and kind of skinny. That name — Judy, we called him — I don't know how he got it. He was from Boston, you know, and he brought the name down with him."

Then there were his outside interests. "We would have devotions on the quadrangle around the statue of Our Lady," recalled LeFevre, "Each day a student would be appointed to lead. I remember Judy preaching an outstanding sermon, the very finest."

A vocation in the priesthood beckoned, and Martin headed for the seminary. At the same time, however, he managed to play professional ball, pitching for the New Haven and Albany clubs in the Class A Eastern League. His record was hardly stellar (2-4 with a 4.58 ERA), but it put him in the record books. At 28, and on the verge of ordination, the Pittsburgh Pirates offered him a tryout, but Martin declined.

The priesthood didn't mean the end of Harold Martin's love affair with baseball. Assigned to a parish in the Diocese of Ogdensburg in upstate New York, Martin organized the Northern New York League, a semi-pro outfit. He also became its star hurler, taking the mound under the pseudonym, "Doc O'Reilly." Ogdensburg, then as now, was no metropolis, and before long Martin's boss, Bishop Joseph H. Conroy, caught wind of the young priest's moonlighting.

"It was a poor parish," explained Martin, "and I felt that if I could get $100 for pitching a ball game for two hours, it would help the exchequer. I thought I was being cute about it, pitching under an assumed name, but those things get around and eventually I was called in for an explanation.

"I told the bishop I was using the money to start a recreation center for the children of the parish. When I got through, he looked at me, smiled benignly, and said, 'See if they need a $50 first baseman.' "

"O'Reilly" continued pitching for Ogdensburg until the early 1930s. He may have been slowing down a little, but what really ended his career was an act of heroism. Martin rushed into a burning house to aid a trapped homeowner, and his eyesight was permanently damaged by ammonia fumes. Yet, with typical modesty, he never boasted of the deed.

Now permanently off the mound, Martin continued promoting baseball. In the midst of the depression he brought into town Chappy Johnson's All-Stars, a team of down-on-their-luck black barnstormers.

Martin's major venture, though, was the formation of a team in the recently created Canadian-American League. The Ogdensburg Colts were managed by an irascible minor league veteran named George "Knotty" Lee. Lee's claim to fame was that, at the turn of the century, while pitching in the old New England League, he was hit so hard by a line drive that he was pronounced dead.

Martin earned his share of the club by providing the Colts with a place to play, Winter Park, which he had originally developed for parish youngsters to enjoy winter sports. For the team to survive, Martin and Lee had to scout up their own talent and then peddle the best of it to higher leagues. Their outstanding find was a scrawny Detroit kid named Maurice Van Robays, who in 1937 paced the Can-Am League in just about every offensive category (including 43 homers) and was sold to the Pittsburgh Pirates. As a National League rookie in 1940, Van Robays would drive in 116 runs.

Most signings weren't nearly as successful. Pitcher Paul "Daffy" Horonzy blew into town and bragged he wouldn't take a paycheck until he won a game. At one point, he got literally beaten up by the Ottawa team, and compiled a stratospheric 9.54 ERA. (He was quickly released.) First baseman Danny Hargrove, recruited by Martin's Boston contacts, showed up with his hands covered with blisters from his WPA job. He couldn't even grip a bat.

But through it all Martin never neglected the spiritual needs of the Colts. *The Sporting News* records that in 1939 all members of the squad attended a Holy Name Communion Breakfast. Unfortunately, as the team failed to qualify for the playoffs, drawing only 19,000 fans for the season and ending the year by moving out of town, the episode did little to convince nonbelievers of the power of prayer.

The Can-Am League began in 1936. In January 1937, Martin was elected its president. Not only was he the lone cleric in such a post, but he was the only circuit chieftain serving without pay. As league president, Judy Martin had a variety of duties, some mundane — such as scheduling and registering player transactions — and others more difficult — such as propping up tottering franchises or disciplining league personnel.

Yet he always was soft-hearted about meting out punishment. "He'd fine me for anything," recalls Eddie Sawyer, who managed the Yankees' Amsterdam farm club and later piloted the 1950 Phillies to the pennant, "and the next day the same umpires would bring the check back to me at homeplate."

Martin was not shy about boosting baseball. "I occasionally get letters from young folks who ask me if baseball would interfere with a vocation to the priesthood," Martin remarked. "I tell them by no means. So far as baseball is concerned, there isn't a cleaner or more honorable way of making a living on God's earth.

"I contend there is no better solution to the juvenile problem than baseball. Just give them a few bats, some baseballs and gloves, and you won't have to worry about the future."

Stories of his personal generosity are legion.

In 1938 he was transferred from Ogdensburg to tiny Huevelton, New York. Conditions were primitive — and frigid. To survive his unheated rectory, Martin would often drive back to Ogdensburg and sleep in whatever empty bed he could find in the local hospital.

Yet it was never too cold for him to assist those in need. "One day he came in with a fine new overcoat some well-to-do friends had given him," recalled one Ogdensburg journalist. "A few nights later he came in from Huevelton, blue from the cold. We asked him where his new coat was. 'I found someone who needed it more than I,' he replied. That was characteristic of Father Martin."

"He really was the backbone of the league," remarked another sports reporter. "One time he got $10,000 as a personal gift from one of his parishioners. He put it all in the league. He didn't take a dime."

Minor league ball was a hand-to-mouth operation. The Colts were no exception. In 1939 the team folded, but soon Father Martin became part-owner of the Can-Am franchise in Utica, New York. When the Second World War intervened, the Can-Am League went into mothballs, but the Utica team transferred to the higher classification Eastern League. Martin sold out, reaping a hefty profit. In typical fashion, he plowed the total back into Ogdensburg's youth programs.

Father Martin and the Can-Am League parted company in 1944, but the priest's interest in the national pastime continued. In 1946 he and a long-time friend, local banker John Ward, helped organize yet another Class C circuit, the Border League. Martin was named honorary chairman of the board.

"I am trying," he once explained, "to repay baseball in a small measure for what the game had done for me."

Father Martin died in 1958, leaving behind a nation of admirers. "He completely lived the religion he professed," eulogized the *Ogdensburg Journal*. "His greatest happiness and satisfaction was in helping the poor, the sick, the lonely, the defeated, the unfortunate. He had a host of prominent friends who gave him money, clothing, food, automobiles — all sorts of things for his own comfort. He never kept any of them any longer than it took him to give them away to those who had what he considered a greater need."

What better memorial could a person have?

UNSER CHOE HAUSER

Babe Ruth hit 60 homers in a season; Roger Maris belted 61. But the only pro player to twice hit 60 or more in a season is the venerable Joe "Unser Choe" Hauser. And no one ever hit more at the minors' top level than Hauser's 69 four-baggers at Minneapolis in 1933. His 299 career minor league homers rank him fifth on the all-time list. Not only is he the only player with two 60-homer seasons, but he is one of only two minor leaguers to accumulate five 40-homer campaigns. *Nobody* ever said Joe Hauser couldn't hit.

"I must have been a pretty good hitter," Hauser, then 94, told *OldTyme Baseball News*' Scott McKinstry in the summer of 1993. "Connie [Mack] always had me hitting clean-up. I was clean-up wherever we played. I'll tell ya, when I hit with a man on third and less than two outs, I was going to score that guy."

Hauser's family came to America from Bavaria, settling in Milwaukee. He, along with his six brothers and two sisters, grew up on Milwaukee's heavily German North Side and was a product of the city's sandlots. "I left school when I was in the sixth grade," he admitted. "I had to work — I didn't have the money to buy school books." He found work in a factory that manufactured cement mixers. Hauser's job was hustling hot rivets to the welders.

Almost immediately Hauser also found a berth on a local semi-pro team. "A fellow recommended me to a local team when I was fourteen," Hauser continued. "They had a good team but no pitching. I won my first game and the older guys on the team began to take to me immediately." He pitched four seasons with that team, Gilly Zunker's "Comers." Then known as "Zip" Hauser because of a blazing fastball, he lost only one game during that span.

By age 18, Hauser had moved over to another semi-pro club at

Waupun, Wisconsin, 60 miles northeast of Milwaukee. He won his first game, 2-0, and struck out 17.

"They recommended me to Connie Mack after I had been with the team a while," Hauser continued. "Connie invited me to the try-outs. I was seventeen and all by myself when I reported to Jacksonville. All I had was a bat in my hand the whole time. Connie called to me and said he wanted to look at me the next day. He watched me take batting practice and then he sent me home in the morning. He gave me $100. He told 'em to sign me up."

Hauser started out with the New International League's Providence Grays. "I reported to Providence as a pitcher/ outfielder," said Hauser. "They knew I had the bat. I joined the club in New Haven. The second day, I pitched. I pitched one inning. I didn't finish it. I walked three and struck out two. I walked the bases full, and the manager took me out. That was the last time I pitched. I was nervous the first game in the minors. Then, it just worked itself out. From then on, I was a hitter. No one had to show me a thing about that. I had it! I knew I had the strike zone, too."

He batted .277 in 1918. That season was a war year, and the New International League was the only minor league to play out the campaign. When that circuit reorganized for 1919, Providence was left out of the league but caught on with the Class A Eastern League. Hauser remained with the club and in 1919 paced the league with 21 triples and six homers. Ironically, in 515 at bats over two seasons with Providence, he hit just seven homers.

His Eastern League performance caused his hometown Milwaukee Brewers to purchase him. Interestingly enough, Hauser's Milwaukee debut came in a two-game April 1920 exhibition series against the defending American League champion Black Sox.

In Hauser's first week with the Brewers, the club started a game with the thermometer registering just 32 degrees. By the fifth inning a blizzard raged, but the umpires refused to call the contest even though four inches of snow eventually covered the ground. Hauser collected five hits including a homer, but fielding was an adventure. "I got two guys out who should have been safe," Hauser once recalled. "They reached first base before I did, but couldn't find the bag. I kicked around and finally found it before they did. The shortstop rolled the ball over to me once and by the time it got to me it was a snowball nearly a foot around."

In spring training of 1921 manager Jack Egan moved him to first base. "Egan took me to a sporting goods store and bought me a first baseman's mitt," Hauser recounted to author Norman Macht. "He told me, 'You play first base and you'll end up in the big leagues next year.' And that's just how it ended up."

But it may have been Joe's brother, a Milwaukee police officer, who had the most lasting effect on his career. He offered him $1 for every home run that he clouted.

"I had my bad days, naturally, like anybody else," Hauser once recalled of his Brewer days. "The 'wolves' would get on me, but I also had a lot of friends in the stands. They were Dutchmen like me — I'm as German as they make 'em — and when these wolves began letting me have it, my friends said to them, don't get on him —it's 'Unser Choe' — 'Our Joe,' and that's how I got the name."

Hauser responded with 20 homers and 110 RBI, and Connie Mack acquired him for $25,000 and four other players. In his rookie season he batted .323 for the seventh place A's but without much power. Combining the 1923-24 seasons, however, he finished seventh in the American League in RBI with 209 and third in homers with 43 (behind only Babe Ruth and Ken Williams). In 1924 Hauser's 115 RBI placed him behind only Ruth. His biggest day came on August 2, 1924 when he collected three homers and a double for an American League record of 14 total bases. The mark lasted less than a year, however, being broken the next May by Ty Cobb's total of 16.

Hauser enjoyed his time in the majors, particularly his teammates on the Athletics. "I always had good roommates," said Hauser. "No poopin' around, drinking or stuff like that. I roomed with Al Simmons when he broke in, and Max Bishop and Jimmy Foxx. All great guys who never gave me any problems. Simmons was an individualist — kinda like Ty Cobb."

As for manager Connie Mack, Hauser had nothing but the warmest regards: "He was a great guy — a great guy, a great guy! You know, he ran that team. No matter where he was — he was in charge. What a wonderful manager."

Back then, Hauser's claim to fame rested in part on his slugging and partly from his physiognomy. He reputedly had the largest mitts in baseball. "His hands are so large," wrote Ernie Lanigan in 1922, "that when he was a pitcher they operated against his chances of success as a slabman, for he could not control the ball."

The future seemed bright for Joe Hauser. But it all came apart when he shattered his kneecap in an April 7, 1925 exhibition against the Phillies at old Baker Bowl. It was one of the oddest of all baseball injuries. Hauser was barely in motion. "I'm in the field running toward first base to take a throw from the shortstop," Hauser told the late oral historian Eugene Murdoch. "A routine play which I had made thousands of time. There was no baserunner, nothing in the way, no chance of a collision. I had taken about three steps toward the base when something snapped in my right knee and I fell in a heap on the ground. When they examined me at the hospital, they found that the kneecap had cracked into two pieces. You could lay a couple of fingers in the gap. The doctors told me that occasionally a quick, muscular contraction caused such a fracture, but that it was not serious and would not lead to any permanent damage. They drilled holes in the two pieces of bone, sewed them together, and packed the joint in a plaster cast."

Out of baseball for the entire 1925 season, he came back in 1926 ("I couldn't bend my knee"), batting an anemic .192 in 91 games. Such a performance wasn't enough to keep Joe in the majors, and the A's sent him down to the American Association's Kansas City Blues. There he smashed 29 homers, drove in 134 runs, and hit a career high .353. And most surprisingly, even with his bad knee (held in place with a brace) he stole 25 bases and led the circuit with 22 triples.

Hauser returned to Philadelphia. "I had a real good spring training that year," he recalled. "I hit something like .400. And when we were about to break camp, Cobb says to me, 'When we get up north, I'll work with you on your hitting.' He says he'll help me.

"He killed me. He wanted me to stand closer to the plate so that I could pull everything, so that I could take advantage of my power. What was I supposed to hit the ball with, my elbows? I had always been a spray hitter. I hit the ball with authority, but I used the whole field.

"Cobb killed me. He did the same thing to a lot of other players. He didn't have many friends. By the time I got myself straightened out, I was back in the minor leagues."

Hauser's average sunk to .260 by season's end, and — over a fairly inconsequential issue — he and Cobb nearly came to blows in the clubhouse. Connie Mack's son Earl asked Joe: "Why didn't you hit the S.O.B?" but on June 3, 1929 it was Hauser, not Cobb, who was waived to Cleveland ("I was hired to be Lew Fonseca's caddy"), where he batted just .250 in 37 games — Fonseca led the AL with a .369 mark — before being demoted to Milwaukee. Even there Joe failed to respond. But in Baltimore the following year, he recovered his batting eye.

He did it by adopting a new stance and a new, lighter bat. "When I reported to Baltimore that spring," he once recalled, "Heinie Sand, the shortstop, suggested I use a lighter bat, about 34 inches long. It was also an ounce or so lighter than the 32-ouncer I had been accustomed to. I found I could get around faster on inside pitches and pull them."

The homers came — in bunches. "Before the season started," Hauser recalled, "New York came to play us at Baltimore. Babe [Ruth] and a bunch of us players were standing around talking on the field. Ruth said, 'Hey, Joe! How many home runs you goin' to hit this year?' He knew I'd probably hit a lot in Baltimore. I said, 'Well, we haven't played any games yet!" I went on to hit 63."

Hauser hit his 63rd on September 20, 1930, breaking Moose Clabaugh's mark of 62 set back in 1926 for the Class D East Texas League's Tyler Trojans. In 1930 Hauser set International League records with 173 runs scored, 113 extra base hits, and 443 total bases — although critics carped that he also led the league with a then-record 117 strikeouts. They also pointed to "friendly, low home fences" in Baltimore's Orioles Park. Chicago Cub scout Jack Doyle merely drawled, "another pop fly," when he saw Hauser poke one more homer into Baltimore's right-field bleachers. Yet others noted that Orioles Park's right-field barrier (313 feet) was deeper than at seven contemporary big league parks (Braves Field, Ebbets Field, Baker Bowl, Forbes Field, the Polo Grounds, Yankee Stadium, and Cleveland's League Park). Although left field was a mere 287 feet down the line (and deeper only than the Polo Grounds, among major league parks), for the left-handed Hauser, it was right field that was his natural target.

Hobbled by a pulled muscle and out for a month, Hauser "slumped" to .259 and 31 homers the following year, although he still led the International League in the latter category. The Orioles responded by selling him to the American Association's Minneapolis Millers.

Hauser rebounded by leading the league with 49 homers in 1932 while batting .303 and driving in 129 runs. Still injuries plagued him, and he accumulated those impressive numbers even though he was out of action for the last month of the season.

The following year was Hauser's career season, recording the then-professional record of 69 homers, along with 182 RBI, while batting .332. That same year he set the still-standing American Association mark of 108 extra base hits and 439 total bases. Some of those homers came off familiar names — Paul Dean, Bill Lee, Duster Mails, and Emil Yde. He hit three in a September 4 Labor Day doubleheader to reach 65, a new professional record. He collected his 68th and 69th homers on what was to have been the next-to-last day of the season, but lost his chance for 70 when the last scheduled game of the season was washed out.

The same old criticisms dogged Hauser. "Some wiseacre in the audience yells out that wasn't such a great feat in Minneapolis because of the bandbox of a ballpark they had there," he recalled. "I called back to him, 'When I was hitting, they were all bandboxes.'"

Truth to tell, however, Minneapolis' Nicollet Park was even more to Hauser's liking than Orioles Park — 279 down the line to right and 328 to the right-center power alley, although there was a 25-foot-high fence in right, and Hauser says in his defense, "Most of [my homers] cleared the screen and landed on the rooftops across the street." Still 50 of his 69 homers came at home.

Nicollet Park or no Nicollet Park, no player had ever before accomplished what Hauser had. He did not get rich in the process. Recalled Unser Choe: "They gave me a new car — a Studebaker — in Baltimore the year I hit 63. When I hit 69, I got $500 and a few gifts. I remember them telling me it would have been more, but they didn't have any money. . .

"I done all that for $400 a month. It was right after the depression. The next year Mike Kelley, the owner of the club told me that was all he could pay, the same thing I got the previous year. He said take it or leave it. I asked 'Mama,' my wife, whether I should take it or leave it, and she said to me, 'What else can you do?' So I took it."

The following year Hauser had the opportunity to return to the majors. He didn't take it. "I had a chance to sign with the Boston Braves in 1934," he once explained, "but they were offering me the same money I was making in Minneapolis [$400 a month]."

He looked like he might break his record in 1935 and was hitting homers both at home *and* away: "I hit 20 homers in the first 21 games.

In Kansas City, I hit five home runs in two games over a temporary fence they had put up, and the next day they took the fence down." Off Kansas City's Henry Johnson, Hauser was, in fact, the first to clear the Muehlebach Stadium's right-field barrier and land one on neighboring Brooklyn Avenue. Fans were so impressed that 28,000 showed up the next day to see if Unser Choe could do it again. Remarkably, he did, and fans passed the hat. "A guy took up a collection. I got about $400," Hauser told Norman Macht, "and I gave him $50 for his trouble."

"I thought I was going to hit a hundred but I broke my leg," says Hauser, who injured his good left knee on July 20, 1934, oddly enough, while visiting Kansas City.

Hauser lasted with the Millers until 1936, when he was still able to clout 34 homers and drive in 87 runs. After that, however, he became a semi-pro player-manager in Sheboygan, Wisconsin. Hauser was still able to hit .344 and .320 in 1937 and 1938 respectively. In 1940 the club entered organized baseball, becoming part of the newly formed Class D Wisconsin State League. Hauser remained as manager and also played some first base, batting .302 in 1942, his last active year. At that point Hauser was 43 years old. His Indians captured the playoffs in 1941 and won both the 1942 pennant and playoffs.

World War II shut down the Wisconsin State League, but Hauser returned as Sheboygan's nonplaying manager when the league re-formed after V-J Day. He was wildly successful, capturing pennants in 1947, 1948, 1951, and 1952. The WSL became a casualty of television following the 1952 season, but Hauser continued to bounce around minor league ball for the rest of the decade, managing the Class C Longhorn League's Artesia Drillers in 1953, the Class D Kitty League's Union City Dodgers in 1955, and the Class C Northern League's Duluth-Superior White Sox from 1956 through mid-season 1958. He won the playoffs in 1956 and the first-half flag and post-season competition in 1957.

Hauser retired to operating a Sheboygan sporting goods store, and although he joshed about poor business ("Nobody comes in to buy anything. I struggle along like a .210 hitter."), he did well enough. In 1967 he was elected to the Wisconsin Hall of Fame. Two years later, at age 70, he made his last appearance in uniform at a Minneapolis Old-Timers' game. In 1993 he was honored at St. Paul's Municipal Stadium.

Hauser's wife, Irene Kaye Hauser, whom he married in 1924, died in January 1987. Nonagenarian Hauser remains in Sheboygan, still ready to reminisce about the old days, to puff on a good cigar or to take a sip or two of Aristocrat Brandy. "I keep myself alive with this," is how Unser Choe puts it.

JOE HAUSER

Year	Club	LG	G	AB	R	H	2B	3B	HR	RBI	SB	Pct.
1918	Providence	EL	39	130	17	36	5	6	1	-	4	.277
1919	Providence	EL	107	385	64	105	20	21	6	-	11	.273
1920	Milwaukee	AA	156	549	94	156	22	16	15	79	7	.284
1921	Philadelphia	AL	167	632	126	200	26	9	20	110	12	.316
1922	Philadelphia	AL	111	368	61	119	21	5	9	43	1	.323
1923	Philadelphia	AL	146	537	93	165	21	10	16	94	6	.307
1924	Philadelphia	AL	149	562	97	162	31	8	27	115	7	.288
1925	Philadelphia	AL	(Did Not Play—Broke Leg on April 7)									
1926	Philadelphia	AL	91	229	31	44	10	0	8	36	1	.192
1927	Kansas City	AA	169	617	145	218	49	22	20	134	25	.353
1928	Philadelphia	AL	95	300	61	78	19	5	16	59	4	.260
1929	Cleveland	AL	37	48	8	12	1	1	3	9	0	.250
1929	Milwaukee	AA	31	105	18	25	2	0	3	14	2	.238
1930	Baltimore	IL	**168**	617	**173**	193	39	11	**63**	175	1	.313
1931	Balimore	IL	144	487	100	126	20	6	**31**	98	1	.259
1932	Minneapolis	AA	149	522	132	158	31	3	**49**	129	12	.303
1933	Minneapolis	AA	153	570	**153**	189	35	4	**69**	**182**	1	.332
1934	Minneapolis	AA	82	287	81	287	7	3	33	88	1	.348
1935	Minneapolis	AA	131	409	74	107	18	1	23	101	3	.262
1936	Minneapolis	AA	125	437	95	117	20	2	34	87	1	.268
1937-39		(Out of Organized Baseball)										
1940	Sheboygan	WSL	79	204	48	53	16	3	7	32	11	.260
1941	Sheboygan	WSL	77	233	53	67	13	5	11	54	10	.288
1942	Sheboygan	WSL	77	242	57	73	17	4	14	70	7	.302
Majors			629	2,044	351	580	103	29	79	356	19	.284
Minors			1,854	6,426	1,430	1,923	340	116	399	1,353	109	.299

STEVE BILKO

"If Rochester was New York City, Steve Bilko would be in the Hall of Fame." So wrote Fred Harris and Brendan Boyd in the cult classic *The Great American Baseball Card Flipping, Trading and Bubble Gum Book*, and that about summed up the career of this over-weight first sacker.

Steve Bilko could hit a ton in the minors. He also weighed a ton. But almost every time he reached the majors, his batting average went on a diet of Ultra-Slim Fast.

Bilko hailed from tiny Nanticoke, Pennsylvania, in the heart of the anthracite country just outside of Wilkes-Barre. Nanticoke was your basic working class community. Bilko later recalled what it was like in the town's bars: "When those miners walked in , they asked for one of three things — a straight shot, or beer, or both. If you asked for a creme de menthe, you'd get thrown out."

The scouts first spotted Steve Bilko when he was a 16-year-old, working out at Wilkes-Barre's Military Park. Even then he was huge. "What is that fellow at first doing? Is he keeping the place warm for his son?" thought Cardinals scout Benny Borgman.

While Borgman viewed the youngster as a bit hefty, he was also stunned by the hitting display he put on. He determined to track Bilko down, and when he did at a ballfield in Sugar Notch, Pennsylvania, there were three other major league scouts already there.

Bilko didn't disappoint his audience. The first time up he homered to center, a blast that would have escaped Yankee Stadium's Death Valley. The next two times up he didn't quite get around. He merely hit a pair of opposite field four-baggers.

The other three talent hunters made a mad dash for Bilko. Borgman had another idea: "Listen, it didn't take a genius to figure out that

162

the kid was under age. I figured they could have him. What I wanted was the father. I drove him home and we talked for hours. What we talked about was the Cardinals."

Finally, at 1 A.M. Steve arrived back at the Bilko homestead. With him was a Phillies' scout, who quickly knew he was beaten. Within an hour Bilko had signed a St. Louis contract.

"I was convinced that I had made history," exulted Borgman. "I was convinced that here was a guy who would one day hit 65 home runs in a single season."

The Cardinals started Bilko with Allentown of the Class B Interstate League. Before long he was tearing up pitching with Salisbury of the Eastern Shore League and Winston-Salem of the Carolina League. He really began to hit his stride though in 1948 with the Piedmont League's pennant-winning Lynchburg Cardinals in 1948 when he led the league with 34 doubles, 20 homers, 260 total bases, and a .333 average. His 92 RBI weren't shabby either. The performance earned him the Most Valuable Player Award.

In 1949 he made the first of his *six* stops with the Rochester Red Wings. That year he teamed with outfielder Russ Derry in a formidable one-two punch. Derry led the International League with 42 homers and Bilko slugged 34 for manager Johnny Keane. Bilko paced the league with 125 RBI.

"He was a good baserunner," recalled Derry in 1978, "maybe not the fastest, but a lot of savvy. And for a righthander, he could field his position well.

"He was maybe his own worst enemy when it came to eating, but if he were playing today, he'd certainly get a better chance in the big leagues.

"And I got to say this. He was one of the friendliest ballplayers I ever knew. Everybody liked him. He never had an enemy."

The Cards brought him up to the National League, and he made his debut for manager Eddie Dyer's club on September 22, 1949.

Throughout the early 1950s Bilko bounced back and forth between St. Louis and Rochester. He launched numerous homers at Rochester's Red Wing Stadium, but his most notable blast might have come over the far distant center-field barrier at Montreal's Delormier Downs. "The Montreal players were aghast," recalled Rochester Business Manager Mike Carpenter.

By 1953, however, Bilko seemed to have solved major league

pitching. True, he only batted .251, but his 21 homers and 84 RBI were more than respectable. But he also struck out far, far too often for the mores of the day. In fact he led the National League with 125 whiffs, coming dangerously close to the major league mark of 127 set back in 1940 by the Boston Braves' forgettable Chet Ross. On May 28, 1953 Steve fanned five times in a 10-inning contest. The next day, however, he redeemed himself by hitting two doubles in a single inning. He eagerly awaited the coming season — but he looked forward even more eagerly to eating everything in sight and reported to camp grossly overweight.

Eddie Stanky, who had replaced Dyer as Cards pilot, was shocked and ordered Bilko to undertake a crash diet. "I got rid of about 40 pounds in six weeks," recalled Bilko. "When we played in Philadelphia right after the season opened, my mother came to a game and she didn't even know me."

Stanky, a tough customer, kept the pressure on Bilko. "When we were on the road, someone always went to dinner with me," Bilko continued. "I'd order potatoes and I'd get a slap on the arm. It was like that all the time. At lunch I'd get an ice cube or two, really. I was so weak I could hardly walk."

Bilko barely played and when he did he left his bat in the dugout, hitting just .143 in eight games. Adding to his problems was St. Louis' acquiring of first baseman Tom Alston (their first black player) for $100,000. The Cards peddled Bilko to Stan Hack's seventh-place Cubs on April 30, 1954, but he continued to drift, batting just .239 the rest of the way.

The Cubs decided to stick with the immortal Dee Fondy at first base and packed Bilko off to the Los Angeles Angels in the Pacific Coast League. There, Bilko would gain the status of cult hero.

The Angels were the PCL's flagship franchise. In 1921 William Wrigley, Jr., had purchased the club for $150,000. In 1925 he built concrete-and-steel Wrigley Field, a showplace park but also a cozy one. Although its basic dimensions — 340 to left, 412 to center, and 339 to right — were appropriately distant, they were misleading. Wrigley Field's power alleys were disproportionately short. They were *made* for a slugger like Steve Bilko.

In 1955 Bilko tore the PCL apart, leading it with 37 homers, driving in 124 runs, and batting a hefty .328. At Oakland on May 4, one

Bilko homer travelled 552 feet. He captured the first of three Coast League MVP awards and the hearts of Los Angeles fans.

Still cut off from major league baseball, Angelinos looked to their own local diamond heroes. The overstuffed Bilko was made to order for the role. The papers loved him, despite — or maybe because of — his girth. "**NOT EVEN MRS. BILKO KNOWS HIS WEIGHT**," screamed one headline. He received more write-ups than even Hollywood's celluloid heroes. "There wasn't a movie star that could touch him," recalled George Goodale, then the Angels' PR man. "I know. I kept count myself."

Bilko influenced a whole generation of West Coast kids. "He was the first fat guy my friends and I ever had for a hero," remembered author John Schulian, "the first fat guy we ever wanted to grow up to be."

Columnist Jon Carroll felt the same way. "I was 9 years old, living in Pasadena near Cal Tech and trying to figure out *life*. I knew Linus Pauling; I used to go to picnics where Pauling would organize sack races. He had already won one Nobel Prize and was working on number two; he had wild, frizzy hair and a squeaky voice. He could have been my hero.

"But he wasn't. . . Steve Bilko hit 56 home runs; he was an adult whose accomplishments I could appreciate. I had tried to hit a baseball: I knew how difficult it was to make contact. And to actually put the ball in the cheap seats . . . *ooh!*"

In fact, Bilko's name was so often in the news it stuck in the head of a young Hollywood writer named Neil Simon. The result: Phil Silvers' immortal Sgt. Ernest T. *Bilko* of television's "You'll Never Get Rich."

Bilko (Steve, not Ernie) followed up his 1955 season, with an even bigger one, demolishing Coast League pitching and pacing the circuit in runs scored (163), hits (215), homers (55), RBI (164), and batting (.360). Not only was he again named MVP, but *The Sporting News* designated him as Minor League Player of the Year.

The 1956 Angels were perhaps the strongest team in franchise history. Manager Bob Scheffing's club went 107-61 and bested second-place Seattle by 16 games. Joining Bilko at L.A. was second baseman Gene Mauch (.348, 20 homers, and 84 RBI), third baseman Gene Freese (.291, 22 homers, and 113 RBI), left fielder Bob Speake (.300,

25 homers, and 111 RBI), and right fielder Jim Bolger (.326, 28 homers, and 147 RBI). As a team the Angels hit .297 with 202 homers.

During that season Bilko and Angels General Manager John Holland discarded Bilko's old contract and negotiated a new one. In one sense, it was a fabulous coup. Some said Bilko was now getting $20,000 a year. Scheffing boasted Bilko was the game's third highest-paid first baseman — behind only Stan Musial and Ted Kluszewski. Some observers felt this ignored a fellow named Gil Hodges, but why quibble?

However, the key clause to the new pact was not monetary but procedural. Inserted into the contract was a provision (allowable under then-current baseball law) exempting Bilko from the next major league draft. Stout Steve thought it would aid his return to the majors. He was dead wrong.

"I signed the waiver," Bilko told *The Sporting News*, "because I felt sure if some major league club bought me, it would therefore prove it was *really* interested in me, believed I could help, and would give me a thorough chance to prove myself since it had put up a good sum of money to buy my contract. As for myself, I was positive if I got that opportunity, and could play regularly, I could be of value to any club. But I *have* to play regularly. Otherwise, I just don't get going. Riding the bench in 1954 with the St. Louis Cardinals and with the Chicago Cubs proved that conclusively."

Signing the no-draft clause *might* have worked for Bilko. Teammate Gene Mauch had signed a similar contract but was sold to the Red Sox even before the season ended. But Mauch was going relatively cheap. The Angels were reportedly asking a hefty $200,000 for Stout Steve.

A discouraged Bilko returned to Los Angeles in 1957 but responded with another fearsome season. He led the league with 56 homers and 140 RBI. Oddly enough, he reached the 56-homer mark on September 6, closing within four of Tony Lazzeri's single season PCL record, but failed to connect in his last 11 games.

Bilko finally was sold back to a major league club on October 8, 1957, going to Cincinnati. Selling Bilko to the Reds hardly did him a favor. First base was occupied by George Crowe, and Bilko had to share the position with the Negro League veteran. But Steve didn't do too badly. Hitting .264 with four homers in 31 games, on June 15 Bilko was traded to the Dodgers with righthander Johnny Klippstein for the rapidly fading Don Newcombe. It should have been a triumphant return to Los Angeles. It wasn't. Stuck behind Gil Hodges, Bilko batted just .207 for the rest of the season.

Having flopped once more in the majors, Bilko returned to his Pacific Coast League safe haven, this time to Fred Hutchinson's Seattle Rainiers. The Rainiers were nothing to write home about, but Stout Steve continued to amuse fans, leading the PCL with 92 RBI.

His performance got him *yet* another shot at The Show, this time with Seattle's parent club, the Tigers. With Detroit Bilko flopped again. Bigger than ever in weight (but not in batting average), Steve was on the Denver Bears roster when the American League held its first ever expansion draft on December 14, 1959. He would return to the majors for one last shot — where else? — in Los Angeles.

Despite Steve's frequent failures in the big leagues, he was unconcerned about his latest chance to flop: "When I reported to the Angels . . . I was a relaxed man. There were two first basemen, Ted Kluszewski and me. I knew I would get a chance to play. If I couldn't hit, I would say good-bye and go back to my bar full time.

"Well, under those circumstances, there was no pressure on me, and I hit the ball pretty good."

Appropriately, pinch-hitting on the final day of the 1961 season, Bilko hit the last homer in Wrigley Field's history. It was his 20th roundtripper and gave the Angels five players in the 20-homer club — which would have tied a major league record, except for the small matter of the 1961 Yankees who did them one better.

Of course, there remained questions about Bilko's defense. One Angels fan was musing about the Wrigley Field PA announcer's warning that anyone touching a ball in play would be ejected from the park. "Does that mean you too?" he asked Steve, looking for some rational explanation for the first baseman's lack of range.

About this time, Bilko and outfielder Rip Repulski finally sold the bar they had owned in St. Louis. The establishment was located in a largely-Irish neighborhood about a dozen blocks from Busch Stadium. For a place run by two guys named Bilko and Repulski, it was ironically named "The Shamrock Cocktail Lounge."

"We would be playing, say, in Boston or Chicago," observed Bilko, "and I would run into guys who would say, 'I was in your joint not long ago. It was jammed.'

"Well for a place always jammed, we figured we should be making a fortune. But the more business we got, the closer we came to going broke."

Nineteen sixty-two saw Bilko rooming with a brash rookie named Bo Belinsky, but an even greater distraction was the emergence of power-hitting first baseman Lee Thomas. Although still swinging the bat fairly well, by 1963 Bilko had returned to Rochester for his sixth and final tour of duty.

Stout Steve retired from baseball and eventually took a job with a Wilkes-Barre perfume company, working there for 11 years. Bilko retired in 1977. In March 1978 Bilko, remembered as a decent man by all who knew him, passed away.

STEVE BILKO

Year	Club	League	G	AB	R	H	2B	3B	HR	RBI	SB	PCT
1945	Allentown	Int. St.	1	1	0	1	0	0	0	0	0	1.000
1946	Allentown	Int. St.	1	1	0	0	0	0	0	0	0	.000
1946	Salisbury	East. Sh.	122	441	73	121	28	4	12	90	6	.274
1947	Winston-Salem	Carolina	116	438	109	148	26	3	29	120	12	.338
1948	Rochester	IL	12	41	5	6	1	0	0	0	0	.146
1948	Lynchburg	Piedmont	128	463	89	154	**34**	6	**20**	92	3	**.333**
1949	Rochester	IL	139	503	101	156	32	5	34	**125**	1	.310
1949	St. Louis	NL	6	17	3	5	2	0	0	2	1	.310
1950	St. Louis	NL	10	33	1	6	1	0	0	2	0	.294
1950	Rochester	IL	109	334	71	97	18	6	15	58	0	.182
1951	Columbus	AA	26	74	13	21	2	0	1	6	0	.290
1951	Rochester	IL	73	273	41	77	14	6	8	50	1	.282
1951	St. Louis	AA	21	72	5	16	4	0	2	12	0	.222
1952	Rochester	IL	82	286	55	92	22	5	12	55	0	.322
1952	St. Louis	NL	20	72	7	19	6	1	1	6	0	.264
1953	St. Louis	NL	154	570	72	143	23	3	21	84	0	.251
1954	St. L.-Chi.	PCL	55	106	12	24	8	1	4	13	0	.226
1955	Los Angeles	PCL	168	622	105	204	35	3	**37**	124	4	.328
1956	Los Angeles	PCL	162	597	**163**	**215**	18	6	**55**	**164**	4	**.360**
1957	Los Angeles	PCL	158	536	**111**	161	22	1	**56**	140	4	.300
1958	Cinc.-L.A.	NL	78	188	25	44	5	4	11	35	8	.234
1959	Spokane	PCL	158	478	76	146	24	1	26	**92**	0	.305
1960	Detroit	AL	78	222	20	46	11	2	9	25	2	.207
1961	Los Angeles	AL	114	294	49	82	16	1	20	59	0	.279
1962	Los Angeles	AL	64	164	26	47	9	1	8	38	1	.287
1963	Rochester	IL	101	261	41	68	17	1	8	37	1	.261
Majors			600	1,738	220	432	85	13	76	276	2	.249
Minors			1,533	5,349	1,053	1,667	293	47	313	1,157	42	.312

JOE ENGEL:
Baseball's Barnum

Before there was a Bill Veeck there was a Joe Engel. Tucked away at Chattanooga, Engel did it all: trading a player for a turkey, raffling off houses, holding "elephant shoots" and "ostrich" races — and even hiring a female pitcher to face Babe Ruth and Lou Gehrig. In his era, Joe Engel brightened up many a day at the ballpark.

"I always try to look on the light side of things," he said in summing up his philosophy, "and I live every day just as if it were New Year's Eve."

The Germanic Engel boasted descent from baronial stock in the Hamburg region. Originally, he claimed the family name was *von* Engel, but when his father Wilhelm Alexander Engel came to the United States, the aristocratic prefix was dropped. Wilhelm Engel was given a letter of introduction to William Pabst, the proprietor of Milwaukee's famed brewery, but instead settled in Washington, D.C., where he ran a tavern featuring Herr Pabst's adult beverages. After the onset of Prohibition's Noble Experiment, Engel, Sr., managed several hotels in the city, the Engel, the Ebbet, the St. James, the Reno, and the Johnson.

Joe — the second of six children — was born on March 12, 1893. It was an ambitious brood. Brother Francis became an executive with the Radio Corporation of America (RCA); sister Charlotte, the president of the Women Bankers of America. The Engels lived just a block and a half from the White House, and Joe palled around with Kermit and Alice Roosevelt, T.R.'s children, often riding ponies with them. He also recalled fairly regular sightings of Presidents McKinley, Taft, and Wilson.

Joe's parents had a career picked out for him. But it wasn't base-ball; it was music, and they bought him a violin for that purpose. That project quickly ended when Joe's instrument was pilfered while he was doing what *he* wanted to do —playing baseball. He pitched for a team called the "Little Red Devils," and even then was a nascent pro-moter, raffling off cheap — and generally unreliable — watches to raise funds for bats, balls, and uniforms.

Joe first attended Washington public schools and then matriculat-ed at St. John's College, a preparatory school. On graduation from St. John's, Engel enrolled at Mount St. Mary's College in nearby Em-mitsburg, Maryland.

Engel proved to be an exceptional college athlete, winning letters in baseball, basketball, football, and track. In one track and field com-petition he won the 100-yard dash as well as 220, 440, and 880-yard events.

In his junior year he pitched a no-hitter against Susquehanna University, and threw three straight shutouts. He also defeated a local professional team, 1-0, breaking their winning streak of 29 straight. James Cardinal Gibbons, archbishop of Baltimore, presented him with a medal as the school's outstanding athlete.

He was impressive enough for Washington's Clark Griffith to bring him directly to the Senators, but this was not Engel's first con-nection with the team. From 1907 through 1909 he served as its bat-boy. Now, as a major leaguer, Engel roomed with Walter Johnson and formed a lifetime friendship with the great hurler.

"What a pitcher he was," exclaimed Engel. "And what a gentle-man! People used to wonder at our close friendship — said we were so different. Walter didn't drink or smoke and was more or less on the serious side. I liked my fun and as a youngster was something of a hell-raiser. But, we just clicked. I spent many happy hours in his com-pany, especially when we'd go on hunting trips at the end of the sea-son. We both were proud of our pack of fox hounds. And, after the hunts, we'd sit around the fire, talking of Johnson's early years in the American League and the personalities on the Washington club who played for [Joe] Cantillon, Jimmy McAleer, and Griffith."

Aside from having the honor of being spiked by Ty Cobb, Engel's most notable accomplishment while in the majors actually had noth-ing to do with the Senators. In 1913 he helped discover Babe Ruth, when he returned to Mount St. Mary's for a nostalgic Commencement Day visit (he had that luxury because Washington did not allow Sunday baseball). "I went there to pitch in an old-timers' game," he once recalled. "And before our game the freshmen played. That's when I saw this big left-hand pitcher."

That pitcher was George Herman Ruth, and Engel was first of all impressed by his haircut ("roached," was the term for the style) and only later by his arm. "He really could wheel the ball in there," Engel later recalled, "and remember, I was used to seeing Walter Johnson throw. This kid was a natural pitcher. He had everything. He must have struck out eighteen or twenty men in that game." After completing his mound duties, Ruth joined the school band where he amused himself on an enormous bass drum.

The following day on the train back to Washington, Engel sat next to Baltimore Orioles owner Jack Dunn. "I told [him] that he ought to sign the boy," recalled Engel, who remarked that Ruth had "real stuff," and parenthetically that "he can also beat the hell out of a bass drum." The following year, Dunn (who was also receiving other glowing reports on Ruth) did just as Engel recommended.

At Washington Engel never quite matched his roommate, Johnson. His stats were clearly lackluster:

	IP	H	W	L	SO	BB	ER	ERA
1912	75.0	70	2	5	29	50	33	3.96
1913	164.2	124	8	9	70	85	56	3.06
1914	124.1	108	7	5	41	75	41	2.97
1915	33.2	30	0	3	9	19	12	3.21

Those figures may not seem all that bad, but bear in mind Engel worked in a pitcher-dominated era. Washington team ERAs for those four seasons were minuscule: 2.70, 2.73, 2.54, and 2.31. "I was just too wild," he later admitted. In mid-season 1915, Griffith demoted Engel to Pongo Joe Cantillon's Minneapolis Millers, where he went 5-3 in helping the Millers to the 1915 American Association pennant. He remained in Minneapolis until the middle of the next season, when Joe Lannin's Red Sox acquired him and farmed him out (along with Herb Pennock and Vean Gregg) to the International League's Buffalo Bisons, a team Lannin also had a financial interest in. With the pennant-winning Bisons, Engel was 9-7 with a respectable 2.55 ERA, but his most memorable day came when the great Napoleon Lajoie belted the tar out of one of his offerings.

Lajoie, then 42 and playing out the string with Toronto, walloped one right back through the box. It hit Engel right over the heart. "It knocked me flat," said Engel, "and I saw the ball trickling away." He had enough left in him to make a desperate play to nab a runner trying to score, but his teammates had to carry him off the field. "The ball had me spitting blood for a week," Engel recalled.

One member of the Bisons was particularly egotistical, and when manager Patsy Donovan made him team captain, he became particularly insufferable. "Whenever he saw a fellow who seemed to take himself too seriously, Joe was deeply concerned," recalled teammate Chippy Gaw, a former major league righthander and a future coach at Boston University. "He didn't rest easy until something was done about it. You know how much a captain amounts to on a ball club. Not much. But this fellow began to swell up right away. It was a crime how officious that fellow got."

Engel wouldn't stand such nonsense and launched an elaborate ruse. Conspiring with equally chagrined teammates, he retreated to his hotel to forge a mash note from a mythical female fan, "Pauline B." to the Bisons' new captain. The note implored him to meet "Pauline" at downtown Buffalo's corner of Main and Genesee, concluding, "Oh, you home run kid, I can hardly wait until tonight!" To add a touch of authenticity to the document, Engel had one of his fellow player's girlfriends inscribe it in feminine hand and purple ink. A little *parfume* was dashed over it for good measure.

That evening Captain Buffalo put on his best suit and headed for the promised land of Main & Genesee. His teammates, however, hotfooted it over there and arrived first, lurking in various doorways and waiting for him to arrive. After he appeared they strained to contain themselves as he nervously paced back and forth, perusing each woman to ascertain if she was his mysterious admirer.

Finally, one player called out "Paul-line!" opening up a floodgate of similar noises from virtually every doorway in ear's reach. "That name," recalled Gaw, "stuck to him from then on."

Engel had a cup of coffee with the Reds in 1917, but spent most of the season with sixth-place Buffalo (for whom he was 13-17). At year's end Washington signed him, but he was soon allowed to make his own deal with the Atlanta Crackers. Engel wrangled a $4,000 signing bonus plus an $800-a-month salary. His primary assignment that year, though, was with the United States military. "I pitched only

172

two games for them," said Engel, "one of them a 1 to 0 victory over Mobile, when the Army got me. Charley Frank, the Atlanta president, yelled bloody murder, about the $4,000 he paid. He wanted it back. But I couldn't have given it to him if I had wanted to. I had spent it."

Following Armistice Day, Engel was released from the service. In 1919 he hooked up briefly with Cleveland, but literally couldn't get anybody out, leaving town with an ERA of infinity plus. Next Engel graced the Jersey City Skeeters roster, although he never appeared in an International League game and then basically called it quits (although he performed briefly for Washington in 1920), turning to his mentor Clark Griffith who hired him as a scout. Griffith respected Engel's eye for talent and had something tangible to base it on. Back in 1915 when the Old Fox had shipped Joe to Minneapolis, he asked Engel to report back on what two players he should get in return. One of them, catcher Eddie Gharrity, was quite a find.

In his new career, Engel's first discovery was shortstop Stanley "Bucky" Harris, who led the Nats to pennants in 1924-25. In fact, Engel unearthed many of the players on those championship teams, including third baseman Ossie Bluege, outfielder Goose Goslin, first baseman Joe Judge, and pitcher Fred Marberry.

Despite these pennants, Engel's most vivid memory of Harris involved Bucky's October 1926 wedding, a real society affair. The bride, Miss Mary Elizabeth Sutherland, was the daughter of Alien Property Custodian Howard Sutherland. The affair was such an event that among the attendees were President and Mrs. Coolidge.

"Bucky, you know, had come to the Washington club right out of the coal fields," said Engel. "He was real tough. He was a good manager, but we were all surprised when we found out he was going to marry into Washington society.

"Well, I went to the wedding with Walter Johnson. We were all sitting there when all at once we turned to look at Bucky coming down the aisle and he was wearing a pair of those Lord Fauntleroy knee pants. We got laughing so hard we hard to leave the church and never did see the wedding."

Those were great times for Washington. "I always admired Griff," recalled Engel. "During one of the lean years after World War I, when I was just scouting, Griff called me and asked if I could go along without a salary for a while. I told him I would.

"After the Senators had won the World Series from the Giants in

1924, Griff gave me a full World Series share, but also a bonus of $10,000. That's the kind of square shooter he was."

Of course, it should be noted that Engel was not *completely* self-sacrificing in going without a salary. "That's okay, Griff," he told the Old Fox, in agreeing to wait for his paycheck, "just so long as you don't bother that expense account."

Engel continued to scout for Griffith. Perhaps the best player he ever delivered was Hall-of-Famer Joe Cronin. To say the least, Griff was not exactly initially thrilled with Cronin.

"When I first spotted Cronin playing at Kansas City [in 1928], I knew I was watching a great player," Engel later recalled. "I bought Cronin at a time when he was hitting .221. When I told Clark Griffith what I had done, he screamed, 'You paid $7,500 for that bum? Well, you didn't buy him for me. You bought him for yourself. He's not my ball player — he's yours. You keep him and don't either you or Cronin show up at the Washington ballpark.'"

Cronin, of course, developed into a great player who managed the Senators to their last pennant in 1933 — and became something more to Clark Griffith — family. "But I left something out," added Engel, "when I'd called in to tell Griff about Cronin, a real sweet and pretty girl named Mildred, whom he'd adopted, answered the phone. I told her, 'Mildred, I'm bringing in a boy who's going to be Washington's new shortstop and your husband. And that's exactly the way it turned out. Mildred has been Mrs. Cronin for many years. But that time I had to sneak Joe into town, because Griff was still all steamed up about the deal."

One prospect Engel passed on was Salt Lake City outfielder Paul Strand, winner of Pacific Coast League Triple Crowns in 1922 and 1923. "He'll never make it in the majors, Griff," Engel sniffed about Strand who in 1923 also set the still standing organized baseball record for hits in a season (325). Connie Mack, however, didn't share Engel's opinion and shelled out $100,000 for Strand. When newspapers reported on Mack's great catch and how he would demolish big league pitching, Engel feverishly began to second guess himself, and his panic grew worse as Strand tore up grapefruit league offerings.

When the A's and Senators met, Engel's old friend, Walter Johnson, was scheduled to pitch. Engel beat a path for The Big Train, begging him to make Strand look bad: "Please bear down on this guy."

Johnson went all out, fanning Strand four times. Griffith was convinced and gave Engel a warm vote of confidence after the game.

The 1920s were an era of mixed blessings for Engel. The Senators did well and, befitting his boisterous personality, Engel even did a turn on the Keith-Orpheum vaudeville circuit, trodding the boards from 1926 to 1929. He was manager and narrator in a pantomime boxing act that helped set an attendance record in a Salt Lake City theater. Of course, the box office might have been helped more by one of the bill's other acts, a young crooner named Bing Crosby. As part of Engel's penchant for show biz publicity, during the "Era of Wonderful Nonsense," he even led an elephant down Washington's Pennsylvania Avenue. But there was a down side. Finances were often chancy and to help make ends meet Engel operated a couple of steamboats on the Mississippi River for his grain dealer father-in-law.

By 1929 Engel —even though he was seriously considering the movie business — was itching to get back into baseball full-time. Initially he focused on buying Rel Spiller's Atlanta Crackers, but the deal fell flat. So he moved slightly north and, at Clark Griffith's behest, purchased the Chattanooga Lookouts from one-time major leaguer Strang Nicklin. Nicklin, the son of former Southern Association president Captain John B. Nicklin, had once coached baseball at West Point and boasted Omar Bradley was his center fielder.

Engel not only bought the franchise but vowed to demolish old Andrews Field and build a park that would be a credit to both Chattanooga and the entire Southern Association.

The result was Engel Stadium, one of the minors' finest facilities. Located at the corner of Chattanooga's Fifth and O'Neal Streets, the 10,000-seat park was a spacious facility, with a 471-foot distance to center field, 22-foot-high fences, and a 44-foot-high scoreboard.

Engel captivated Chattanoogans, enlivening life in a city deeply mired in the Great Depression. "He was both loved and envied for his unmatchable ability to bring a ray of sunshine into the lives of everyone," remembered sportswriter E. T. Bales. "Many had forgotten how to laugh and really enjoy living."

When the 1930 season opened, hostile Atlanta fans remembering Engel's unsuccessful efforts to buy the club, greeted him with a banner reading: "To hell with Joe Engel. We are backed by 16 millionaires." The following Opening Day at Atlanta, Engel retaliated, sporting a caved-in top hat and shabby swallow-tail coat, he drove a beat-up old Ford onto the field. On the hood of his jalopy he painted the slogan, "Chattanooga's Only Millionaire."

Before Engel arrived Chattanooga had a reputation of a poor baseball town. He immediately reversed that. In 1929, the Lookouts' last pre-Engel year, attendance was a paltry 78,000. With the depression worsening — but with Engel promoting like hell — it surged to 146,000 in 1931 and 172,000 in 1931. And Engel did it the hard way, *without* night baseball. The rest of the minors had quickly converted to arclights in 1930, but Clark Griffith stubbornly refused to install lights at Engel Stadium until 1936.

One of Engel's first moves had been to expand the club's "Knothole Gang," letting youngsters in for free. All he required from young fans was a certificate attesting to regular and Sunday school attendance. Beyond that Engel gave generously whenever youngsters — and oldsters — needed a helping hand. "Many of the most successful men in Chattanooga were in one of his early knothole gangs…" commented local Judge Riley Graham in 1970. "But there isn't a man [here] today who hasn't in some way felt the kindly hand of the Joe Engel who has done so much for the kids in this city. He would be a millionaire if he had saved and wisely invested the money he has spent on bats, balls, and uniforms for youngsters, as well as the cash he's given down-and-out ballplayers who came to him."

One reason for his generosity to Chattanooga's youngsters was a tragedy in his own life, the 1932 death of his only son, nine-year-old Joe Bryant Engel, run over in Washington by a drunk driver.

Among Engel's most famous stunts involved the March 1931 signing of female pitcher, Jackie Mitchell — "the girl who struck out Babe Ruth."

Virne Beatrice "Jackie" Mitchell was just 17. She had been a sickly child. In fact, she was a premature baby, weighing just four pounds at birth, but her parents followed doctor's orders and saw that she got plenty of exercise. "I was out at the sandlots with father from as long as I could remember," said Mitchell. At age seven she even received a few tips on pitching from Brooklyn's Dazzy Vance.

By age 17 she had grown to 5'7" and 130 pounds — certainly big enough for a 17-year-old girl in 1931, but *not* very big for a professional pitcher. Nonetheless, she played ball around Chattanooga and in one amateur contest fanned nine male batters. Coincidentally, the club she played for was called the Engelettes and sponsored by our hero. That March she attended an Atlanta baseball camp run by former big league shortstop Norman "The Tabasco Kid" Elberfeld. Engel now saw new possibilities in the young southpaw.

That same month he signed Mitchell to a Lookouts' contract. Her goals were modest. "All I want is to stay in baseball long enough to get money to buy a roadster," she revealed to reporters.

The press, of course, was more than interested in the story. From the *Chattanooga News* to the *New York Daily News*, coverage was plentiful —particularly when Engel announced Mitchell would appear in an exhibition against the already legendary New York Yankees. Engel succeeded beyond his wildest dreams in generating headlines, but one paper held out from the publicity avalanche. The conservative *Sporting News* refused to buy into the gambit. "Quit your kidding," they wired their local correspondent. "What is Chattanooga trying to do? Burlesque the game?"

Engel originally scheduled Mitchell to pitch on April Fool's Day 1931, but rain delayed the contest. The following day, however, Mitchell got her chance. Former major league righthander Clyde "Foots" Barfoot started for the Lookouts but surrendered a leadoff double to Earle Coombs and a run-scoring single to Lyn Lary. Manager Bert Niehoff signalled for Mitchell to enter the game.

The first batter facing her was none other than Engel's old discovery, Babe Ruth. "Yes, I think I can strike him out," Mitchell had breezily informed the press just the day before.

For his part, Ruth earlier told reporters: "I don't know what's going to happen if they begin to let women in baseball. Of course, they will never make good. Why? Because they are too delicate. It would kill them to play ball every day."

Mitchell's first offering was outside for a ball. The Bambino swung wildly at the next two pitches, although both were probably also outside the strike zone. The next pitch was a called strike three. Ruth, noted one witness, "kicked the dirt, called the umpire a few dirty names, gave his bat a wild heave and stomped off to the Yanks' dugout."

Lou Gehrig now stepped up to bat. The Iron Horse lamely swung three times and missed three times. Mitchell had faced the two foremost sluggers in the game and struck out both — although there was some doubt they were giving their best. Such criticism nettled Mitchell. Years later, she saltily told an interviewer: "Why, hell yes, they were trying, damn right. Hell, better hitters than them couldn't hit me…Why should they've been any different?"

Better hitters than Ruth and Gehrig? On what Planet?

Tony Lazzeri followed Gehrig to the plate. If there was any doubts regarding Ruth's and Gehrig's intentions, there was none regarding Lazzeri's. He was determined to get on base, bunting the first pitch foul. Then Jackie couldn't find the plate, throwing four straight balls. After "Poosh-em-Up" trotted down to first, manager Niehoff strode to the mound and put Barfoot back in the game.

Most thought Mitchell would continue with the Lookouts as the regular season opened and a few saw her prospects as bright. *The New York Times* editorialized: "Cynics may contend that on the diamond as elsewhere it is *place aux dames*. Perhaps Miss Jackie hasn't quite enough on the ball yet to bewilder Ruth and Gehrig in a serious game. But there are no such sluggers in the Southern Association, and she may win laurels this season which cannot be ascribed to mere gallantry. The prospect grows gloomier for misogynists."

But the exhibition was the end of Mitchell's "professional" career. Judge Landis voided her contract and banned her from organized baseball, agreeing with Ruth that the sport was "too strenuous" for women. Engel, however, was not through with Mitchell, signing her to play for the travelling semi-pros "Lookout Juniors" managed by Elberfeld.

Engel was the father of the flamboyant giveaway. While others feared turning baseball into a circus, Engel worried that three rings weren't enough. Numerous times, he pumped up attendance by giving away an entire house. When night ball finally came to Chattanooga on May 1, 1936, a record 24,639 fans showed up at the 16,000-seat park to see Engel raffle off a domicile. The crowd so overflowed the stands that before gametime Engel froze his supply of baseballs to lessen their chance of being hit into the throng.

On another instance, a youthful, $12-per week grocery store clerk won an Engel home and auto. "He sold the house and car, bought out his boss and went into business for himself," noted a satisfied Engel.

Engel's most famous trade, one of the most famous trades *anywhere*, for that matter, involved shortstop Johnny Jones. The Charlotte Hornets were eyeing Jones, and Engel informed them the infielder was available. "Felix Heyman, who owned the Charlotte club, was a butcher," said Engel. "I told him he could have my boy for the biggest turkey in his shop."

So for a 25-pound bird, the deal was made. Ever cognizant of the value of publicity, Engel invited the local press over for a turkey dinner, an event that proved somewhat of a disappointment. "I still think

I got the worst of that deal," Engel ruefully remarked. "That was a mighty tough turkey."

Engel seemed to have a fixation with birds. In the 1930s he hung 50 cages full of canaries in the grandstand. On another occasion he brought out five fake stuffed "ostriches," which proceeded to lay giant "eggs" at second base. Engel —sporting a gardenia in the lapel of his garish green suit — then escorted a huge "duck" onto the field who then proceeded to drop an even larger "egg."

Engel also pioneered the gimmick of having fans dash for cash on the diamond. "There were some quarters and silver dollars in the tub," Engel revealed, "but you can bet most of those coins were nickels."

Among the more fondly remembered Engel promotions were his so-called "elephant hunts." Rarely, however, are these described. When they are, one can readily see why they are *not* held today. Wrote the *Chattanooga Times*' Wirt Gammon in 1938: "In the elephant hunt, 14 colored lads, dressed only in white shorts and carrying long spears, danced to three tom-toms. After six hunters, wearing bamboo hats, carrying automatic shotguns and riding wooden hobby horses, appeared the 'cannibals' rounded up the herd of elephants — made of cloth — and then began the bombardment. Almost 50 shots were fired before an elephant was bagged and only two were 'killed' during the chase."

Equally objectional by today's standards was Engel's staging of "Custer's Revenge." Somewhere along the line Engel had acquired a native American pitcher, Chief Woody Arkeketa. In the surrealistic world of Engel promotions, this translated into the following: To the strains of the "Beer Barrel Polka," Engel's ground crew erected a tepee on the pitcher's mound. Engel then "lured" Arkeketa into the structure with a jug of fire water. Waiting inside was "Custer." After Engel and Arkeketa entered the wigwam, all hell broke loose. Five separate explosions rocked the tent. Blood-curdling screams filled the air. Then out ran Chief Arkeketa, wearing a bald wig. Not far behind was "Custer," with a butcher knife in one hand and a wig in the other.

And because Engel's stunts covered all the bases, one even involved the Southern Association's first Chinese-American hurler, a New York-born pitcher named George Hoy. After Hoy joined the club, Engel marched out before the first game of a doubleheader and announced: "Hoy can't play in this one. He's upstairs doing my laundry. But he'll play in the second game."

Not every day saw a full house at Engel Stadium. During one frustrating dry spell, a desperate Engel hung a sign from the park's gate: "This park is not quarantined."

It was times like those that made Engel a tough adversary in a contract dispute. A pitcher once wrote back to him, demanding, "You'll either have to double my salary or count me out."

Engel calmly wired back:

"1, 2, 3, 4, 5, 6, 7, 8, 9, 10."

Engel stories are legion. Lookouts' radio announcer Tom Noble once got himself embroiled in a street fight with Southern Association umpire, Augie Guglielmo, later a National League arbiter. Engel not only failed to get upset with Nobel, he rewarded him with a three-day paid vacation. "If he had won the fight," quipped Engel, "I'd have given him a week."

On another occasion a puzzled Engel spotted Southern Association ump Buck Campbell sitting in the Chattanooga stands. He asked Campbell what he was up to, and discovered that he had been scheduled to work a game at Knoxville but it had been postponed. Engel ordered his scoreboard operator to post half-inning results from Knoxville as if the game was actually proceeding. Campbell was beside himself until learning the truth.

Yet another time, Engel took his complaints about Southern Association officiating right to the top. Before a crowd of 10,000 fans he introduced a special guest thusly: "Ladies and gentlemen, I want you to meet the man who is responsible for the Chattanooga club being in last place. I want you to meet the man that is responsible for all the lousy umpiring you have seen this year. Give the biggest boo you know how to give to the president of the league, Charlie Hurth."

In 1938 the Washington Senators, who had spent an estimated $248,000 on the club, decided to finally unload it on local backers. Engel, who put $50,000 of his own cash into the scheme, got busy rounding up investors — 1,700 in all, at $5 a share. He loudly trumpeted the concept of community-ownership. "Give minor league ball back to the people and the towns," Engel exulted. "That's where it belongs, instead of to some far-off major league magnate. Give the fans the incentive of loyalty to their team, so that they follow it proudly as 'my team.' That cannot be done under the farm system…

"If we make a go of it this season, you will see fan-owned clubs bobbing up all over the country next year."

Chattanoogans bought the club from Griffith for an estimated $125,000, and Engel received $25,000 in severance pay from the Washington club. The transaction aroused the suspicions of Commissioner Landis. He suspected a kick-back. "What does that mean? Do you think that money was really a gift?" he demanded of one of the club's new owners.

"Judge, I thought enough of the deal to invest $15,000 in it," was the response. "You don't think I feel that there's anything wrong, do you?"

Well, there probably wasn't, but fan-ownership proved to be a bust in Chattanooga. Despite a pennant in 1939, the club went bankrupt, and a couple of years later the Senators had to resume ownership.

During World War II Engel chipped in to aid the war effort. To raise interest in a bond drive, he vowed to jump into the Tennessee River if their goal was met. It was, and Engel hired a bus to transport him and observers down to the river. Local authorities intervened, however, and prevented Joe from carrying out his promise — much to the relief of the second Mrs. Engel.

During Engel's tenure the Lookouts won their first Southern Association pennant ever (their previous flags had come in the old Southern League and South Atlantic League). In capturing the 1932 championship, he was aided by a decision handed down by Judge Landis. With the season winding down, the Southern Association's Board of Directors refused to allow the Lookouts to reschedule a critical rainout contest. If the game were not played, Chattanooga had no chance at all of defeating Tom Watkins' Memphis Chicks for the championship. Watkins and Engel, once close friends, became adversaries when Engel came into the Southern Association and took over Chattanooga. Landis overruled the league, and the Lookouts won that game, 12-4, and the flag by two percentage points.

To celebrate his victory, Engel had a team photo taken of the champion club. In typical Engel fashion, each player was shown in black tie, tuxedo, and wing collar. So was Engel, except, he was also adorned with a shiny top hat, perched rakishly atop his head.

Two more pennants came — in 1939 and 1952. Along the way Engel developed more talent for the Griffith family. On Kid Elberfeld's recommendation, he signed 16-year-old Cecil Travis in 1931.

Travis was so unsophisticated he didn't even own spikes, but Engel inked him anyway. Travis responded with a .424 average in 13 games, and the Senators bought his contract at season's end. Also produced at Chattanooga were Alvin Crowder, Buddy Meyer, Bing Miller, Sid Hudson, Early Wynn, Charlie Dressen, Buddy Lewis, Doc Prothro, Sammy West, Pete Runnels, Bob Allison, Ted Abernathy, and Harmon Killebrew.

Numbered among Lookout managers in the Engel years were Kiki Cuyler (who won a pennant in 1939 in his first year as a manager) and Rogers Hornsby. Hornsby had a much-deserved reputation as one who loved to play the ponies —something which greatly displeased vociferously anti-gambling Commissioner Landis. When Hornsby took over as Lookouts pilot, Engel had a jockey present a sway-backed nag to the Rajah at homeplate. Hornsby was not amused, and neither was Landis. "I do not think your latest stunt a bit funny," the commissioner telegraphed Engel. "If anything like that happens again, you will be in big trouble."

Engel's last years in baseball were not happy ones. Washington backed out of Chattanooga in 1960, but Engel obtained a Phillies' working agreement. Under Frank Lucchesi, the Lookouts won the Southern Association pennant, but in the deal Engel had lost much control over the club. Adding to his misery, the Southern Association folded after the 1961 season.

Engel and the Lookouts returned to baseball in 1963 with a South Atlantic League franchise, finishing sixth under manager Jack Phillips. In 1964 the circuit changed its name to the Southern League, but under new manager Andy Seminick the Lookouts remained a second-division operation. In 1965 they attracted just 25,707 fans, the lowest gate in the circuit. After that season the club again lost its working agreement and folded.

The Griffith family remembered their old friend, listing him as their scouting supervisor. Engel would find an excuse to visit the old ballpark every day, as he fiddled with a dwindling volume of correspondence. Occasionally, he would walk out onto the field and sadly "look into the past."

Engel died June 12, 1969 at Chattanooga's Campbell Hospital.

"I really feel he was one of the finest people I ever met, a great humanitarian," eulogized Cal Ermer, the Lookouts' manager from

1952 through 1957, "He would help anyone and everyone, and you will never find another like him.

"I think it was best said by a veteran baseball man in the recent baseball draft, 'since Joe is out of running the Lookouts, you never hear about Chattanooga, when he ran the team there was always a dateline coming out of Chattanooga and going all over the country.'

"I feel I have lost a wonderful friend and I think not only will the area miss him, but all baseball."

THE MAD RUSSIAN:
Lou Novikoff

He was the stuff of legends, although today his name hardly remains the proverbial household word. But in his time Lou "The Mad Russian" Novikoff provided sportswriters with copy that was simply too good to be true, a veritable cottage industry of anecdotes.

Yes, Novikoff was the quintessential prospect. He tore up every minor league he played in, but couldn't quite seem to click in the majors. When it came to facing big league pitching, reality had a way of rearing its ugly head for Mr. Novikoff.

That hardly made him unique. Check the listings for Frank Leja or Clint Hartung. Prospects quickly become suspects when big league curves start breaking.

But the Mad Russian had color — major league color — although it was trapped in a minor league body.

You want proof? Let's go to the secret FBI dossier and see what the Novikoff file turns up:

Fielding:

Just plain atrocious. Among the worst. "The way balls used to bounce off my head would have Babe Herman cockeyed with envy," Novikoff once bragged, not without some justification.

Baserunning:

Once while with the Cubs, Novikoff tried swiping third with the bases loaded. Veteran manager Jimmie Wilson was properly aghast at

184

the rookie's boneheadedness. "I know it was a dumb thing to do," Lou admitted when he trudged back to the bench — and the doghouse, "but I had such a good jump on the pitcher I just couldn't resist."

Gourmand:

The increasingly rotund Novikoff once polished off 13 helpings of fried chicken in a single sitting.

Animal Rights Advocate:

The Russian Novikoff fed his pooch — a Russian wolfhound, natch — genuine caviar.

Entertainer:

One of the most famous Novikoff stories involves the Mad Russian and one of his long-suffering Cub managers. Depending on the teller, the pilot is either Charlie Grimm or Jimmie Wilson, but their protagonist is always Novikoff.

The manager — whoever he was, and who can blame a fellow for wanting to be part of such an interesting tale? — was awake one evening in Boston. Unable to sleep with the clock well past midnight, he turned on his radio and heard a live broadcast from a local night club and heard the master of ceremonies intone: "And now, ladies and gentlemen, here's Lou Novikoff of the Chicago Cubs, singing 'Trees.'"

Grimm (or Wilson) threw on his clothes, hailed a cab, stormed into the nitery and fined the Mad Russian for violating curfew.

If Jesse Helms were the manager, they would call it censorship.

Born in Glendale, Arizona, on October 12, 1915, the Mad Russian was one of 12 children. The Novikoff household was so crowded there was no room for a second language. Young Lou spoke only Russian until he was 10.

Appropriately, Novikoff took a somewhat convoluted path to a baseball career. Even before being signed by the PCL's Los Angeles Angels in 1937 the 5'10", 185-pound Novikoff earned fame (under the name of Lou Nova) as a fast pitch softball pitcher. In one eight-inning contest he struck out 22 batters. Yet he was also one of softball's greatest hitters. Years later he was asked how he would have faced himself as a pitcher. "I either would have brained me with a pitched ball or killed me with a line drive."

The Angels must have envisioned the latter scenario and converted the 21-year-old to the outfield. They optioned him to a quintessential minor league stop, the Ponca City Angels. His .351 mark missed leading the Class C Western Association by just three points. That earned Lou a promotion to the Three-I League's Moline Plowboys, where he began his string of leading minor circuits in batting, hitting a league-leading .367 and adding 19 homers for good measure.

Novikoff started the following season with the American Association's Milwaukee Brewers but after 11 games was demoted to Tulsa in the then pitcher-friendly Texas League. With the Oilers Lou responded with a league-leading .368 mark, seven homers and 77 RBI. Even there he was colorful. Once while visiting Shreveport, Novikoff instructed homeplate umpire Art Passarella, "Call the first two pitches strikes." Passarella did just that as Lou indicated his contempt for the opposing pitcher. The home crowd booed the Mad Russian lustily, but that only encouraged him to greater hamminess. As he stepped from the batter's box, Lou clapped his hands together and finally pointed to left field. Then came the next pitch. He swung away — and the ball sailed clear over the fence. Shreveport's once hostile fans were more than won over.

On August 20 the Angels recalled their hottest prospect and he responded by hitting .455 with eight homers and 37 RBI in just 36 games. *The Sporting News* named him Minor League Player of the Year.

Nineteen-forty saw Novikoff simply rip the Pacific Coast League apart. Aiding Novikoff's slugging was a bit of reverse psychology. His wife Esther would sit in the stands and razz him mercilessly. "Novikoff, you bum," she'd screech, "You can't hit worth a damn! You stink!"

The strategy more than worked. "Novikoff will hit as long as they make baseballs and bats to hit them," gushed Angels manager Bill Sweeney as Lou won the PCL Triple Crown (.363, 41 homers, 171 RBI), establishing himself as a West Coast legend as he also paced the circuit with 259 hits, 147 runs scored, and a league record 438 total bases.

Nineteen-forty was Novikoff's year so completely, that he even avoided the ravages of baseball superstition. Normally when fans honor a player with a "day," he is invariably jinxed, but when "Lou Novikoff Day" was proclaimed to allow the Mad Russian to obtain Minor League Player of the Year honors, he homered in the first game and in the nightcap threw a runner out at homeplate, then homered again in the last inning for the game's only run. As Novikoff received his trophy he even serenaded teammates and fans with the strains of "My Wild Irish Rose," and "Down By The Old Mill Stream."

Yet, unbelievably, Seattle first baseman George Archie (.324, eight homers and 95 RBI in 179 games) captured MVP honors. Archie, it seemed, possessed one skill The Mad Russian sadly lacked: he could field.

The Cubs, salivating at the thought of having Novikoff to swat homers out of the *real* Wrigley Field, shelled out $150,000 for him and 21-year-second baseman Lou Stringer and dreamed the Slugging Soviet would lead them to a pennant. Newspapers and magazines such as *Look*, *Collier's*, *Esquire*, and *The Saturday Evening Post* heralded him as the second coming of Babe Ruth. One praised him as the "greatest righthanded hitter since Hornsby." Some even claimed his abysmal fielding had been improved greatly by coaching from legendary Coast League outfielder Jigger Statz. And Novikoff didn't hurt his reputation any by consistently walloping spring training pitching.

"It didn't make any difference what kind of pitching was served him," wrote Cubs historian Warren Brown. "He hit good pitching and he hit bad pitching. It wasn't even necessary for a pitcher to get the ball over the plate to him. He was likely to swing on a ball thrown behind him and cripple an infielder with the resultant drive." Brooklyn's Larry MacPhail — no mean judge of talent — visited the Cubs' Catalina training base and generously offered to take him off the Cubbies' hands. They turned down an offer well in excess of their original investment.

Despite all the hoopla, once the season opened the Mad Russian quickly became the Bad Russian. Through June he batted just .241 with a measly five homers and 24 RBI. Nor was his fielding any better. In fact, it was worse, as he seemed completely flummoxed by Wrigley Field's picturesque ivy.

"I thought maybe he had hay fever, so I got some samples of golden rod and proved to him we didn't grow those kinds of vines," said Jolly Cholly Grimm, then a Cubs' coach. "I talked to Jim Wilson, the manager, and even to [club secretary] Bob Lewis. Bob had a bright idea. He said maybe Novikoff thought it was poison ivy. I took him out there again, grabbed some of the stuff off the wall, and rubbed it over my face and hands. I even chewed a few leaves. All Novikoff could say is what kind of a smoke they might make!"

Teammate Len Merullo had an explanation for Novikoff's failure to live up to expectations: "Boy, he could tomahawk the ball. But he wasn't getting his sleep. In the minor leagues, you're playing all night baseball. He could sleep all day and get out to the ballpark. In Wrigley Field, unfortunately we never had lights. Most of the time you'd be away from the ballpark before four-thirty. Louie would get a head start and he'd be up all night. Louie was as good a hitter as there was around in those days, but never in the condition they hoped he would stay in."

The Mad Russian had his own theory: "I can't play in Wrigley Field because the left-field foul line isn't straight like in other parks; it's crooked."

It was hardly surprising when General Manager Jim Gallagher optioned him to Milwaukee in the American Association. Going with him was Grimm, who became Brewers manager.

Fledgling Milwaukee owner Bill Veeck had requested Novikoff's presence. Veeck had just purchased the club from Harry Bendinger, and it was in a horrible situation. The Brewers performed in rickety old Borchert Field, a relic dating from 1888, and their record on Veeck's arrival was a putrid 19-43. Grimm went to work on Novikoff to get him back on track. Each night he would point to the stands and give the Mad Russian the following pep talk: "Look at all those people. Do you think they're out here to see our lousy ballclub? No sir! They came to see you hit. You wouldn't let them down, would you?"

Novikoff responded, batting .370 in 90 games. He won his fourth straight minor league batting crown in his fourth different circuit.

Still he was a management nightmare. Grimm claimed this happened one day at Borchert Field: "From our dugout we couldn't see the left-field corner of the ball park. Lou was playing left and the ball was hit out there. He was gone so long that I got off the bench and went out to see what happened. Finally I see Lou coming out from behind the concession stand with a hot dog in one hand, a coke in the other — but no ball."

"Lou was never one of baseball's great thinkers," added Veeck. "He would sometimes drive us crazy by bunting with the bases loaded or by hitting away when a bunt was clearly called for."

Novikoff once groused that Borchert Field's left field was particularly bumpy. Grimm ordered the groundskeeper to flatten it out, but in the very first inning of the next game, Novikoff let not one, but two line drives bounce past him for triples. When he loped back into the dugout, a no-longer Jolly Cholly instructed him, "Lou, I just figured it out. There are two ways you can play those balls. Fall down in front of them or wait until they've stopped rolling, then go after them. But remember — throw to third base, and we'll cut 'em down to doubles."

How Novikoff won his American Association batting title is quite a story. He and Columbus' Lou Klein went into the season's final day tied in the batting race. Yet, as the Brewers assembled at Borchert Field, the Mad Russian was nowhere to be found. While the last-place Brewers' fans were properly excited about their hero's chances, the three-time minor league batting champ was clearly blasé over the situation.

With a doubleheader to play on that final day, Novikoff was in fact so uninvolved he didn't even bother to show up. Veeck rang Novikoff's hotel room, but no one answered. He then frantically phoned every gin mill the Mad Russian might have holed up in (well, maybe not *every* one). Again, no luck. Finally Sportshirt Bill asked a hotel bellman to go into Novikoff's room. There our hero lay, sprawled out on the bed and feeling no pain.

"Get him under a shower and get him dressed," Veeck ordered. "I'll send a gateman to drive him out."

Stalling for time, the ever-inventive Veeck closed down all but two of the Milwaukee ticket windows and then pled with umpires to delay the game because of the "crush" of fans outside. The ruse worked, and finally Novikoff arrived. "Look," implored Grimm, "you got to get a few base hits today. A few base hits today and you win the batting title."

Novikoff still wasn't very impressed, but trudged out anyway and went 5-for-8 (including a double and triple), outpointing Klein for the batting crown.

The Mad Russian returned to Wrigley Field in 1942. Management turned a blind eye to his abysmal fielding and even to some woeful stickwork. On June 10 Novikoff was batting a mere .206. In one city series White Sox manager Jimmy Dykes told Novikoff: "I know why they call you the Mad Russian. If I couldn't hit any better than you, I'd be mad too." But once again wife Esther came to the rescue. Her usual vitriolic "rooting" failed to work, so she instead retreated to the kitchen and emerged with a magic elixir — a Russian delicacy called "hoopsa" —hamburger and cabbage served up on a bun.

Coincidentally or not, Lou's hitting perked up immediately. Through a four-week stretch beginning in late July, he batted more than .375. He finished the season at an even .300.

It might be thought that the Cub brass would be pleased with Novikoff's .300 performance, or at least harp on him regarding such obvious matters as a lack of power (seven homers) or his by-now traditional defensive deficiencies. Instead, both owner Philip K. Wrigley and General Manager Gallagher complained that Lou was taking too many called third strikes.

Wrigley even offered Novikoff $5 for each time he struck out swinging. Once with the bases loaded and two outs, Novikoff fanned on a pitch over his head. "You must be awfully short of dough," chided a Cubs' coach as Lou trudged back to the dugout.

Maybe Novikoff *was* staring at too many called third strikes, but that could hardly be confirmed by his overall "K" total. Columnist Dan Daniel pointed out that Novikoff struck out only 28 times in 483 at bats, a creditable total compared to, say, Pete Reiser's 45 in 480 at-bats or Dolph Camilli's 85 whiffs in 524. "It looks," summed up Daniel, "as if Chicago doesn't take Mr. Novikoff seriously enough."

Not all of Novikoff's diamond adventures were the stuff of merriment. In September 1942 his Cubs became involved in a raging beanball war with Leo Durocher's Dodgers, who — unlike Chicago — were engaged in battling the Cardinals in one of the century's great pennant races.

Cubbies were hitting the deck all day. At one point Novikoff homered, but when he advanced to the plate for his next at bat, he was distinctly nervous about the fate awaiting him. "I came to bat with a baseball in my hip pocket," Novikoff related, "Mickey Owen asked me what I had. I said, 'Owen, if Higbe throws at me this time, I'm going to take this ball out of my pocket and hit you with it. And you tell Higbe that when he sees me throwing at you, he better start running."

The anxiety even carried over to his home life. "Y'know, I love chicken," he continued. "And nobody can cook it like my wife cooks it. Every day I came home from the ball game and she puts it in front of me for dinner. And I go to work on it.

"But that afternoon in Chicago after that game with the Dodgers, when they threw those dusters at us, I went home and when my wife put the plate down, I pushed it aside. I couldn't eat it. That's bad. I've got a wife and two children, and pitchers start throwing at my head. I ask you — is baseball worth that?"

Yet, Novikoff's response was not to hide on the bench but to gain revenge on the Lips' headhunters. "So please, Jimmie, put me back in there today," he begged manager Jimmie Wilson. "I personally want to make sure the Dodgers don't win the pennant." They didn't.

In the spring of 1943 Novikoff staged a holdout. He calculated his .300 average was worth $10,000 per annum, and not the piddling $6,500 in chiclets Mr. Wrigley was offering. "Well, I've always been told baseball is a big business — so I'm making it big business," Novikoff mused. "Al, Paul, and Jack, my brothers have all gone in the Army. No one's left to support ma and the two youngsters but me. I have a wife and wee kids of my own to look out for. So I held out for the money I thought I needed.

"I expect to hit over .300 for the Cubs. My legs feel fine."

But as the season opened, neither side budged sufficiently, and Lou remained out on the West Coast. He thought he'd pass the time playing for a semi-pro club, but after appearing in just one game was reminded that such moonlighting was illegal. The Cubbies, however, were getting desperate, losing 19 of their first 26 games without their flamboyant left fielder. The club and Lou agreed to compromise at $8,500, and Novikoff reported for action in late May.

He had lost none of his style in the field. Shortly after returning, he gathered up enough nerve to actually brush the ivy, but saw the ball bounce over his head for an extra-base hit. The next batter lined a single to left. The ball caromed off Novikoff's chest and skittered away. "If you aren't the lousiest ballplayer I ever saw," Esther Novikoff screamed from the stands. She may have meant it.

With Peanuts Lowry and Andy Pafko up from the minors, Novikoff received less and less playing time. He finished the season at .279 with no homers and 28 RBI. The following year, he rode the Cub bench despite a respectable .281 average. The Cubs — on their way to a rare pennant — shipped him back to Los Angeles for the 1945 season.

"He had a nice family, a wife, and a couple of daughters," summed up Len Merullo, "and he was not a hard drinker, but he loved to have as much beer as he could get in him and really enjoyed being around a crowd. He had that big moon face and a big smile, just a very likeable type of guy. He'd tell you stories, he'd lie like hell. You knew he was lying, but he was entertaining."

Back in the Pacific Coast League, Lou was again in his element, going 10-for-22 in his first five games, but his batting eye was clearly fading. He hit just .310, with nine homers and 52 RBI in 101 games. Yet, that was good enough to earn him a ticket back to the majors — or at least to the Phillies. With Ben Chapman's fifth-place club, Novikoff was used primarily as a pinch hitter, and managed to bat .301 in 17 games, but the Phils exiled him to the PCL's Seattle Rainiers, where he batted .325. The following year he chipped in with an identical .325 average, 21 homers, and 114 RBI. He was hitting .327 in mid-season 1948 when the Newark Bears acquired him, but Lou's days of Triple-A glory were nearly over. For the Bears he batted .327 again, but drooped to .258 the following year and was demoted to Houston in the Texas League. There he swung the bat at a pathetic .230 pace.

He descended further down the minor league ladder in 1950, playing with the Yakima Bears and the Victoria Athletics in the Class B Western International League. There — at 34 years of age — he batted a respectable .326.

That was the end of the line for Novikoff, but a rebirth for Lou Nova. The Mad Russian returned to his roots — and to softball, playing into his early 50s. In fact he became the first inductee into the International Softball Congress Hall of Fame.

Yet despite his softball accomplishments, Novikoff knew he had squandered a wealth of potential. "I knew people expected a lot of me, and I tried awfully hard to produce," he once sadly reminisced. "But I just couldn't hit the way everyone thought I should and I guess I should have been a better fielder."

Novikoff's final years were hardly happy ones. He worked on the California docks as a longshoreman, and while still in his 50s, he developed emphysema. Down on his luck, his friends threw a benefit for him. The event helped him financially, but did little for his morale, only reminding him of his misfortune. "It makes me ashamed, " he admitted. "I am a man and this is what I have come to. All I have left now is my pride."

Still Lou Novikoff has attained a baseball immortality of sorts. While Frank Lejas come and go, we have still not seen anyone to compare with the Mad Russian.

LOU NOVIKOFF

Year	Club	League	G	AB	R	H	2B	3B	HR	RBI	SB	PCT
1937	Ponca City	Western Association	124	510	98	179	43	6	16	112	14	.351
1938	Moline	III	125	507	110	**186**	26	**23**	19	**114**	5	**.367**
1939	Milwaukee	AA	11	42	6	9	4	0	1	3	1	.214
1939	Tulsa	Texas	110	419	72	154	26	9	14	77	7	**.368**
1939	Los Angeles	PCL	36	135	36	61	11	4	8	37	2	.452
1940	Los Angeles	PCL	174	714	**147**	**259**	44	6	**41**	**171**	3	**.363**
1941	Chicago	NL	90	203	22	49	8	0	5	24	0	.241
1941	Milwaukee	AA	62	203	22	49	8	0	7	64	0	**.370**
1942	Chicago	NL	128	483	48	145	25	5	7	64	3	.300
1943	Chicago	NL	78	233	22	65	7	3	0	28	0	.279
1944	Chicago	NL	71	139	15	39	4	2	3	19	1	.281
1945	Los Angeles	PCL	101	390	60	121	27	6	9	52	5	.310
1946	Philadelphia	NL	17	23	0	7	1	0	0	3	0	.304
1946	Seattle	PCL	84	312	24	94	13	2	2	34	4	.301
1947	Seattle	PCL	171	647	90	210	44	7	21	114	1	.325
1948	Seattle	PCL	64	168	13	55	9	1	3	30	1	.327
1948	Newark	IL	70	260	43	85	14	0	15	53	0	.327
1949	Newark	IL	57	213	35	55	8	0	16	48	0	.258
1949	Houston	Texas	59	217	17	50	9	2	1	24	2	.230
1950	Yakima-Victoria	Western Int. Lg.	86	322	53	105	21	1	12	79	2	.326
Major League Totals			356	1,081	107	305	45	10	15	138	4	.282
Minor League Totals			1,362	5,221	857	1,758	322	73	186	1,040	47	.337

RALPH KINER:
A Hall-of-Famer
Remembers the Minors

Very few players have ever made the majors without starting in the minors. Playing in the minors is virtually a rite of passage for major leaguers. Of course, there have been exceptions — Walter Johnson, Dave Winfield, Dick Groat, Ted Lyons, Frankie Frisch, Eppa Rixey, and Sandy Koufax are notable examples. For a while Connie Mack made a hobby of recruiting collegians, with Chief Bender, Eddie Plank, and Jack Coombs, being among the most noteworthy. Ernie Banks and Larry Doby jumped directly from the Negro Leagues to the majors.

But most major leaguers and most Hall-of-Famers — even Ruth and Cobb — started in the minors. This is the story of one of them, slugger Ralph Kiner.

The Hall-of-Fame Mets broadcaster was reminiscing following a late season Shea contest, recalling the start of his baseball career over a half century ago with the Eastern League's Albany Senators at old Hawkins Stadium, recollecting teammates and rivals and a place called Albany, New York.

There's been a lot of water over the dam since he made his pro debut against the Binghamton Triplets on April 23, 1941: seven consecutive home run crowns — the major league record. A home run frequency second only to the mighty Bambino. The general managership of the Pacific Coast League's San Diego Padres. A distinguished career as the voice of the New York Mets from their disastrous inception in 1962 through their various glory days and their crash to earth in the early 1990s. And, yes, Cooperstown.

Baseball's been very, very good to Ralph McPherran Kiner.

Kiner was just wrapping up a September Sports Channel telecast and was receptive, even eager to talk about the place where he had started his professional career.

How had this slugger, most famous for his dictum — "Singles hitters drive Fords. Home run hitters drive Cadillacs." — gotten to Albany in the first place? Kiner had graduated from high school in Alhambra, California, where he majored in Long Ball (10 homers in 24 games). He faced three choices for a professional career: the local Hollywood Stars, the Yankees, or the Pirates. The Stars offered Kiner 50 percent of whatever they would get when they sold him to a big league club. New York, on the other hand, had underwritten Kiner's sandlot club, the Yankee Juniors. Kiner had even worn the old uniform of outfielder George "Twinkletoes" Selkirk. Signing with New York, however, had a big drawback. Their system was so deep in talent, Kiner might get lost in it. In fact, if he signed a Yankees' contract, he would start at a Class D club for $60 a month.

The Pittsburgh Pirates won the bidding war by shelling out a then magnificent $3,000 signing bonus plus a guarentee of $5,000 more if he made the majors. They further promised Ralph he would start out no lower than the Class A level.

It was the first time the New Mexico-born Kiner had been east of the Mississippi. He left home with a friend, Bobby Jones, who was reporting to the Lake Charles Skippers in the Class D Evangeline League. Along the way the duo picked up a hitchhiker. Ralph, in turn, picked up a case of measles from him, which delayed his debut on joining the Senators' spring camp in Barnwell, South Carolina. Once recuperated, though, Kiner smashed a 440-foot homer in his first game.

"I enjoyed it," said Kiner of his Albany days, as he reached for a cigar the size of a Louisville Slugger. "It was my first time away from home. The people in Albany treated me wonderfully, and we had a good ball club, and I just enjoyed the whole thing."

Albany had enjoyed professional baseball off and on since the 1870s. In 1936 the city's International League franchise had collapsed. The following year Albanian Thomas F. McCaffrey moved a New York-Penn (Eastern) League franchise, the Brooks, from Allentown, Pennsylvania.

"Tom McCaffrey was a great owner," observed Frank Staucet, the Senators' shortstop from 1948 to 1955. "He could visualize a ballplayers' needs. He wasn't a selfish guy. When he came into a town where we were playing, you knew he'd be picking up the tab for dinner that night. He was an owner in the image of Yawkey and Wrigley. He was in it for the love of the game, not to just make a buck."

Such was the atmosphere young Kiner found himself in 1942. "I lived in a private home," he recalled. "I forget where. It wasn't much. It was something like $3 a week and I got my meals there, and it was near the ballpark, old Hawkins Stadium. The next year I was there, I lived in the Ten Eyck Hotel and made a deal there that we could have the room for $3 a day. I roomed with Jimmy Cullinane, who was the third baseman, and we had a closet we could put our clothes in when we went on the road and lock 'em up. So it was a really good deal, living at the Ten Eyck, which was a great hotel at that time.

"In those days they assigned you to a minor league club, and you could be in the minor leagues for a total of seven years. So they could really bury you down there. It's not quite the same as it is now, and at the end of the year when the major league club could go to a 40-man roster, they called up and said I was placed on the major league roster, and we went home at the end of the season, and if I had been called up, it would have been a big money deal for me later on, because I would have gotten credit for 42-43-44-45 in the pension plan, because that would have been a major difference in my retirement pay."

"When the 1942 season was over, Ralph Kiner and I were both bought from Albany," Cullinane once recounted in an interview. "We were roommates and we got word at the Ten Eyck Hotel where we stayed. The same telegram bought both of us."

"Both Jimmy and I went into the Naval Aviation Program," added Kiner. "He ended up flying blimps,and I ended up flying PBMs."

Kiner was a slugger even in those Hawkins Stadium days, though his totals of 11 dingers in 1941 and 14 in 1942 seem mighty low by Kineresque standards.

"Well, they were low," Ralph readily admitted in the cozy Shea Stadium Press Room as he sipped what he and Tim McCarver might term an "adult beverage." "My 11 home runs for the first year — I think a fellow named Larry Barton led the league with something like 17. It was a pitchers' league. They had a dead ball, big ballparks most of the way. If you recall Hawkins Stadium, it was tremendously big in center field, and they had outstanding pitchers and bad lights. Pitchers like Early Wynn [at Springfield] and Warren Spahn [at Hartford], and

I'll never forget the Wilkes-Barre pitching staff. They had the hardest throwers I'd ever seen in my life pitching for them.

"Mike Naymick was there. He was one of their hard throwers. Big. Tall. About 6'8", and they had a fellow named Earl Center that just really threw the ball hard, a whole bunch of hard throwing pitchers. William Embree was there. He might have been the best pitcher in the minor leagues at the time. He really had a great rising fastball.

"Those were the reasons. They just had good pitching, and it was a dead ball."

And Kiner didn't even mention another member of the 1942 Wilkes-Barre staff, righthander Alley Reynolds, who led the circuit with a 1.56 ERA and 193 strikeouts and threw 21 complete games, 11 shutouts, and a no-hitter. His no-hitter came on September 1. He lost it, 1-0, on an 11th-inning single. And if Kiner had trouble hitting pitchers of that ilk, consider the case of the Springfield Indians — as a team, they hit just *two* homers over the course of the entire season — both by a second baseman named Eddie Popek.

Kiner continued: "I lead the league with 14 homers and that year, 1942 — only one player in the whole league hit .300, and that was Steve Souchock for Binghamton, and I think he hit .306 [actually .315]. Nobody else hit .300 in the whole league, so you can tell it was a pitchers' league." So much so, that when the Eastern League opened its season on April 29, 1942, there were four 1-0 games, with Wilkes-Barre, Elmira, Binghamton, and Hartford triumphing against the rest of the circuit.

Kiner was never noted as a fielder, but until the advent of the DH, anyway, fielding was a part of the game for everyone, and Ralph was expected to put on a glove no matter how many Spalding products he sailed over the fence.

Surprisingly, in 1942 he led the whole Eastern League with 338 putouts — a mark one would not readily guess. He also led in errors with 17 ("I don't remember that").

"I played center field," continued the now-heavyset broadcaster, "I could run in those days. I started out as a center fielder and actually played center field in my first days in the major leagues, so I could run."

Future Hall-of-Fame pitcher Bob Lemon was then an infielder with the Wilkes-Barre Barons. "Bob Lemon tells the story," said Kiner, "and he says, 'When I first saw Ralph Kiner, he was a skinny kid who used to bunt for base hits!' and I guess when I went there [Albany] I was 19 and probably weighed about 160 pounds and was 6'1". Then, of course, I played two years with Albany. I started the season with Toronto and then went into the service, and I came out of the service, and I was about 200 pounds. Of course, when you put on 40 pounds, I guess you lose a little of your speed."

Ralph, despite his much-ridiculed "Kinerisms," is actually a keen student of the game, and while on the old Senators had the opportunity to learn under a couple of crafty veterans: managers Specs Toporcer and Rip Collins. "I played the first year for Specs Toporcer, who was the great infielder [the first major league shortstop to wear glasses], and he was our first manager. He was very good, but the one thing I remember about him was that he used to fine us $5, which was a lot of money. I was making $150 a month then, and I was paid pretty well. He fined us if he ever caught you eating a hot dog. He thought they were bad for you. So that's why I remember him so distinctly.

"My next year I played for Rip Collins. I believe it was his first year as a manager. He had just retired as a baseball player, and Rip was our manager that year, a switch-hitting playing manager, and we won the championship in 1942."

The Senators took the Eastern League pennant by four games over the Scranton Red Sox, which featured righthander Harry Dorish and outfielder Leon Culberson. Albany's squad was a light-hitting unit (team batting average: .244) led by Kiner; his roommate, Jim Cullinane (.277); manager Collins (.276); and outfielder Bill Nagel (11 homers). On the way down was former Pittsburgh infielder Bill Brubaker, who managed a mere .249 average in 91 games.

Cullinane might have joined Kiner on the Pirates, but fate intervened. "One fall [after the war]," recalled one former teammate, "he was working around his house, putting up storm windows, and a window fell on his throwing hand, his right hand, and he had the finger next to his small finger smashed. And he lost about half of his finger. Now, that affected Jim's throwing in the field. Unquestionably, the guy could hit like hell, but that injury screwed his chances of becoming a major leaguer because he couldn't throw the ball to first base."

Leading the Senators' pitching staff was future Pirates righthander Xavier "Mr. X" Rescigno (23-6; 1.76 ERA). Southpaw Don King went 11-8 with a 1.59 ERA. As strong a team as Kiner's Senators were, they washed out in the first round of the playoffs, losing to the Yankees' Binghamton Triplets farm club three games to two.

At interview's end, Ralph stood up and turned the tables, posing a few questions about Hawkins Stadium (he was aware it had been demolished to make way for a shopping center, but didn't know that the shopping center itself had gone under and the place was now the headquarters of the NYS Workers' Comp Board), the Ten Eyck Hotel (torn down as well and now the site of an Omni Hotel), and old Union Station (now a bank's corporate headquarters). Ralph shook his head to learn today's trains no longer stop in Albany, but across the river in Rensselaer.

Yes, time gallops on, particularly in regard to the financial rewards of a baseball career.

"I remember they gave us a wallet for winning the championship," Kiner added, almost as an afterthought. "I had that wallet for years, and I guess it was the biggest prize I ever had in my career until I got to the major leagues."

And they call them the "Good Old Days"!

Declaration of Independence:
The Northern League

For decades the number of minor league clubs had been limited by how many major league working agreements could be parcelled out. For most of that time period, rationing made sense. Bush league ball was a losing proposition financially, and without big league help it made no sense to operate a minor league club.

That began to change in the 1980s when cities clamored to obtain new minor league franchises and vied with one another to build better ballparks to house them. Suddenly, the minors were *in*, but supply was hardly keeping up with the demand.

Back in 1988 SABR-metrician and historian Bill James, in an essay titled "Revolution," called for kicking over the entire minor league system. James reasoned that if minor league clubs were liberated from the grip of their major league masters, they would flourish, much as college football and basketball teams do based on genuine local rivalries and competitiveness. James also posited that such a freeing of minor leagues would also tend to drive down superstar salaries as big league clubs could then recruit replacement players from a wider talent pool.

Not surprisingly, no one in the majors paid any attention.

However, as the majors continued to squeeze the minors — both in terms of financial considerations and onerous new ballpark requirements — a number of individuals *were* taking the idea very seriously.

Starting in 1993 the Northern and Frontier leagues set up shop as independent entities, free to win or lose, soar or flop, as they would — without major league interference or assistance. Emboldened largely by the Northern League's flamboyant prosperity (and to a smaller extent by the threadbare Frontier League's mere survival), other renegade circuits opened for business in 1994.

The Northern League was the brainchild of *Baseball America* publisher Miles Wolff. On leaving the Navy in 1971, Wolff secured a job as the $600 a month general manager of the Dixie Association's Savannah Braves. After bouncing around in other minor league front office and broadcasting jobs, in 1980 he scraped together $2,500 (plus $30,000 in working capital) and purchased the Carolina League's Durham Bulls. It wasn't always easy (the team's uniforms were stolen the day before Wolff's first opener), but Wolff prevailed and eventually bought a second club, the Appalachian League's Burlington Cubs. Following the 1990 season, he sold the Bulls to Raleigh broadcast executive Jim Goodmon for $4 million.

With Wolff's background and his numerous contacts in the game he was able to put together an operation that, unlike many enthusiastic but ill-thought out baseball enterprises, benefitted from an extraordinarily able leadership team.

"We've had the right people at the right place at the right time," commented Northern League Executive Director Tom Leip. "Most of the people in our league have had experience in pro ball, either major or minor leagues. That's why Miles chose the people he did — they've been around."

That team included: St. Paul owner Marvin Goldklang, an attorney and investment banker who at one time or another had a piece of the Utica Blue Sox, Pittsfield Cubs, Williamsport Mets, Charleston Rainbows, Erie Sailors, and the Miami (and later) Fort Myers Miracle; Rochester Ace owner Charlie Sanders, who headed the Atlanta farm system; Sioux Falls Canaries owner Harry Stavrenos, who operated in the California League; Thunder Bay President Ricky May, a former minor league general manager and one-time director of sports marketing for Valvoline; Duluth-Superior Dukes General Manager Tom Van Schaack worked for the New York-Penn League's Watertown Indians; Sioux City President Cord Pereira, a former vice president of the Northwest League's Boise Hawks; and St. Paul General Manager Mike Veeck, who had turned around the once moribund Miami Miracle franchise.

Wolff demanded no franchise fees from Northern League investors — *initially*. What he did ask for was a $100,000 line of credit and
proof of expertise in running minor league clubs. If, after two seasons,
a franchise still wanted to remain in the Northern League, a $50,000
franchise fee was required.

"To an extent," explained Goldklang, "many of us at the minor
league level have been viewed as theater owners. Someone else pro-
duces and distributes the film, and we open the doors, charge admission, sell some popcorn and soda and sell the film. That's it.

"The Northern League is baseball, not theater. A lot of us are finding it's more fun this way. It's not about thumbing your nose at anybody. It's about being in the business of baseball, rather than opening
theaters."

Also aiding the Northern League experiment were a number of
veteran field managers such as Singin' Ed Nottle, Tim Blackwell,
Frank Verdi, and Mal Fichman. All had been banished from organized
baseball after quite successful careers.

Fichman had toiled for such independent clubs as the Salinas
Spurs and the Erie Sailors. Verdi, a former Yankee farmhand who
washed out after tearing his rotator cuff, had previously managed in
the Oriole and Red Sox system. Back in 1987 he had piloted another
independent franchise, the California League's San Jose Bees, including such major league outcasts as Daryl Sconiers, Brian Harper, Ken
Reitz, Elias Sosa, and Warren Brusstar — as well as an influx of Japanese personnel. Despite finishing 61 games back, Verdi survived the
trauma to hook on with the Boston chain. After a losing season at
Elmira in 1990 he was cut loose.

Blackwell had been let go after six years in the Mets' organization, two straight pennants, and a lifetime winning percentage of .560.
"I was shocked," he admitted. "Dumbfounded. Those were my only
words I can come up with." Blackwell thought he was finished in
baseball until St. Paul's Mike Veeck offered him a job. "I hope to be
somewhere else next year," the walrus-mustachioed former catcher
admitted. "Like everybody else here, I hope to use this league as a
steppingstone to bigger things."

Blackwell was lucky. Ed Nottle had been out of the game for two
and a half seasons before the Northern League came into being. Nottle once had a promising career, being named *Baseball America*'s
Minor League Manager of the Year in 1982, and he confidently

thought he was in line for the job at Fenway Park. "Basically, I wore out my welcome," Nottle admitted. "I probably went too far with the flippant remarks and with telling the Red Sox what I thought. Actually, it was more like telling them and telling them."

This band of outcasts was not interested in merely lurking in the corners of the baseball map. The Northern League's St. Paul franchise dared to invade major league territory, that of the Minnesota Twins. For their part the Twins seemed unimpressed by the challenge. Sniffed then Minnesota General Manager Andy MacPhail: "I suppose it's professional baseball in that they pay their players, but I view them more as a sophisticated summer league." He would soon rue those words.

Also beginning operations in 1993 was a not very well structured operation called the Frontier League. It was the brainchild of Bud Bickel of Huntington, West Virginia, former general manager of the Appalachian League's Huntington Cubs.

Bickel explained his rationale, thusly: "Over the last six years, I've gone to the Winter Meetings. Each time I've gone, there's been any number of communities trying to get into minor league baseball. Despite the fact the minors are taking off, it's a closed market. That's one of the factors that motivated me to start the Frontier League."

Each team would carry 20 players, paid an average of $500 a month. Frontier League franchises starting the initial 1993 season were: the Zanesville Greys, Kentucky Rifles, Ohio Valley Redcoats, Chillicothe Paints, Tri-State Tomahawks, Portsmouth Explorers, Lancaster Scouts, and West Virginia Coal Sox.

Assisting Bickel in finding talent was former major leaguer Al Oliver, now coaching at Shawnee State University at Portsmouth, but otherwise there was no comparison with those running the Northern League.

Conditions in the various Frontier League parks were, well, frontier-like. In Lancaster, the basepaths were covered with gravel. In Ashland, the bullpens contained no pitching mounds, and players were advised not to run on the infield grass "to save wear and tear."

An omen of disasters to come occurred on Opening Day when country star Wynonna (a native of Ashland, Kentucky), backed out of throwing out the first ball for the Ashland-based Tri-State Tomahawks.

Just three weeks into the season the Tri-State and West Virginia franchises folded. West Virginia averaged just 117 fans per game;

Tri-State a mere 170. They should have known. Before Opening Day the League had sent 700 season ticket applications into the two towns and received just one order.

On July 30, Ohio Valley fired pilot Lee Mrowicki, ostensibly for stealing baseballs. "What I'd been doing," Mrowicki explained, "was throwing the game balls umpires tossed out of play into our depleted BP box. I'm not sure what I was expected to do." Referring to vague "personal and philosophical differences," Kentucky Rifles manager Roy Cutright and his coaches resigned on August 10. When Rifles players arrived at the park later that day, they found no one in charge of their club.

League owners canned founder Bickel in mid-season. "There are all kinds of financial problems," said one official. "It's a mess." Official statistical record keeping was also amateurish, late, and often inaccurate. Some teams never paid their modest $3,000 league franchise fee.

"As far as we're concerned, Bud is ex-commissioner of the Frontier League," said Portsmouth General Manager Steve Sturgill. "In a league like this, you need outstanding leadership and Bud wasn't giving it."

A third independent circuit was the Texas-Louisiana League. Masterminded by Dallas businessman Byron Pierce, a former outfielder at Dallas Baptist University, the league was announced in November 1992 and contemplated clubs in the Texas cities of Abilene, Amarillo, Beaumont, Lubbock, Tyler, and Waco as well as Lafayette and Monroe in Louisiana.

Pierce was less willing to go it alone than either Wolff or Bickel and actively sought working agreements with major league clubs. In any case, the Texas-Louisiana League never got off the ground in 1993.

But back to the Northern League.

Leavening the circuit's mix were a number of former big league players, including two of more than passing interest — sluggers Pedro Guerrero and Leon "Bull" Durham.

Bull Durham hadn't played professional ball since 1989. Plagued at one time by drug problems, he had turned his life around and now ran a printing firm in Cincinnati. The lure of baseball proved too much for him, though. In the spring of 1993 he tried out unsuccessfully for the White Sox and was considering offers to play in both Mexico and Japan. He opted instead to remain stateside.

Said Durham: "I'm here to turn some people on, throw some memories back into their mind. I want to show them the old Bull can still hit like he did in Wrigley. If people see that, maybe I'll get another chance in the majors."

For the season Durham hit .292 with 11 homers and 59 RBI in 226 at bats.

Guerrero, then 36, started the season with the Mexican League's Jalisco Cowboys. After earning a 10-day suspension for confronting a heckler, Guerrero was cut loose. The Northern League was his last chance.

After signing with the Sioux Falls Canaries, Guerrero grumbled: "How do I like being here? I don't like it here. But I'm here to play. I'm here to try to make my way back to the big leagues. I know I can still play...

"My shoulder feels good. I'm in good shape, but I have to work now to get in better shape. I haven't played for a while, and my legs are rusty. It's like training camp."

Guerrero batted .278 with three homers and 33 RBI in 151 at bats. As the season progressed, his attitude about the Northern League mellowed to the point that he was inquiring about buying the Thunder Bay Whiskey Jacks.

Other ex-major leaguers in the circuit included Rochester's Jeff Bittinger and Curt Ford, St. Paul's Brent Knackert and Jim Eppard (a five-time minor league batting champ), and Sioux Falls' John Mitchell. Mitchell was sold in mid-campaign to the Red Sox' organization. Knackert went to the Mets.

At season's end each Northern League franchise had peddled at least one player to major league organizations. Even before the season concluded, the Rochester Aces had sold batting champion Kash Beauchamp to Cincinnati. In the Northern League Beauchamp hit .367. For the Reds' Southern League farmclub Beauchamp hit .400 with five homers in 60 at bats.

"More and more scouts have been coming to our games," Leip bragged. "It started after the first guy was sold. Other major league teams said, 'We better pay attention, too.' Our league provides a good alternative if an organization has a hole to plug on a team that's in a pennant race."

Northern League play also sported a bit of an international flavor. Aside from rescuing Guerrero from Mexico, it boasted players from Japan and Cuba.

Shortstop Rey Ordonez and pitcher Eddie Oropesa were members of the Cuban National Team. In July, while in Buffalo for the World University Games, they defected by jumping over a 12-foot-high chain link fence. Why defect? "The simple reason was freedom," Ordonez explained through a translator. "I just wanted to be free and play baseball. Like all Cubans, freedom is very important to me. It's very difficult there. And it was very difficult to leave everything behind."

The Saints signed both Ordonez and Oropesa in mid-August. Ordonez responded with a 4-for-5 debut (including three doubles) against Thunder Bay. In his first appearance the left-handed Oropesa no-hit Duluth for four innings until he developed a blister on his throwing hand. With St. Paul Ordonez batted .283 in 15 games; Oropesa posted a 1.93 ERA. Saints owner Marvin Goldklang was ecstatic over Ordonez's chances, calling him a "blue chipper. That's what he is. He had a whole bunch of scouts look at him when he was playing for the Cuban National team, and the consensus was he's right now better defensively than any shortstop in the American League."

At season's end, eight big league clubs expressed an interest in signing the two players. Oropesa went to the Reds; Ordonez to the Mets. "His bat is the question," said Mets Scouting Director John Barr of Ordonez. "With his defensive makeup, we project him as playing in the middle infield in the big leagues."

One of the key elements in the Northern League's success has been a fellow with a familiar name — Mike Veeck, son of the legendary Bill Veeck, and for good measure the grandson of a one-time Cub general manager.

Bill Veeck did it all. As owner of the American Association's Milwaukee Brewers and the majors' Browns, Indians, and White Sox, he took the staid out of stadium. From hiring baseball clowns like Jackie Price and Max Patkin to sending midget Eddie Gaedel up to pinch-hit to making scoreboards explode, Bill Veeck eventually promoted his way into the Hall of Fame.

During Bill's last major league gig, with the White Sox, young Mike was at his side. Not all of his memories were pleasant, however. The ultimate disaster was Mike's Disco Demolition Night brainstorm. On the face of it, the idea was commendable: let any fan with a disco record in to a Sox doubleheader for 98 cents. Fifty-five thousand fans showed up. Between games the younger Veeck (a former rock and roll singer) had collected 10,000 records by Bee Gees' wannabes, placed them in a dumpster at the center of the diamond, and set them afire. What was not commendable was the riot that followed. Fans went berserk. Thousands more records flew across the stands. The field was wrecked, and Chicago was forced to forfeit the nightcap.

Strike two against Mike came when White Sox announcer Jimmy Piersall called his mother, Mary Frances, "a colossal bore" — or something very close to that. The exact wording is still disputed.

"He called my mother a word I don't use," claimed Mike. The two either did—or did not — engage in a fistfight. According to the volatile Piersall, Veeck "came up with somebody else and grabbed me from behind." In any case, as Mike Veeck admits, "the papers murdered me."

The third strike was simply being Bill Veeck's son. When Veeck, Sr., sold the White Sox, it meant that Mike Veeck would be banished from the major league scene. He tried running a jai alai fronton in south Florida and hung dry wall. His marriage, frayed from Mike's increasingly heavy drinking, fell apart. "I had nothing left," Veeck admitted. "My marriage was gone. My life was gone. My self-respect was gone."

Veeck got a hold of himself and stopped drinking. When Marvin Goldklang put together an investment group that included entertainers Bill Murray and Jimmy Buffett and took over the Florida State League's Miami Miracle in 1990, Mike got a second chance in baseball.

The franchise was a disaster. It wasn't even in Miami anymore, having fled Bobby Maduro Stadium to a site in Pompano Beach. It had no working agreement, and the 1989 season attendance stood at a minuscule 14,972. No other Florida State League team drew less than 28,009.

Under Veeck, attendance climbed to 43,580 that first year and to 56,362 in 1991. Then the franchise moved to Fort Meyers, where despite a last-place finish, the club drew 105,578 in 1992.

In the Florida State League, Veeck honed the ballyhoo that would serve him in good stead in the Northern League. To broadcast games he hired color man Don Wardlow, the game's first *blind* announcer. Also put to work was Jericho, the club's golden retriever mascot. Clad in Miracle jersey and cap, Jericho trotted out onto the field with

Gatorade and towels for the umpires. On hand in the stands were personnel who provided shoe shines and hair cuts. Veeckian promotions included Babes in Toyland Night (where kids scamper onto the field to pick out any two of the 1,000 toys strewn across the outfield) and the Blue Review. The Blue Review was a variation of Bill Veeck's Grandstand Manager, where fans voted on what moves they wanted Browns manager Zack Taylor to employ. In the Blue Review fans voted on the antics of three vociferous Miracle season ticket holders as they taunted umps and visiting players.

"It ain't brain surgery," Veeck admitted. "All I'm trying to do is entertain."

One of young Veeck's stunts was definitely in the family tradition: dragging out aged Minnie Minoso for one last hurrah. On June 30, 1993, the 70-year-old Minoso became the first player to appear in pro ball over six different decades.

Appropriately enough, the well-preserved Minoso faced the Northern League's youngest player, Thunder Bay's 19-year-old Yoshi Seo. Anticlimactically, Minoso grounded back to the box.

Veeck promoted all year. For Irish nights, the Saints used green bases. For just $5 a fan could have a massage from an Honest-to-God nun, Sister Rosalind, or for $10 obtain a hair cut behind homeplate from a hair stylist, "the lovely Gina." Sound familiar? How much it would cost to have your locks trimmed by the nun was not revealed.

Guerrero attributed the calming of his troublesome back spasms to Sister Rosalind, who was more than happy to be at the park. "I can feel the family spirit here," she said. "It's very powerful. They make a fun thing here. There's not a down moment. It's alive, not plastic. The humanness is missing from a place like the Metrodome. Here, it's for real."

Every St. Paul Saints game in August and September 1993 was sold out (22 straight sellouts). On a season-long basis 97 percent of all available seats at 5,069 seat Municipal Stadium were sold out.

Summed up Veeck, "I love St. Paul. They've embraced the silliness, and in the process this place has already stolen a piece of my heart."

At season's end the Saints netted an estimated $500,000. The nearby Twins reportedly lost money.

Mike Veeck could take comfort from what he had created, the

hoopla and the razzmatazz, but he knew there were definite limits to his advance. "I can't work in the big leagues," Veeck admits, "At one time that hurt me terribly. But now I know my place."

About the only negatives to the Northern League's banner inaugural season involved the failure of an experimental 10-second clock (designed to speed up the game) and the state of circuit umpiring.

Admitted league Executive Director Tom Leip, concerning the ill-fated timer: "The problem was we left the plate umpires in charge of it. Well, they've got a game to run. Often, they didn't notice the clock expire. Next year, we'll put a horn on the clock, like the shot clock in the NBA."

In regard to umpiring in general, there were wide-spread complaints. Most blamed the situation on two-man crews, often drawn from college ranks. They were "brutal," contended Bull Durham.

Only the Rochester Aces, playing in decrepit Mayo Park, lost money. After the 1993 season the franchise shifted to Canada, becoming the Winnipeg Goldeyes. The first campaign's attendance ran as follows:

Club	Attendance	Per Game
Duluth-Superior	105,954	3,116
Rochester	50,803	1,452
St. Paul	167,956	4,940
Sioux City	112,971	3,800
Sioux Falls	86,187	2,535
Thunder Bay	127,581	4,116
TOTAL	651,452	3,209

In 1994 Durham was back, and joining him were ex-major leaguers "Oil Can" Boyd (soon to be sidelined with arm problems), southpaw Joe Kraemer, and catcher Carl Nichols. Also joining in was veteran minor league center fielder Ted Williams. This Williams had a bit more speed than his famous namesake and was known to Duluth-Superior fans as "The Splendid Sprinter."

And topping things off were nine exhibition (30 games were originally scheduled) contests against the first women's professional team in 30 years, the Colorado Silver Bullets. Their initial matchup, an ESPN-2 telecast Mother's Day mismatch between the Silver Bullets and the Northern League's All-Stars, ended as a 19-0 blowout, with

Bull Durham collecting two homers. "These ladies acknowledge the game," said Boyd. "They love and respect it, just like we do."

In the Northern League's 1994 campaign, the circuit smashed through the all-time short-season league attendance record, breaking the Northwest League's mark of 786,801 set just the previous year. The Northern League hit the 797,993 level with 29 games to go and bettered the old record in 99 fewer games than were necessary to set the "old" record.

Elsewhere on the independent front, the trend was similarly positive. Leagues were springing up all over the map. The limping Frontier League planned on carrying on and was joined by a number of new operations. Byron Pierce's Texas-Louisiana League announced that it was finally getting off the ground in 1994, with franchises in Beaumont, Tyler, Alexandria, Corpus Christi, Amarillo, Edinburg-McAllen (Rio Grande), Alexandria, Mobile, and Lafayette. Buoyed by Mike Veeck's St. Paul success, Pierce also invaded organized baseball territory, in his case, San Antonio, challenging the Texas League's Missions who in 1994 were moving to a new stadium. The Texas-Louisiana League's Tejanos slipped into the Missions' old V.J. Keefe Stadium.

"San Antonio is a large metropolitan area with more than 1.3 million people," advanced TL League Vice President Doug Theodore. "We feel there are enough people in San Antonio to support two teams."

Joining Texas-Louisiana League's managerial lineup were former major leaguers Alan Ashby (Rio Grande White Wings), Pete Falcone (Alexandria Aces), Charlie Kerfeld (Beaumont Bullfrogs), Mark Wasinger (Corpus Christi Sand Crabs), Ross Grimsley (Amarillo Dillas), Ed Jurak (Mobile Bayrunners), and Bill Stein (Tyler Wildcatters). The once-volatile Kerfeld was a somewhat surprise choice for a managing position in any kind of a league. "Charley's mellowed out," said league General Manager Jack Lazorko, an ex-major league righthander, who had barnstormed with Kerfeld on the Hollywood Stars. Lazorko continued, "He had fun when he played. He was loose. But now he's real serious. And he's from Beaumont, where he'll be managing. It should work out great."

The Texas-Louisiana League mandated a $20,000 per month salary cap per club, but it should have no problem writing checks. Bankrolling Pierce's circuit is Dallas businessman, Carl Westcott, whose personal fortune was estimated at $100 million.

Most significantly, perhaps, Pierce and Westcott were returning to an old, discarded idea: syndicate baseball. The circuit would own all franchises and control all aspects of marketing, player development, talent distribution, etc.

"Everything will be under one roof," explained Lazorko. "Instead of each team having separate owners, we have one league ownership. It's an innovative concept. We can have league-wide sponsors."

Literary agent and author Jay Acton also swung into action in 1994 with the much more modest Northeast League. Although it was originally announced that this four-team circuit (the Mount Vernon Hoot Owls, New Rochelle Bears, White Plains Devils, and Yonkers Blue Bandits) would play from July 1 to August 31, at one site in Westchester County, New York, just north of New York City, that plan soon changed, scaling down to a one-week tournament in 1994 (another plan soon junked) and a six-team league (the Albany-Colonie Diamond Dogs, Glens Falls Bobcats, Newburgh Night Hawks, Sullivan Mountain Lions, Little Falls Landsharks, and Yonkers Hoot Owls).

Acton, whose National Association experience included involvement with Utica, Watertown/Welland, South Bend, and Peninsula, frankly described his scheme as "a direct imitation of what Miles [Wolff] is doing but at a much lower level." Only local college players would be recruited; no per diems would be paid or overnight travel incurred. Players would hold jobs during the day and play all their games at 7 P.M. All clubs would be held under league ownership ("vertically integrated" is how Acton phrased it). To honcho his circuit, Acton secured the services of former Mets center fielder Lee Mazzilli as league commissioner. Former major league pilot Doc Edwards was retained to manage at Albany; Ron LeFlore at Newburgh; Dave LaPoint at Glens Falls; Paul Blair at Yonkers; and Ken Oberkfell at Sullivan.

In old Dixie, cable and ski executive Richard Grottanelli launched a Mid-South Baseball League. Franchises were eyed for Greenville and Meridian in Mississippi; Clarksville, Ohio; Jooplin and Springfield, Missouri; Owensboro and Paducah, Kentucky; and Pine Bluff, Arkansas.

Further west, another independent circuit, the Golden State Baseball League, had hoped to start play in 1994, but later drew back, postponing its debut until 1995. GSBL President Bob Weinstein awarded franchises in Antelope Valley, Paso Robles, Merced, Chico, Indio, and Brawley.

In the Pacific northwest, a Northern League veteran, former Duluth-Superior general manager Bruce Engel was organizing an independent Western League, with teams proposed in Bend, Grays Harbor, Long Beach, Palm Springs, Salinas, Sonoma County, Surrey (BC), and Tri-City (Richland-Kennewick-Pasco). The WBL boasted such managers as ex-Brewers skipper Tom Trebelhorn, Jeff Burroughs, Bill Supdakis, and Nate Colbert.

"We'll be a lot like the Northern League," vowed Engel, a Portland lumber baron. A unique feature of the Western League, is that it was the first league to own a franchise in another circuit, operating the Erie Sailors of the 1994 Frontier League.

"This is the future of minor league baseball," summed up Mal Fichman, who had managed at Duluth-Superior in the Northern League in 1993 and would pilot the Frontier League's Johnstown Steal in 1995. "In five years, I'll bet 50 percent of the clubs will be independent. Really. This is great. It's Rotisserie League Live."

STRIKE INSURANCE

What if they gave a Major League Baseball strike and nobody cared?

At times in the late summer of 1994, that's exactly what appeared to be happening as fans and the press took the walkout by Don ("The Grinch Who Stole The World Series") Fehr's multi-millionaire minions with unexpected equilibrium.

Was it denial on their part, a false sense of bravado to mask a "Big Hurt?" Or genuine lack of interest? Or was it because *real* fans — the live and die with the game variety — had (at least 'til Labor Day or thereabouts) an ace up their sleeve: minor league ball?

From Portland, Maine, to High Desert, California, strike-angered fans turned to bush league ball. As one Pawtucket fan scrawled across a banner, "The Players Can Strike Forever. We'll Always Have The PawSox."

Such loyalty translated into a healthy 11 percent jump in minor league attendance in 1994 to 33,355,199 paying customers, the highest total watching bush league ball since 1949. Stoking interest in the minors in the fateful — if somewhat short — 1994 season, after all, was The Jordan Factor. In January, Michael Jordan puzzled NBA fans, baseball fans, and just about everybody else in the universe by coming out of his brief retirement to return, not to the Chicago Bulls, but to a career in baseball. Jordan, who had lost his father in a brutal murder the previous August, defended his decision. "I'm serious," he vowed. "My father thought I could be a major-league baseball player, and I'm sure that right now he can see me trying. He's watching every move that I make."

Never mind that the 30-year-old hoop superstar hadn't actually played the National Pastime since high school in Wilmington, North

Carolina. Never mind Jordan couldn't even beat Tom Selleck at the home run hitting contest at the 1993 All-Star Game. After a mediocre spring training, the White Sox (the team that brought you Bo Jackson's artificial hip and tried to bring you septuagenarian Minnie Minoso) assigned Jordan to the Double-A Birmingham Barons.

Despite his meager $850 a month paycheck, Michael was still a superstar. When asked in spring training if he would be riding the buses in the minors, Jordan replied, "I'm not too adjusted to royalty that I can't ride a bus as long as it's a luxury bus." He wasn't kidding. When crunch time came for the 6'6" Jordan's knees, he responded by buying the Barons a $350,000 luxury bus just like those used by rock and country music stars. The Jordan-mobile featured 35 reclining seats, six televisions, and a VCR, plus a little something extra — a lounge with a wet bar in the rear of the vehicle.

Jordan got off to a respectable start including a 13-game hitting streak, but soon pitchers caught on that they were dealing with a *really* big strike zone and took full advantage of it. The ex-NBA superstar struggled to finish the season over .200, batting just .202 with three home runs, 51 RBI and 30 stolen bases. In 436 at-bats he fanned 114 times. In the field he committed 11 errors.

Still, Jordan felt he had made progress. "I just understand my fundamentals a little better," Jordan told *Baseball Weekly* as the season was winding down. "It took me a whole season to do that, so my batting average went down from .300 down to where it is now. But I feel more equipped…I'm a lot better as a batter than when I was hitting .300."

But Jordan's pallid batting average meant little to Southern League — or even to non-Southern League — fans. Games featuring Jordan's Birmingham Barons accounted for a spectacular 40 percent of attendance in the 10-team Southern League, including two Nashville crowds of nearly 17,000 fans each. Chattanooga saw its biggest crowd (13,416 fans) since Joe Engel last raffled off a house. Birmingham itself set an all-time club attendance record, of 467,867 fans (an average of 6,983 fans per game), breaking its old mark of 445,926 set in pre-TV 1948 with a monster Saturday night crowd of 16,247 at Hoover Metropolitan Stadium — a stadium record. Their improbable season total placed them sixth on the all-time Double-A list.

"You know, we've had Cal Ripken and Jose Canseco and Bo Jackson and Mark Langston and everyone else come through this league," chortled Southern League President Jimmy Bragan. "But like I was telling Michael, there's never been a player that had the effect on attendance that he has."

And when the strike came, and ESPN turned to telecasting minor league games, for some reason a Birmingham game was the first scheduled. Jordan, however, disappointed network magnates by sitting out the game with an injured left shoulder. "We were joking around that with Mike getting hurt, we were afraid that ESPN was going to run the amateur ping-pong tournament or something," said Barons southpaw Bob MacDonald, a former Tigers and Blue Jays hurler.

Nonetheless, ESPN's Sunday night broadcasting team of Jon Miller and Joe Morgan crowded into the tiny press box at Memphis' Tim McCarver Stadium, trying to talk for three hours about situations they were totally ignorant of. Come to think of it, that hardly placed them in a situation unique to network announcers.

Still, it was a great opportunity for bush league baseball. "For minor league baseball this is real important," Memphis Chicks General Manager Dave Hersh commented. "It's a shame that it takes a strike to put the limelight on a business that draws 30 million people a year...Two thousand guys play this game in anonymity, and I think it's great for them."

Aiding interest in the minors were some savvy management moves as the strike deadline approached. A number of prospects were demoted to the minors and would thus be unaffected by the stoppage, continuing to gain valuable playing experience. The Orioles farmed out southpaw Arthur Rhodes, who had pitched shutouts in his last two big league starts and been named American League Player of the Week. The Giants demoted Bill VanLandingham, who was 8-2 with San Francisco. Yankee left-handed starter Sterling Hitchcock, also was sent down to protect his development, as was promising Cub righthander Steve Trachsel, 9-7 with a 3.21 ERA before being despatched to Iowa.

And then there was the case of Kevin Elster. Elster's year had an overall unreal quality to it. With his career on hold from a chronic bad right shoulder as the 1994 season opened, he was edgily sitting at home in California. The Yankees needed shortstop help, however, and to give the smooth-fielding Elster a shot at a comeback, assigned him to their Eastern League farm at Albany-Colonie. After a slow start Elster was called up to the Yankees in July, and was playing regularly

for manager Buck Showalter when he reinjured his shoulder. On a re-
hab assignment on August 1, Elster returned once more to Albany-
Colonie's shabby Heritage Park.

"My shoulder is fine," Elster remarked after the strike started. "If
they weren't on strike, I probably wouldn't be here, but I've got to
play the 20 days out. Then, I walk out."

"I got nine days pay, and they didn't," Elster continued. "I feel
lucky in that sense, but as far as lucky goes, if I didn't get injured
years ago I'd be making tons of money and be happy as hell."

Nine days was nothing to sneeze at. Based on Elster's $200,000
major league salary he was pulling down $1,092 per day for perform-
ing at such venues as Reading, Pennsylvania, and New Britain, Connecticut.

Besides Elster and conveniently "demoted" players, fans could
find a number of other familiar names performing in the minors, although some were noted more for their "names" than anything yet
accomplished. Nolan Ryan's son Reid could be found pitching for the
Rangers' Hudson Valley Renegades farmclub; Ken Griffey, Jr.'s
brother Craig was at Jacksonville, while Greg Luzinski's son Ryan
caught for Vero Beach, and Pete Rose's son Pete, Jr, was spending his
season with the Prince William Cannons. "It's not like I've been released 55 times," said Rose, Jr, a six-year minor league veteran. "I
was traded to Chicago the first time because *they* wanted me. I was
drafted by Cleveland because *they* wanted me. When the Indians released me, the White Sox were calling me by the time I got back to the
hotel."

And if those names were on the way up, or at least hoped to be,
others had already been there. Former Astros slugger Glenn Davis
was roughing up American Association pitching at Omaha. Thirty-
seven-year-old Leon "Bull" Durham was spending his second season
in Miles Wolff's Northern League and former Pirate knuckleballer
Tim Wakefield was earning — or at least trying to earn — his
$170,000 salary at Buffalo. Joining him on the Bisons' staff was
former Baltimore 18-game winner, southpaw Jeff Ballard.

The Dodger system was loaded with once-and-perhaps-future big
leaguers. Starting pitcher Darren Dreifort and reliever Chan Ho Park,
the first native Korean major leaguer, held forth at San Antonio. Errat-
ic fielding shortstop Jose Offerman and former Astros relief pitcher
Al Osuna hoped to turn things around at Triple-A Albuquerque.

Even Mike Kekich found a home with Albuquerque. Mike

Kekich? Yep, *that* Mike Kekich, the Fritz Peterson Mike Kekich; the Mike & Susan & Fritz & Marilyn Mike Kekich. No, he wasn't part of the Dukes' starting rotation; the club had merely signed him up to pitch batting practice to its hitters.

And at Indianapolis, fans could pretend they were in a time warp with Indians' roster featuring former big leaguers shortstop Kurt Stilwell, catcher Barry Lyons, outfielders Casey Candaele, and Kevin Maas, and pitcher Rick Reed. "I'm glad that I'm playing here. I'd hate to be out," Maas said, even though both he and Candaele supported their striking major league brethren. "Certainly the money would be better if I was up in the major leagues the whole year, but since I've been here most of the year, I want to finish it out."

The Texas Rangers turned to their American Association affiliate, the Oklahoma City 89ers to fill their magnificent — but empty — Ballpark in Arlington. Thanks to eastern media dominance nobody seemed to notice that The Ballpark in Arlington (TBIA for short — or TCBY for the terminally confused) was the best ballpark around, superior even to Baltimore's beautiful Camden Yards. To give local fans a last look at the place (Texas general partner George W. Bush had pessimistically predicted an end to the season as soon as the strike broke out), the Rangers called in the calvary.

The horse soldiers, in this case, were the men of their top farm team, the AAA Oklahoma City 89ers, who they brought in to play the Omaha Royals. With respect for minor league sensibilities, ticket prices were heavily scaled back (back in many cases below what it would cost to just *tour* a major league ballpark, let alone normally see a game in one), ranging from $2 to $8. "The Rangers are very pleased to take part in this event," said Rangers President Tom Schieffer. "It will give our fans the opportunity to watch our top minor leaguers in action while affording the 89ers' fans a chance to see our beautiful ballpark."

In minor league towns near major league cities, such as Modesto or Bowie or New Haven, the strike afforded bush league clubs the opportunity to show big league fans exactly what the minors were up to. "I think it will take about 10 days to hit, for fans to go through their withdrawal period," commented General Manager Tim Marting, whose Modesto A's were about 75 minutes from the Bay Area.

"At first, I think people will treat it like the Athletics and Giants are on a road trip," Marting said as the strike began. "Then, I think people will be like, 'Hey, I haven't heard them on the radio for a while.' Already, though, I'd say every third call we're getting now is from the Bay Area, asking for a pocket schedule."

One of Modesto's attractions was pitcher Bob Bennett, Lakota Sioux in ancestry and a very distant in-law of famed Sioux chief Crazy Horse. To honor his heritage Bennett refused to trim his shoulder length hair. Oakland finally told him his locks were OK — as long as he kept them under his cap when he pitched. Except during games when he left it in his locker, Bennett also carried an eagle feather with him. Not surprisingly his Lakota name Wanbli Wanji translates as One Eagle.

At Toledo, just after the strike hit, 21-year-old Tiger farmhand Jose Lima no-hit the visiting Pawtucket Red Sox on August 16. The righthander struck out 13 and came within one walk of a perfect game, but that wasn't the evening's real story. The punch line came after the game, when the down-to-earth Lima spent the next 45 minutes signing autographs for all comers. Then after he had showered and changed he signed for *another* 200 fans. Explained Lima: "I say, 'These people cheer for me.' I could never say no."

Don't tell Don Fehr about this guy.

But fans didn't need a Bob Bennett or a Jose Lima to attract them to the minors. "People who come to the games very rarely ask, 'Who's pitching?' and 'Who are we playing?' said Chuck Domino, general manager of the Eastern League's Reading Phillies. "They just want to be a part of the minor league experience because they've heard so much about it. It's the ambience, the affordability and the accessibility of the players, everything."

"I'm not happy for the industry to see a strike," added Pittsfield Mets General Manager Richard Murphy. "If the major league strike creates stimuli for people to come...we're going to greet them with open arms."

"We had a lot of people that came out in the last week or so and said, 'Geez, we didn't realize minor league baseball was exciting,' " said Henry Stickney, general manager of the California League's already very successful Rancho Cucamonga Quakes. "We make it exciting. The minor leagues now are intent on starting a new generation of fans."

During the strike, the minors continued proving they had promotions the majors couldn't — or wouldn't — touch. In the ever-inventive, *very* independent Northern League, the Sioux City Explorers were proving that you didn't need to have a Veeck family member at the helm to come up with something, er, different.

Pitching for them on one August night was none other than 39-year-old righthander Mujiber Rahman, better known to television fans as one of the two Bangladeshi storekeepers operating around the corner from "Late Night with David Letterman."

It was not only Mujiber's professional debut, it was also his *amateur* debut. But after a feverish 30 minutes of pre-game on-the-job training by Sioux Falls pitching coach Dan McDermott, Mujiber was ready for action.

Well, almost ready.

On reaching the mound, Mujiber displayed *nearly* perfect form. Still a little shaky on the basic rules and strategies of the game, he was ready to aim his offerings at first base rather than the more traditional target of homeplate.

"Once we got him pointed towards the plate and not throwing to first base, it looked like he would be all right," commented Sioux Falls interim manager Mark Schlemmer, a man of obviously low expectations. "If we would have had another hour with him before the game, I think we would have had him throwing strikes." But after Mujiber's first pitch sailed over the head of the St. Paul Saints' Doug Kimbler, Schlemmer alertly saw something was amiss and marched to the mound. "He just didn't have enough time before the game and he developed tightness in his elbow," Schlemmer explained. "In the interest of his career, we felt that it was best to take him out before any further damage was done."

Farther to the west the Las Vegas Stars were plotting their own brand of mayhem, resurrecting an old Charlie Finley stunt but adding a Philip K. Wrigley "Double Your Pleasure"-twist to it. With the season rapidly winding down, Stars manager Russ Nixon planned on shifting outfielder Keith Lockhart and catcher-second baseman Kevin Higgins around to all nine positions in a Thursday night game against the PCL's Tacoma Tigers. "I think it's a fun idea," Nixon said. "It's a great way to display their talents."

In the majors only Bert Campaneris and Cesar Tovar had pulled that trick, but not in the same contest. The minors — as always (well almost always, thanks to Lou Gehrig) — have already done the majors at least one better. On September 4, 1991, Rochester Red Wings Tommy Shields and Shane Turner had performed at all nine positions as the Red Wings triumphed, 8-0, over the rival Syracuse Chiefs.

However, that was nothing compared to what happened in the Northwest League in 1976. Portland and Grays Harbor *both* had *all nine* players switch around to all nine positions in the same game.

The Las Vegas experiment went pretty well as the Stars outlasted the Tigers, 10-7. Lockhart held Tacoma scoreless in his one-inning mound stint and collected five RBI. Higgins went 2-for-3 at the plate and scored twice.

One of the venues closest to a big league park was Prince George's County Stadium, home to the Bowie BaySox, a farm team of the near-by Orioles. The Sox were a relatively new Eastern League franchise but, depending or your musical or theological preferences, had been operating either like the Flying Dutchman or Moses in the Desert.

After the PBA went into affect, the Orioles' old Eastern League affiliate, the Hagerstown Suns, were set on the move. Municipal Stadium wasn't a bad park. It had its charms, but it was nowhere near to meeting the new standards for Double-A, and the city fathers weren't about to shell out enough money to make it conform.

So the team went looking for a new home, and although it never went very far, it went often. Officially, they shifted from Hagerstown in central Maryland to suburban Bowie, just down the pike from Camden Yards. The area was prosperous, growing and full of Orioles fans. There was only one problem.

It had no ballpark.

In 1993 the club played out of Baltimore's old Memorial Stadium, hoping their permanent home would be ready before the start of 1994. It wasn't. The BaySox kept moving around, from Memorial Stadium to a field at the nearby Annapolis Naval Academy, before finally sliding over to Prince George's County Stadium.

Again, there was *one* problem. It wasn't finished. It wasn't anywhere near finished. Oh, they had bases and foul lines and free parking and lights and seats (very nice seats with cup holders if you were lucky enough to get a reserved seat), but they didn't have much of anything else.

Skeletal steel greeted fans on their arrival. Food was being vended out of trailers. Porta-johns provided the only sanitary facilities. The planned restaurant was nowhere to be seen. Ditto for the play area in right field and the carousel that was to go with it.

It was the revenge of Hagerstown.

Still, it wasn't a bad place to watch a ballgame. Bowie fans didn't seem to mind. If you even just *start* to build it, they will come. And come they did. In droves.

After all, they were fans of the big Orioles, and Bowie (or Annapolis or wherever they were) featured some interesting talent, like Alex Ochoa who had a rifle for an arm in right field. Or righthander Armando Benitez who threw the ball at 102 miles per hour and struck out 14 in 10 innings with Baltimore. Or stocky infielder Jose Millares. He didn't hit much, but he sure was fun to watch as he broke the bat over his knee after striking out on a pitch up in his eyes.

The most familiar name at Bowie, however, was outfielder Jack Voigt, an outfielder of major league quality whom the Orioles no longer had room for once they signed Lonnie Smith. By rights, Voigt should have gone to the Birds' Triple-A farmclub at Rochester, but he decided he'd rather keep his Baltimore-area apartment and commute to Prince George's County.

So he did just that.

Even before major league players struck, the BaySox were drawing 4,000 fans per game. With the strike, attendance doubled. "I don't care if I see another Orioles game this season," said BaySox fan Ralph Komives, who performs document searches at the National Archives. "Here I can give the kid $5 and he's happy; otherwise, it would be $50 at Camden Yards. Before the strike they were attracting 4,000 a game. Now it's six or seven thousand."

Komives was speaking on the last Sunday afternoon of the 1994 Eastern League season, and what an afternoon it was at Prince George's County Stadium. A line of fans literally two blocks long waited to gain entrance to the half-finished park. There was no Michael Jordan to attract them. No Max Patkin or Dynamite Lady. No free souvenir mugs or batting helmets. The club had already gained entrance into the league playoffs.

It was a meaningless Double-A game, and over 10,000 fans *paid* their way in.

Bowie's situation was hardly unique. "People need their baseball fix," summed up Everett Giants General Manager Melody Tucker. "We're hearing from them every day. The fans call and say they need to come and see games.

"A major league strike isn't good for anyone, we know that. But for those who miss their baseball, at least the minor leagues are still here."

To say the least.

THE MINOR LEAGUE BIBLIOGRAPHY

Acton, Jay, with Bakalar, Nick, *Green Diamonds: The Pleasures and Profits of Investing in Minor League Baseball*, Zebra, New York, 1993

Ashenbach, Edward and Ryder, Jack, *Humor Among The Minors*, Donahue & Co., 1911

Beverage, Richard E., *The Hollywood Stars: Baseball In Movieland 1926-1957,* The Deacon Press, Placentia (CA), 1984

Beverage, Richard E., *The Los Angeles Angels*, The Deacon Press, Placentia (CA), 1981

Blake, Mike, *The Minor Leagues: A Celebration of the Little Show*, Wynwood, New York, 1991

Bosco, Joseph A., *The Boys Who Would Be Cubs: A Year in the Heart of Baseball's Minor Leagues*, William Morrow, New York, 1990

Brooks, Ken, *The Last Rebel Yell*, Seneca Park Publishing, Lynn Haven (FL), 1986

Browning, Wilt, *The Rocks: The True Story of the Worst Team in Baseball History*, Down Home Press, Asheville (NC), 1992

Bryson, Bill and Housh, Leighton, *Through the Years with the Western League Since 1885*, 1951

Cauz, Louis, *Baseball's Back In Town*, Controlled Media Corporation, Toronto, 1977

Chrisman, David F., *The History of the International League (1919-1960)*, Maverick Publications, Bend (OR), 1981

Chrisman, David F., *The History of the Piedmont League (1920-1955)*, Maverick Publications, Bend (OR), 1986

Chrisman, David F., *The History of the Virginia League (1900-1928, 1939-1951)*, Maverick Publications, Bend (OR), 1988

Clifton, Merritt, *A Baseball Classic*, Samisdat, Richford (VT), 1978

Clifton, Merritt, *Disorganized Baseball*, Samisdat, Richford (VT), 1982

Dews, Robert P., *The Georgia-Florida League 1935-1958 (Extra Innings)*, Rebel Books, Edison (GA), 1985

Dews, Robert P., *Southeastern Disorganized Baseball*, Rebel Books, Edison (GA), 1987

Dobbins, Dick and Twichell, Jon, *Nuggets on the Diamond: Baseball in the Bay Area From the Gold Rush to the Present*, Woodford, 1994

Dolson, Jack, *Beating The Bushes*, Icarus Press, South Bend (IN), 1982

Etkin, Jack, *Innings Ago*, Normandy Square Publications, Kansas City (MO), 1987

Fatsis, Stefan, *Wild and Outside*, Walker & Co., New York, 1995

Filichia, Peter, *Professional Baseball Franchises: From the Abbeville Athletics to the Zanesville Indians*, Facts on Files, New York, 1993

Finch, Robert L. and Addington, and Morgan Ben (editors), *The Story of Minor League Baseball: A History of the Game of Professional Baseball in the United States, with Particular Emphasis on its Development in the Smaller Cities and Towns of the Nation — The Minors*, National Association of Professional Baseball Leagues, Columbus (OH), 1953

Fireovid, Steve (with Wingardner, Mark), *The 26th Man*, macMillan, New York, 1991

Foster, John B., *History of the National Association of Professional Baseball Leagues*, National Association of Professional Baseball Leagues, Columbus (OH), 1926

Foster, Mark, *The Denver Bears: From Sandlots to Sellouts*, Pruett, Boulder (CO), 1983

Gammon, Wirt, *Your Lookouts Since 1885*, Chattanooga Publishing Co., Chattanooga, 1953

Greenberg, Steve, *Minor League Road Trip: A Guide to America's 170 Minor League Teams*, Stephen Greene Press, Lexington (MA), 1990

Gunther, Marc, *Basepaths: From the Minor Leagues to the Majors and Beyond*, Scribners, New York, 1984

Hampton, Bing and Petree, Patrick, *Old Times to the Good Times: Oklahoma City Baseball*, Oklahoma City 89ers Public Relations Department, Oklahoma City, 1981

Hemphill, Paul, *Long Gone*, Viking, New York, 1979

Holl, James P., *The Canton Terriers 1936-1942: The Middle Atlantic League Years*, Daring Publishing Group, Canton (OH), 1990

Irving, Elliott, *Remembering the Vees*, Cumberland Printing, Farmville (VA), 1979

Johnson, Arthur, *Minor League Baseball and Local Economic Development, University of Illinois Press*, Champaign (IL), 1993

Johnson, Harry "Steamboat," *Standing the Gaff: The Life and Hard Times of a Minor League Umpire*, University of Illinois Press, Champaign (IL), 1994

Johnson, W. Lloyd and Wolff, Miles, *Encyclopedia of Minor League Baseball: The Leagues, the Cities, the Leaders, 1902-1992*, Baseball America, Durham, 1992

Johnson, W. Lloyd, Minor League Register, Baseball America, Durham, 1994

Kahn, Roger, *Good Enough To Dream*, Doubleday, New York, 1985

Keetz, Frank M., *1899: Schenectady's First Complete Season*, Schenectady (NY), 1980

Keetz, Frank M., *"Doff Your Caps To The Champions!"* — *Schenectady: A Case Study of a Minor League Baseball Franchise in 1903,* Schenectady (NY), 1984

Keetz, Frank M., *Class C Baseball: A Case Study of the Schenectady Blue Jays in the Canadian-American League 1946-1950*, Schenectady (NY), 1988

Keetz, Frank M., *They, Too, Were "Boys of Summer": A Case Study of the Schenectady Blue Jays in the Eastern League 1951-1957*, Schenectady (NY), 1993

Kettle, Jerry (with Ed Addeo), *Low & Outside: The Confessions of a Minor Leaguer*, Coward-McCann, New York, 1965

Kirkland, Bill, *Eddie Neville of the Durham Bulls*, McFarland & Co., Inc., Jefferson (NC), 1993

Lamb, David, *Stolen Season*, Random House, New York, 1991

Lange, Fred W., *History of Baseball in California and Pacific Coast Leagues, 1907-38: Memories and Musings of an Old Time Baseball Player*, Oakland, 1938

Linthurst, Randolph, *The 1947 Trenton Giants*, West Trenton (NJ), 1982

Linthurst, Randolph, *Newark Bears (1932-38): Baseball's Greatest Minor League Team*, West Trenton (NJ)

Linthurst, Randolph, *Newark Bears (1939-44): The Middle Years*, West Trenton (NJ)

Linthurst, Randolph, *Newark Bears (1945-49): The Final Years*, West Trenton (NJ)

LinWeber, Ralph E., *Toledo Baseball Guide of the Mudhens*, Toledo, 1944

Lyttle, Richard B., *A Year in the Minors: Baseball's Untold Story*, Doubleday, Garden City (NY), 1975

Mackey, R. Scott, *Barbary Baseball: The Pacific Coast League of the 1920's*, McFarland & Co., Jefferson (NC), 1995

Mayer, Ronald A., *The 1937 Newark Bears: A Baseball Legend*, Vintage Press, East Hanover (NJ), 1980

Maywar, James R., *The 1926 Port Huron Saints*, Port Huron (MI), 1984

McCombs, Wayne, *"Lets Gooooooooooo Tulsa!": The History and Record Book of Professional Baseball in Tulsa, Oklahoma, 1905-1989*, Tulsa, 1989

Mowbray, Bob, *The ESL Encyclopedia: Eastern Shore League of Professional Baseball Clubs and Other Delmarva Baseball Testimonials*, Cambridge (MD), 1989

Nagle, Walter H., *Five Straight Errors on Opening Day*, Caxton Printers, Caldwell (ID), 1965

Newman, Zipp and McGowan, Frank, *The House of Barons*, Cather Bros., Birmingham (AL), 1948

Nufer, Doug, *Guide to Northwest Minor League Baseball*, Sammamish Press, Issaquah (WA), 1990

Obojski, Bob, *Bush League: A History of Minor League Baseball*, MacMillan, New York, 1975

Okkonen, Marc, *Baseball in Muskegon: An Illustrated Chronology of the National Pastime in West Michigan's Port City*, Muskegon, 1993

O'Neill, Bill, *The American Association: 1902-1991*, Eakin Press, Austin, 1991

O'Neill, Bill, *The International League: 1884-1991*, Eakin Press, Austin, 1992

O'Neill, Bill, *The Pacific Coast League 1903-1988*, Eakin Press, Austin, 1990

O'Neill, Bill, *The Southern League: Baseball in Dixie, 1885-1994*, Eakin Press, Austin, 1994

O'Neill, Bill, *The Texas League: 1888-1987*, Eakin Press, Austin, 1987

Overfield, Joe M., *The 100 Seasons of Buffalo Baseball*, Partners' Press, Kenmore (NY), 1985

Palmer, Howard, *The Real Baseball Story*, Pageant Press, New York, 1953

Paradis, Jean-Marc, *100 Ans de Baseball a Trois-Rivieres*, Trois-Rivieres, Quebec, 1989

Parker, Al, *Baseball Giant Killers: The Texas Spudders of the '20's*, Nortex Press, Quanah (TX), 1976

Patkin, Max (with Hochman, Stan), *The Clown Prince of Baseball*, WRS Publishing, Waco (TX), 1994

Patton, Jim, *Rookie: When Michael Jordan Came to the Minor Leagues*, Addison-Wesley, New York, 1995

Perlstein, Steve, *Rebel Baseball*, Onion Press, Minneapolis (MN), 1994

Pietrusza, David, *Baseball's Canadian-American League*, McFarland & Co., Jefferson (NC), 1990

Postema, Pam (with Wojciechowski, Gene), *You've Got To Have B*lls To Ump In This League*, Simon & Schuster, New York, 1992

Price, Jim, *Indians: A Century of Baseball in Spokane*, East Washington State Historical Society, Spokane, 1986

Rappoport, Ken, *Diamonds in the Rough*, Grosset & Dunlap, New York, 1979

Reddick, David B. and Rogers, Kim M., *The Magic of Indians Baseball: 1987-1987*, Indianapolis, 1988

Remington, John L., *The Red Wings — a Love Story: A Pictorial History of Professional Baseball in Rochester, New York*, Rochester, 1969

Rogers, John and Reynolds, Henry, *Fifty Years with the Memphis Chicks*, Memphis Chicks, Memphis, 1952

Rorrer, George, *Redbirds: Thanks a Million*, Courier-Journal, Louisville, 1983

Ruggles, William B., *The History of the Texas League of Professional Baseball Clubs*, Dallas, 1932

Ryan, Bob, *Wait Till I Make The Show*: *Baseball In The Minor Leagues*, Little, Brown, Boston, 1974

Schott, Art, *70 Years With The Pelicans 1857-1957*, New Orleans, 1987

Shearon, Jim, *Canada's Baseball Legends*, Malin Head Press, 1994

Snelling, Dennis, *The Pacific Coast League: A Statistical History 1903-1957*, McFarland & Co., 1995

Society for American Baseball Research, *Minor League Baseball Stars*, Cooperstown, 1978

Society for American Baseball Research, *Minor League Baseball Stars*, *Volume II*, Kansas City (MO), 1985

Society for American Baseball Research, *Minor League Baseball Stars*, *Volume III*, Cleveland, 1992

Spalding, John E., *Always On Sunday: The California Baseball League, 1886 to 1915*, San Jose (CA), 1992

Spalding, John E., *Pacific Coast League Stars: 100 of the Best, 1903-1957*, San Jose (CA), 1994

Stadler, Ken, *The Pacific Coast League: One Man's Memories, 1938-1957*, Marbel Publications, Los Angeles, 1985

Sullivan, Neil J., *The Minors: The Struggles and the Triumph of Baseball's Poor Relation From 1876 To The Present*, St. Martin's Press, New York, 1990

Summer, Jim L., *Separating the Men from the Boys; the First Half-Century of the Carolina League*, John F. Blair, Winston-Salem (NC), 1994

Tarvin, A. H., *70 Years on Louisville Diamonds*, Schulmann Publications, Louisville, 1940

Thornley, Stew, *On to Nicollet: The Minneapolis Millers*, Nodin Press, Minneapolis, 1988

Violanti, Anthony, *Buffalo: How The Dream of Baseball Revived a City*, St. Martin's Press, New York, 1991

Waddingham, Gary, *The Seattle Rainiers 1938-1942*, Writers Production Service Co., Seattle, 1987

Wolff, Rick, (edited by Phil Pepe), *What's a Nice Harvard Boy Like You Doing in the Bushes?*, Prentice-Hall, Englewood Cliffs (NJ), 1975

Zingg, Paul J., and Medeiros, Mark D., *Runs, Hits and an Era: The Pacific Coast League, 1903-58*, University of Illinois, Press, Champaign (IL), 1994

About the Author

David Pietrusza, author of *Minor Miracles*, is national president of the Society for American Baseball Research (SABR), the world's largest sports research organization.

Minor Miracles is his third published work on baseball, following *Baseball's Canadian-American League* and *Major Leagues*. He is also managing editor of *Total Baseball*, the official encyclopedia of Major League Baseball, and served as research assistant on *Mickey Mantle's All My Octobers*.

He has published articles on baseball in such publications as *USA Today Baseball Weekly*, *The National Pastime*, *Baseball America*, *Catholic Digest*, *The Baseball Research Journal*, *New Mexico Magazine*, and *Elysian Fields Quarterly*. His column, "Beating the Bushes" appears regularly in *Oldtyme Baseball News*.

Pietrusza served as a consultant for the "Baseball Online" component of PBS' educational on-line service Learning Link. He is also the producer/screenwriter of the documentary, "Local Heroes" for public television station WMHT (Schenectady, NY).

Pietrusza, a former member of the Amsterdam (NY) City Council, is also the author of *The End of Cold War*, *The Invasion of Normandy*, *The Battle of Waterloo*, and *The Mysterious Death of John F. Kennedy*.

Pietrusza now lives in Scotia, NY, with his wife Patricia, their Labrador retriever Maggie, and their somewhat moody lovebird, Sunny.